Transdisciplinary Journeys in the Anthropocene

T0382928

Transdisciplinary Journeys in the Anthropocene offers a new perspective on international environmental scholarship, focusing on the emotional and affective connections between human and nonhuman lives to reveal fresh connections between global issues of climate change, species extinction and colonisation. Combining the rhythm of road travel, interviews with local Aboriginal Elders and autobiographical storytelling, the book develops a new form of nature writing informed by concepts from posthumanism and the environmental humanities. It also highlights connections between the studied area and the global environment, drawing conceptual links between the auto-ethnographic accounts and international issues.

This book will be of great interest to scholars and postgraduates in environmental philosophy, cultural studies, postcolonial theory, Australian studies, anthropology, literary and place studies, ecocriticism, history and animal studies. *Transdisciplinary Journeys in the Anthropocene* may also be beneficial to studies in nature writing, ecocriticism, environmental literature, postcolonial studies and Australian studies.

Kate Wright is a Postdoctoral Research Fellow at the University of New England, Australia. She is currently immersed in an experimental, multispecies research project that involves developing and coordinating an Indigenous community garden in collaboration with Armidale's Aboriginal community.

Routledge Environmental Humanities
Series editors: Iain McCalman and Libby Robin

A full list of titles in this series is available at: www.routledge.com/series/REH

The *Routledge Environmental Humanities* series is an original and inspiring venture recognising that today's world agricultural and water crises, ocean pollution and resource depletion, global warming from greenhouse gases, urban sprawl, overpopulation, food insecurity and environmental justice are all *crises of culture*.

The reality of understanding and finding adaptive solutions to our present and future environmental challenges has shifted the epicentre of environmental studies away from an exclusively scientific and technological framework to one that depends on the human-focused disciplines and ideas of the humanities and allied social sciences.

We thus welcome book proposals from all humanities and social sciences disciplines for an inclusive and interdisciplinary series. We favour manuscripts aimed at an international readership and written in a lively and accessible style. The readership comprises scholars and students from the humanities and social sciences and thoughtful readers concerned about the human dimensions of environmental change.

Transdisciplinary Journeys in the Anthropocene

More-than-human encounters

Kate Wright

LONDON AND NEW YORK

from Routledge

First published 2017
by Routledge

2 Park Square, Milton Park, Abingdon, Oxfordshire OX14 4RN
711 Third Avenue, New York, NY 10017

Routledge is an imprint of the Taylor & Francis Group, an informa business

First issued in paperback 2018

British Library Cataloguing-in-Publication Data
A catalogue record for this book is available from the British Library

Library of Congress Cataloging-in-Publication Data
A catalog record for this book has been requested

ISBN: 978-1-138-91114-7 (hbk)
ISBN: 978-1-138-61519-9 (pbk)

Typeset in Goudy
by Keystroke, Neville Lodge, Tettenhall, Wolverhampton

'Storied places and companions infuse this deeply moving book of earthly encounters. This is not travel writing in any conventional sense, but home writing attuned to the bumptious motions of living and dying together of diverse human and non-human peoples. These are stories that can nurture response-abilities in our urgent times.'

Donna Haraway, University of California, Santa Cruz,
author of *When Species Meet*

'"This book," Kate Wright observes, "is written on home ground, where my places of memory and warm familiarity are also places of colonial violence and dispossession." Such is the fate of those across the planet who find themselves born into settlement cultures. Responding to her plight, the author engages in "recuperative work," rooting out structures of violence and dispossession still embedded in her beloved New England tablelands of Australia, in order to be true, as much as she can, to the "original storying of the place where my own stories were born." Her study is intimate and moving, a deeply personal account of her love for this particular place under the sun, even as she engages in a tough-minded, critical rethinking of her entanglement in a history permeated with genocidal and ecocidal legacies. Her embrace of transdisciplinary method, moving fluently and confidently among poetic, philosophic, ethnographic, ecological, historical, and autobiographical approaches to her subject matter, is innovative and always on target. Far too often appeals to the local are dismissed as not providing a rigorous understanding of the large issues and great forces at work in the onset of the Anthropocene. Wright's work here shows just the opposite can and should be the case. We need a lot more studies like this one.'

James Hatley, Salisbury University, Maryland

'This book is a major contribution to the emerging field of the environmental humanities. It is a field founded on the idea that knowledge is forged on troubling journeys, not just applied to problems by masterful humans in order to extract solutions. A new way of being is needed. Instead of the movement of theory to an empirical domain, a subtle yet remarkable ontology is conjured in this book, perhaps for the first time. Kate Wright has invented a kind of subjectivity, with both a mode of knowledge composition, and a tone, that are crafted in interspecies relations. We hear how others know otherwise, voices arguing with different kinds of authority; dialogues *with* Lucy the dog, *with* water and a forest, such that these actors can negotiate equally and supportively. The argument gathers momentum as these others are choreographed by Wright to join forces in this pluridimensional world. The environmental eumanities are here relaunched on a new journey, generating hope through generous thought in a spirit of trust.'

Stephen Muecke, University of New South Wales, Sydney,
author of *Ancient and Modern: Time, Culture and Indigenous Philosophy*
and *No Road: Bitumen All The Way*

'This book radically repositions the role of humans in this world. The author does this by telling wonderful illuminating stories that move the reader to imagine both a new politic and renewing poetics. Wright exemplifies the kind of imaginative intellectual thinking that we need right now to live in a world that depends upon relationality. Sure, this book will make you think differently but it will also make you feel very, very connected!'

Katrina Schlunke, author of *Bluff Rock: Autobiography of a Massacre* for Lucy

Contents

Figures

Photographs are the author's own, except where noted.

Acknowledgements

Having spent years writing from the contact zone between species, as I sit down to write my acknowledgements, I am conscious of a tendency to thank only humans, or at least to thank humans first.

It would be remiss of me, however, to acknowledge only the bipedal creatures who have supported and cared for me along this emotionally treacherous journey, as so many furry and feathered critters have made what is sometimes a cold and hard task warm and worthwhile. It also seems unjust to acknowledge only those beings I have encountered directly, and forget those who have nourished me in countless ways but who I have not met because the limitations of my experience.

So, to begin, I would like to acknowledge all of my 'shadow friends', all those who I have not been able to meet, but who have provided the material conditions for me to be able to spend years pursuing such an unusual task. And of course, there are those critters who I have met, some of whom have made their way directly into this work, some only implicitly. Thanks to Bunny, Barney, Harry and Mac, and the countless other lives I have encountered along the way, particularly those who made my childhood home the perfect place to meet the world. And, of course, thanks to Lucy, who taught me some hard lessons in loss but, most of all, showed me how to really love a home. This book is dedicated to you.

And thank you to all the humans who have supported me throughout the project. I would particularly like to thank Catherine Simpson and Deborah Bird Rose for their ongoing engagement with this work. Both began as my PhD supervisors and have become very dear friends. I am incredibly grateful for the way their thoughts have enriched my own thinking, for feedback that helped craft this book, and for the emotional and intellectual support and encouragement that was, at times, direly needed! Many colleagues and friends have also provided feedback on parts of the text for which I am very grateful, including Thom Van Dooren, Astrida Neimanis, Katrina Schlunke, Baden Offord, Stephen Muecke, Marcus Baynes-Rock, Dinesh Wadiwel and Elaine Kelly. Conversations with Jennifer Hamilton helped inform part of 'Thinking Like A Storm'.

I began this research at Macquarie University in Sydney, and completed it while a Postdoctoral Research Fellow at the University of New England in Armidale. Both institutions have provided a stimulating and supportive environment, and I thank the many colleagues who have offered their kind words of support along the way, especially Jennifer McDonell, John Scannell and Josh Wheatley.

A special thanks to the New England Aboriginal Elders who so generously shared with me their stories, feelings and thoughts: Pat Cohen, Lorna Hague, Christina Kim and Margaret Walford. I'd particularly like to thank Uncle Steve Widders who has become a close friend through our shared commitment to the Indigenous community garden in Armidale. Your words continue to inspire me.

Parts of this book have been published in articles in *Environmental Humanities*, *SCAN: Journal of Media, Arts, Culture*, *M/C: A Journal of Media and Culture*, *Journal of Environmental Philosophy*, *Transformations: Journal of Media and Culture*.

A special thanks to my family: Vic, Edie and Ben. Thank you for all the shared years that led me to begin this project, and all the support throughout it. I love you very deeply.

Thanks to all my dear friends who have supported me throughout this long task. Thanks too to the baby-in-becoming, who I am looking forward to meeting very soon. You have enriched this work in ways I cannot explain.

I like to think that despite our tendency to love a few and forget the many, this love, if it is generous and wise, can lead us to a love for the world and all the lives within it. With that hope, I thank my lover and best friend, Derek, for his laughter, his kindness, his blunt – yet tender – honesty, his patience, his cuddles and his reassuring refrain: 'It'll be worth it – just finish the bloody thing!'

Introduction
Unsettling 'blood's country'[1]

Countrylink

On the train coming up from Sydney the sunset is alchemic – eucalypt leaves turn from green to gold. The train tracks are like veins, the train like pulsing blood. The rhythmic bump of train-on-track makes the horizon dance.

> *South of my days' circle, part of my blood's country,*
> *rises that tableland, high delicate outline*
> *of bony slopes wincing under the winter,*
> *low trees, blue-leaved and olive, outcropping granite –*
> *clean, lean, hungry country.*
> > —Judith Wright, excerpt from
> > 'South of My Days' (1953, p.30)

Running

She knows where the trees are. Without looking her body feels where to turn. She won't trip or stumble because her legs remember the steep inclines and the sharp falls of the earth, the hard patches of dirt, the soft mud, the slight angular turns in the soil. Her face and throat remember the texture of the air, the smell, the sounds. When feet thump against earth this familiar, it's not running, it's rejoining.

The 'Dale

I keep coming back. Each time I go on a research trip I catch the train from Newtown Station to Sydney's Central Station, and then the Countrylink train for another eight-and-a-half-hour ride to Armidale. Dad picks me up at dinnertime, and I start again where I began, on that 35-acre block of land just outside of Armidale where I spent the first eighteen years of my life.

I know the shape of the little place where I grew up, which seems more significant somehow than knowing individual trees or rocks. I know the contours of the land – where gravity feels stronger, where feet become light or heavy. I know the smell of different seasons, and the sounds of birdsong in the wind float through me.

I left home at eighteen, driven in part by a compulsion to escape that familiarity. I always loved the Armidale region, but there was nothing to keep me there. The university didn't have the course I wanted, my closest friends were moving to the cities and there was a fear among many of my peers that if you stayed too long in 'the 'Dale' you'd never leave. Such was the pull of this small city, just big enough to provide some job and study opportunities, but still stifling in that hometown way. Perhaps it is this combination of magnetism and claustrophobia that keeps me tied to the logic of return – that rubber-band effect which snaps me back and forward. I keep going over old ground, and those tracts of pastoral land marking out the distance between Sydney and Armidale now seem as familiar as the places themselves.

The idea of studying the region where I grew up seemed from the start to be an emotionally confronting and risky task, but I couldn't imagine writing with the same conviction about anything else. My closeness to the topic was unsettling. Was I too near to think clearly about the issues? Were there things in this place of my past which I might not want to discover?

I imagined the New England tableland region as a kind of parent in whose own life before and beyond me I had, up until now, been utterly uninterested. How, as an adult, do you approach someone you have already known for years as a child? How do you talk to them as well as listen? How do you respond to the stories of someone who is such an intimate part of your own stories?

My study of the New England tablelands has forced me to face troubling questions about my position in a place I claim to love. The following chapters explore experiences of contact between human and nonhuman life in New England places. I realised as I was writing this book that this contact involves, almost exclusively, introduced species. My own New England life-world has been distinctly non-Aboriginal. Over the following pages I challenge many divides between native and non-native life because of their lack of responsiveness to dynamic environments, and their overly simplistic approach to classifying life. But the idea that my New England experience has been almost entirely non-native raises a serious question about the colonising impact of the story I am writing. As Margaret Somerville asks: 'Does my story write out another story? Does it make room for multiple stories? Can your story be written here? Is it a postcolonial space?' [2]

This book aims toward dialogue rather than monologue,[3] and I hope that it makes space for other tales situated in this rich region. If there is a question about the legitimacy of such a non-Aboriginal engagement within an Australian place, I respond that I cannot change the nature of my experience. The New England world I have written is the world in which I grew up. I cannot deny that my earliest experiences of love for animals were felt toward introduced species, nor that my strongest memories of being in a forest are not of eucalypts, but conifers. At the same time, love is not a zero-sum game. To acknowledge the world I came to love through being part of it is the basis from which I can acknowledge the love others bear toward their worlds of emplaced and encultured experience. In the era of the Anthropocene, an era of global environmental distress, I hope that my journey into a beloved homeplace helps to sing up others' homeplaces and communicates the need to protect beloved spaces of habitation, for human and nonhuman, across the world.

Writing my story into place

Many philosophers have written on the importance of studying what you are closest to.[4] In a move against the illusion of objectivity sustained by emotional distance, proximity is now a new kind of methodology: write about what you know, research what you have stakes in, be honest about your connections. This book is written in the spirit of this kind of faithfulness, where being true to place comes first.

Written with the aim of place fidelity, my goal has been to gain more knowledge through greater immersion in my own childhood life-world, to become more attuned to my home-place and its inhabitants. Philosopher Thomas Nagel writes of the way subjective engagement, rather than distorting reality, can actually bring one closer to the reality of experience as it is lived:

> If the subjective character of experience is fully comprehensible only from one point of view, then any shift to greater objectivity – that is, less attachment to a specific viewpoint – does not take us nearer to the real nature of the phenomenon: it takes us farther away from it.[5]

Adherence to proximity as a kind of methodology is not just about writing the familiar. There is also an imperative of openness. Environmental philosopher Deborah Bird Rose defines openness as a vulnerability to transformative encounter:

> To be open is to hold one's self available to others: one takes risks and becomes vulnerable. But this is also a fertile stance: one's own ground can become destabilised. In open dialogue one holds one's self available to be surprised, to be challenged, and to be changed.[6]

This book is written on home ground, where my places of memory and warm familiarity are also places of colonial violence and dispossession. In the following pages I engage with this ambivalence on a personal level – with the deeply uncomfortable knowledge that my own 'blood country' has been stained with the blood of Aboriginal people. The places I carry with me through my life – those places which have become a part of me – are places that already belong to others, and which are now scarred by the violence of colonisation. Learning about this emplaced trauma has turned my home into 'something less familiar and less settled'.[7]

Travelling along bitumen that has been poured over Indigenous tracks,[8] gazing at monuments which celebrate the violent foundations of a nation as the beginning of progress and civilisation, I am forced to acknowledge that this settler performance of a nation, with all its silences and delusions, both is and is not me.[9]

Like Albert Memmi's coloniser who refuses to accept the unjust economic, political and moral conditions of colonialism, my life is still bound and determined by structural colonial relationships which advantage me (the coloniser) by disadvantaging Australia's Aboriginal peoples (the colonised). The is-/is-not-me conditions of settler identity arise from this structural predicament, because '(i)t is not easy to escape mentally from a concrete situation, to refuse its ideology while continuing to live with its actual relationships'.[10]

While Australia is often referred to as a postcolonial country, this does not mean that it is decolonised. Ann Curthoys makes the point that while 'the term "postcolonial" may refer to a critique of colonial forms of power and discourse', this is not the case in a settler society like Australia where there is no 'clear moment of decolonisation'.[11] This book is written with the goal of seeking out alternatives to continued violence and silence. It is aimed toward decolonisation, undertaken through 'the unravelling of assumed certainties and the re-imagining and re-negotiating of common futures'.[12] Here I take up the task of decolonising a home-place. Engaging with decolonising work in this personal mode promotes dual responsibilities for a beloved place: to acknowledge the violence of the past and to commit to a nonviolent future.

Decolonising a home-place

The process of decolonising a home-place involves 'seeing the familiar as strange',[13] and rethinking established settler identities and behaviours. Part of this process is the development of a 'sentient education' – an attunement to place so that the landscape can speak its own stories.[14] Instead of the settler monologue which silences voices of country, this book aims to create a space for dialogue, and to promote learning to listen to new sounds and songs. This is part of a more-than-human decolonisation.

Because the legacy of colonisation in Australia 'includes both genocide and ecocide'[15] decolonisation must also involve healing steps to recuperate damaged Australian environments. Val Plumwood has observed that the concept of colonisation can be used to describe human relationships with nonhuman life at a general level, 'that the relationship between humans, or certain groups of them, and the more-than-human world might be aptly characterised as one of colonisation'.[16] The decolonising aim of this work therefore extends to the more-than-human world, and aims to 'resituate humans in ecological terms and nonhumans in ethical terms'.[17]

In this book I have aimed toward an expanded ecological engagement with place through the beings that have been closest to me. Revisiting my childhood landscapes, I have often found myself deep in the vestiges of the remembered past. I sometimes wonder if I am writing about a place that no longer exists, an ethnography of what once was. But the memories are sustained in place, and seem to dance with the cadence of time: a collection of experience that flows along gullies, grows into trees, seeps into earth and rock. Margaret Somerville explains the feeling of immersion in a landscape rich with personal memory as being like a dot painting, where each place of memory is a dot which 'can be entered at will to become the whole world'.[18] The taste of New England lingers on my tongue through my own dots of time and place:

Wind at night blowing through the trees.
The smell of the air before rain.
Lightning.
Quiet.
Campfires.
Kookaburras laughing.
The light from the house shining in the middle of dark bush.
The green soccer fields in Armidale.
Snow.
Lying in the grass after too many glasses of red looking at the stars.
Distant blue hills.
Being alone.
Knowing the way.
My dog.
My father.
My brother.
My mother.

My memories form the foundation of this research. The intensely personal nature of this study has made it unapologetically subjective. But I hope that throughout the following pages readers find resonances with their own beloved places. Each dot of experience helps to make a life-world meaningful. I hope that my dots make spaces for others, and begin to map out tracks toward futures as yet undreamed.

Place breathes

The motivations for my research have been experiences of intimacy and personal belonging in the New England tablelands, in particular the areas around my childhood home near Armidale. Because of this inspiration, and my theoretical adherence to proximity as a kind of methodology, the book is grounded in the particularities of one specific place in the world. The intimate coordinates of the local are the lens through which I examine entangled ecological ethics in an era when humans are being asked to position themselves as a species with global, geological impacts – impacts that are often felt and made in the intimate spaces of everyday life. The feelings of homeliness and intimacy I question and celebrate in my study comes from a belonging born of connectivity. The borders of a place, like the borders of a body, are always porous. Place, like skin, breathes.

In contrast to separatist and parochial views of place, I hold the view that while places have integrity of composition, they are also necessarily interdependent. To deny this in a globalised world breeds what Val Plumwood terms a 'false consciousness of place'.[19] While global awareness is certainly important, at the same time, the local should not be negated by, or subsumed into, the universal. The contingencies of particular places, and the difference from one place and another, matter. Furthermore, moving beyond the narrow confines of localism, place-based studies have much to offer.

My own study seeks to use the tangible contingency of knowing one specific part of the world to investigate relationships between human and nonhuman lives in the world at large. I look at how understanding an environment as something composed of connectivities and sustained by intimacy may extend feelings of proximity which can lead to respect and care for the more-than-human world across the globe. This research aligns with the growing inter-disciplinary field of the ecological humanities which cuts across established binaries in Western thought to 'engage with connectivity and commitment' as modes of reasoning in a time of environmental crisis.[20]

Bringing the Anthropocene home

There is much discussion and debate around the reasons why people feel disconnected from climate change and other extreme and precarious environmental conditions that characterise what it means to live in the era of the Anthropocene. This book is an attempt to bring the Anthropocene *home*, to localise the impacts of a rapidly changing world so that we can come to understand our own imbrication with, and responsibility to, severely compromised ecologies.

The Anthropocene is a troubling term for a disturbing era. As a species, humans have wielded such power, and caused such pervasive changes in the more-than-human world, that we are now classified as a 'geological agent' whose activities 'rival the great forces of Nature'.[21] While the Anthropocene demands that we position ourselves and our behaviour within the larger context of the behaviour of our species, it does not implicate, or affect, all humans equally. The Anthropocene has been re-dubbed the Capitalocene because it is not the inevitable inheritance of the human biological species at large, but the sociogenic inheritance of an economic system that promotes exponential growth for the benefit of a tiny minority of the world's population.[22]

The emergence of the Anthropocene is inextricable from a troubling history of colonial violence and invasion and its devastating impact on the more-than-human world. Imperial expansion involved the violent assault of Indigenous peoples and Indigenous ecologies across the globe, an attack that lay the groundwork for the environmental catastrophes we now face as a species. Discussions of environmental recuperation are therefore fundamentally entangled with issues of social justice, especially as climate change and other threatening prospects of our unstable era will disproportionately affect indigenous communities, and the poor more generally.

As I ponder relationships of responsibility and inheritance in a developed, colonial nation I am plagued by the uncomfortable awareness that I, a settler-descended Australian, am implicated in this era's great unravelling, where the patterns and webs that sustain multispecies life on the planet are being unmade by recursive traumas. In this book I engage with Gregory Bateson's concept of 'the pattern that connects',[23] to explore what it means to live responsibly in an entangled world that is undergoing radical change. Bateson used the concept of the 'pattern that connects' to emphasise the vital importance of attending to connectivities in a relational world. Each of the journeys I undertake in the following pages follows a 'pattern of connection', to explore human entanglement with more-than-human life. Following Bateson, I chart the way humans and the more-than-human are at stake in each other, caught up in an intimate 'ecology of mind', where even the seemingly most individualistic parts of the self – thoughts, memories, and feelings – are interwoven with the places we inhabit, and so with the environmental future of the planet.

In many senses the emergence of the Anthropocene signals human neglect of entangled patterns of life that sustain places across the globe. Environmental philosopher and eco-feminist Val Plumwood used the term 'hyper-separation' to articulate the narcissism of a species disconnected from the conditions of their world. Plumwood implored people to treat their 'earth others' with respect, and sought to dismantle the dualistic hyper-separations which devalue nonhuman life and conceptually remove humans from their entangled position in a multispecies earth.

The designation of the 'Anthropocene' era is therefore paradoxical and contradictory. Anthropos, the species who has for so long regarded themselves to be outside and above the rest of the living world, have now been granted their own epoch, seeming to almost celebrate the narrow narcissistic loyalties that have led to the emergence of an era of unprecedented anthropogenic destruction. Yet the Anthropocene also forces a radical shift in how humans understand their relationship to the more-than-human world, as it prompts a geological imagination that positions our actions in the vast matrices of deep co-evolutionary time.

This book takes the Anthropocene as a productive paradox to develop new, creative modes of thinking with and for more-than-human life. In a time of great sadness and devastation, I am looking for hope in the creaturely languages I came to know as a child, and the lessons they might offer for how we are to live well among our earth others in a time of extinction and ongoing waves of loss. My search for meaning in this dark time has been born from childhood passion for the life-world I grew up in. Vinciane Despret has written on passion that it is not 'some parasitic supplement' rather 'it means to make an effort to become interested, to immerse oneself in the multitude of problems...It means to care'.[24] By tracing the 'pattern that connects'[25] through the entanglements that tie me to a place I have come to know and love – my New England home – I hope that I can communicate the vital importance of intimate and emplaced care for more-than-human life in a relational world where delicate patterns of interconnection are woven across the globe: an intimately entangled nest that nurtures the future of our own, and many other, species.

A relational New England

New England is a defined region, with its own character and eccentricities. While my study does engage with the individuality of the New England tableland region to some degree, it is, at heart, relational in its approach. Instead of focusing on essences, I am interested in encounters. Freya Mathews promotes encounter, instead of knowledge, as a way of relating to the world as responsive and alive.[26] My methodology of proximity is phenomenological, beginning with the 'life-world' – the everyday lived experience – and seeking understanding from within entangled positions in living, communicative systems.

I am also conscious of the arbitrary designation of the 'New England tablelands', and the mapping of such a region as part of a colonial cartography which appropriates Indigenous lands and uses imported measurements of place to calculate Aboriginal people out of their sovereign country.[27] These artificial regional boundaries are a violent assault against Aboriginal Australian Dreaming tracks which criss-cross the nation, transforming Indigenous country[28] into a 'checker-board grid of states'.[29] Because of this, the process of decolonising a home-place must seek to overcome or re-imagine colonial cartographies of 'a continent abstracted into a nation-state by the lines on a map'.[30]

Rather than paint the reader a measured and mapped picture of this region – like an aerial photograph that captures each part at equal distance, and gives each form equal attention – this book is a subjective topography of place. I have written of the rich web of relationships that pattern place into the shapes and rhythms we come to know. The characteristics of the area that make it into the writing are those that are most relevant to my purpose of understanding relationships between human and nonhuman life. A pet dog in the outskirts of Armidale is given more attention than New England's historical New State movement, for instance. However, the process of defining something's relevance to the study has not been as easy or as simple as I initially suspected it would be. Particular historical encounters have shaped the region in intricate ways. An important lesson I have learned from this long research journey has been the ways the landscapes of the present are made from events in the past. This teaching has awakened me to the historical contingencies of my New England home.

In July 2010, in a cramped office overcrowded with books on the beautiful University of New England campus, I sat with English professor John Ryan, an expert in New England's local history and folklore, to talk about the place I was writing. We got onto the topic of the non-native deciduous street trees in Armidale, and he informed me that these had all been planted, pretty much, by one man: Alwyn Jones, in the 1950s.[31]

Looking out the window from the passenger seat of my parents' car as we drove home from the campus, I saw the landscape of my youth with new eyes. Every March, this historical moment, where a white man decided to paint an Indigenous landscape in the colours of England, replays. History returns through the bodies of imported botanies that glow orange and red in the autumn. These sorts of coalescences between human and nonhuman lives are central to my understanding of the patterns of connection we share and make with the more-than-human world.

Fernand Braudel explains that natural history is not a mere backdrop to human action, something which can be introduced at the beginning of a historical account and then forgotten, to be left as a kind of material terra nullius,[32] 'as if the flowers did not return each spring, as if flocks [of birds] were frozen in their migrations, and as if the ships did not have to sail on an actual sea, which changes as the seasons change'.[33] Alwyn Jones' returning autumn trees are the tangible expression of a collective agency, and New England's evocative tableland geography actively shapes the kinds of relationships which form between human and nonhuman lives.

A natureculture history of the tablelands

The New England tableland is a plateau that stretches from the Moonbi Range in lower New South Wales to the Queensland border. Its eastern edge is marked by an extremely deep, entrenched gorge system that cuts slices out of the country from Dauan Island in Northern Queensland to the Grampians in Western Victoria. This spectacular country of cliffs and waterfalls feels like a dramatically geometric end of the Earth. To the west the country levels into the northwest slopes where the dirt turns red and the land unfolds like a handkerchief flattening out to the horizon.

The New England tableland, like the rest of Australia, is narrated into being through an Indigenous creation story. The Dreaming story tells of Creator Beings who arose from the soil to shape the land and create the landscape. Before this time, the earth was a barren, empty plain, but beneath its surface were the Ancestors, 'sleeping in a state of potentiality'.[34] At this time humans were also asleep in embryonic forms in a state of proto-humanity. At a certain point the Creator Beings were disturbed and erupted from beneath the earth. They hunted, fought, danced, ran, made love and killed all over the country and their vibrant activity shaped the contours of the Australian landscape. I picture this time as an era of reverberation. After the volcanic explosions of rock the land kept shaking beneath the terribly powerful running-falling-warring-dancing of the enormous creators.

The first white man to 'discover' New England was the English explorer John Oxley. In the midst of a biting cold winter in 1818, Oxley did not envision giant Creator Beings thumping across country, digging out an escarpment before sinking back into Antipodean land forms. Nor did he imagine the shifting tectonic plates of Gondwanaland, breaking up the earth into puzzle pieces, 80 million years before his arrival.

To Oxley and his party, this landscape was a strange inversion of the Alpine-style peaks of Europe and North America. He recorded in his journal that it was an 'upside-down land' of 'natural phenomena' that defy 'all rule' and 'perplex us…greatly'.[35] Oxley's image of the tablelands was a case of 'double vision'.[36] He was incapable of seeing the escarpment except through the frame of Northern hemisphere environments. Jay Arthur uses the term 'double vision' to describe a colonial condition of perceiving Australian land where the settler is aware of two places existing at the same time: 'to see in this double vision the colonised landscape and the landscape of origin'.[37]

As Oxley surveyed the sharp, rocky contours sliced into bush and backcountry, his eyes were foggy with an opaque vision of sublime peaks. In imperial European discourse mountains are pregnant with poetry and religion. Great adventurers embark on journeys of ascent, becoming closer to their Judeo-Christian sky-God. This backwards place must have seemed perverse. Simon Ryan explains that long before explorers entered Australia, in imagination the continent was 'inverted, and representations of this imaginary place hinted at void'.[38] Did Oxley envision his society's inevitable physical and metaphysical descent? As he experienced that almost psychotic vertigo of hovering on cliff edge by steep drop, did he imagine a fiery underworld, where cavities in rock spawn barbarity and savagery?

For Oxley the land was Antipodean, antithetical, yet uncannily familiar.[39] While reflecting on the escarpment Oxley exclaimed '[h]ow dreadful must the convulsion have been that formed these glens!'[40] The thunderous waterfalls, their resounding, immanent echo, the entire exalted scene was a 'massive and sudden emergence of uncanniness'.[41] Though familiar, in 'an opaque and forgotten life',[42] the New England escarpment was threatening and destabilising.

After discovering the Aspley Falls near Walcha, Oxley remarked that he and his party were 'lost in astonishment at the sight of this wonderful natural sublimity'.[43] Edmund Burke describes 'astonishment' as a 'state of the soul, in which all its motions are suspended, with some degree of horror'.[44] Yet the sublime is contained, a way of 'compartmentalising the threatening'[45] by translating an uncanny Other into a stable Eurocentric code.[46] The voice of the Antipodean rock is muted by colonising words and thoughts.

Colonial New England

The very name of the region 'New England' demonstrates that the land was experienced, and still is understood, 'in relation to another place', 'as a *second* experience'.[47] The naming of New England aligns with an assimilationist writing of place which defines land 'in terms of colonial relationships that exhibit Eurocentricity and nostalgia for the European homeland'.[48] Deborah Bird Rose has observed that settlers conceived of themselves as 'agents of disjunction', and their intentions to create new societies and leave the old behind is signalled by their terminology of 'new worlds'. At the same time as they seek to remake the world (*New*), settlers attempt to generate Antipodean continuities (*England*).[49]

Val Plumwood argues that the process of colonisation in Australia began with this disjunctive naming, and that colonial naming practices were 'both anthropocentric and Eurocentric, registering a monological or non-interactive relationship with a land conceived as passive and silent'.[50] Such colonial names signal a detachment from place because they fail to engage in dialogue with the land. These names also write out Aboriginal place-names, and so begin a process of installing colonial histories while forgetting the Indigenous.[51]

An awareness of the many Aboriginal nations and language groups within New England instantly undermines the seemingly settled colonial cartography of the region. Overlapping the New England tablelands, but not entirely contained within its borders, are the Anaiwan, the Dhunghutti, the Kamilaroi, the Gumbaynggirr and the Ngarabal nations.

I am writing from within an amnesiac colonial culture, and I use the problematic name 'New England' throughout to refer to my home region. Rather than dispense with the name altogether, my analysis intends to highlight the unsettled qualities of the 'New England' title by acknowledging the performativity of settler belonging and its reliance on oppression and silence.[52] Where colonial naming of New England induces settler amnesia, the process of researching this book has been a process of 'un-forgetting'.[53]

I had the great privilege of meeting with some of New England's Aboriginal Elders to discuss with them their belonging. From these conversations I was awakened to a place and time that had previously been invisible to me. Even though I searched in gravel pits for stone artefacts as a child, and looked for the carved shape of shields in eucalypt trees, Aboriginal history seemed far away from my own life-world. When I spoke to the Elders in 2011, though, it became suddenly close.

In my high school years I attended Duval High, a local public school named after the mountain it sits behind – Mount Duval. Steve Widders, Aboriginal Elder and traditional descendant of the Anaiwan people, explained to me that Mount Duval has an Aboriginal name, but he has been unable to find out what the name means:

> No one to my knowledge knows the Aboriginal name, and where it comes from, and what significance it had to Aboriginal people. Yet it's very synonymous with Armidale. Everybody relates Mt. Duval to Armidale, and that's named after a French explorer.

Steve's frustration at this loss is part of a larger distress at the destruction of Aboriginal culture in the region, particularly language and the connection to land. Being unable to give the Indigenous name of a landform is a violation of that intimate connection between Australian Aboriginal people and place – a connection which forms the foundation of identity. Steve explains: '[Aboriginal] people say, which hill do you come from? Which mountain's yours? What's your river? I can tell people I come from Mount Duval. I know the Aboriginal name of it, but I don't know the meaning of it'.

A mountain in whose shadow I studied for six years became a powerful symbol of colonisation. I could no longer pretend that the words 'Mount Duval' were endemic or perennial. I am personally implicated in a history of violence, and its aftermath of amnesia.[54]

A harshly situated presence

With the task of decolonising a home-place comes a burden of responsibility for the past. The 'white man' of colonial New England feels much closer to me than the generalised white coloniser of Australia. As I spoke to the Elders about the specific and localised impacts of dispossession I *felt* for the first time that I had lived my life on stolen land. This moral claim of the past called me into a relationship of responsibility in the present.[55]

Over a sandwich and a coffee in a little café in the mall in Armidale, Steve described the dispossession of Aboriginal people from the places I now call my homelands.

> [T]he Aboriginal people had a real connection with the land, before the white man came. He started building here and they were relegated to reserves and missions. So you're not allowed to wander, you're not allowed to hunt your food, you're not allowed to go across the river to visit your other people there. You stay on this side. Because the squatters wanted to come and take the land, use it for their own purposes...That's how a lot of massacres happened. Because the people that were wanting to use it came and took possession of it, and they just killed the people who lived there, wouldn't allow them to hunt for their food.

The violent massacres of the New England frontier have scarred the land, leaving open wounds of cultural devastation.[56] The tablelands were invaded in the great pastoral expansion of New South Wales in the 1830s. The first squatters moved on to the tableland in 1832, and by 1839 the region was fully occupied.[57] Historian I.C. Campbell reports that the period from 1839 to 1842 was 'particularly violent:'

> The districts beyond the limits of settlement were characterised by a significant absence of the more moderating influences of European society: women, families, school teachers and missionaries. It could be presumed that this section of the society would have been more likely to take a sympathetic interest in the native people, and also to maintain something of the restraint of civilisation over the white men, for even the most cultivated and gentlemanly proved themselves capable of great violence and brutality on the frontier...[58]

This was a period known as the time of 'gentlemen squatters' with the region 'considered by far the most aristocratic part of New South Wales'.[59] As the squattocracy[60] constructed a 'new England' on Indigenous country they conformed to their own ideals of high society, while simultaneously slaughtering Aboriginal people, stealing their land and committing the most severe violations of human rights.

Deborah Bird Rose argues that decolonisation requires an ethical dialogue which recognises that both settler-descendent and Aboriginal Australians are situated in the damaged places of colonisation.[61] From the 'harshly situated presence'[62] of being a settler in a wounded country, feelings of homeliness and belonging are unstable and problematic.

An undercurrent of belonging is implicit in many of the arguments presented throughout this book because my discussion is located in a place where I feel my strongest sense of ease and homeliness. Despite this affective quality I use the term belonging with caution in relation to my own being in New England because I resist the way it has been conceptualised in the past. The 'belonging' of the coloniser often continues the amnesiac processes of colonisation that usurp Indigenous lands and relationships to country.[63]

I feel it necessary to contrast my own understanding of belonging with what I regard to be the incommensurate belonging of Indigenous Australians – an Aboriginal belonging which is grounded in ceremony and spirituality. Indigenous scholar Aileen Moreton-Robinson describes this fundamental difference of place relations between the Aboriginal and the non-Aboriginal:

> Our ontological relationship to land, the ways that country is constitutive of us, and therefore the inalienable nature of our relation to land, marks a radical, indeed incommensurable, difference between us and the non-Indigenous. This ontological relation to land constitutes a subject position that we do not share, and which cannot be shared, with the postcolonial subject whose sense of belonging in this place is tied to migrancy.[64]

I acknowledge and accept this position, and share Baden Offord's feeling that the incommensurate ontological belonging of Indigenous Australians is 'something that needs immediate and unreserved acknowledgement',[65] but that 'the ontological belonging of Indigenous Australians, while incommensurable, does not sit in denial to my sense of belonging'.[66] My own feelings of belonging in New England do not seem to me to constitute an ontological state of being of the country, but instead are grounded in relational processes of connectivity.

Inspired by the work of Gregory Bateson, my relational approach to place is predicated on the notion that organism-and-its-environment are an inseparable unit – the unit of survival.[67] This interconnection reveals the vital importance of place to survival, but also the ultimate permeability of self to place. My own experience of growing up in New England follows this logic of connectivity and mutualism. Belonging is not a fixed state, but a movement toward intimacy, connectivity and commitment.

Poet and author Mark Tredinnick's regard of his settler position in his own home-place, the Blue Mountains region near Sydney, resonates strongly with me. He writes: 'I want…to belong very deeply here, and I know I never will…and I know that that matters less than the attempt to belong, which is an attempt…to grow intimate'.[68] If belonging is understood as a sovereign Indigenous relationship to land, then I do not belong, but this does not obviate my intimate and encompassing experience of being in place. My work attempts to write place in a post-humanist mode. Tredinnick observes, in the introduction of his monograph:

> There is a kind of literature that practices...ecological imagination, and we call it nature writing...In those books, most of them consisting of essays (lyric and personal), places come alive on the pages...In Australia, where I live, there is no tradition yet of such writing.[69]

My writing of my homeland attempts this ecological imagining, where words trace over place, responsive to its cadences, and in dialogue with the many voices which inhabit it.

Chapter outline and theoretical background

In contrast to conventional travel writing that moves from place to place, this book holds place constant and travels across the great domains of life. The book is divided into five parts, each of which explore genres of more-than-human encounter – Stone, Trees, Animals, Water, Sky. I write from the contact zones between species, where flesh meets fur, and skin touches bark, and combine personal tales of encounter with cultural, historical and environmental narratives to make sense of an entangled and relational world.

My study draws on many disciplines including cultural studies, postcolonial theory, Australian studies, biology, media and communications theory, cognitive psychology, human geography, anthropology and environmental philosophy. In response to the complexities of place, I draw on multiple theoretical frameworks. This fits the model described by Margaret Somerville as 'trans-disciplinary research'.[70] Such a model does not keep the shape of each discipline, but instead lets disciplinary boundaries become perturbed and interpenetrated. While different chapters emphasise different theoretical modes, all develop around themes of permeability, connectivity and proximity.

More-than-human memory

Throughout *Transdisciplinary Journeys* I emphasise the importance of recuperation through memory in the goal of decolonising a home-place. This involves the remembrance not only of the mass human and nonhuman losses through colonisation, but also remembering and restoring counter-colonial relationships with the land. At the heart of this ethics of remembering is an attention to organic modes of memory beyond human worlds. Inspired by Bateson's concept of an 'ecology of mind' that locates human thought in the complex interactions of wider systems, I approach memory as something that is shared across human and nonhuman bodies, part of an ecology of living thoughts in a dynamic living world.

Recounting personal narratives built on autobiographical memory, I have attempted to situate my own memory within multispecies ecologies in order to recuperate my childhood wonder at nonhuman life, believing that it reflects an openness to be challenged and taught by the world which is so central to the decolonising project.[71]

By associating this openness with childhood, by no means do I wish to suggest that responsiveness to more-than-human agency is somehow childish.[72] Nor am I trying to romanticise a universal innocent child. Instead I am remembering my very real and often painful fleshly material interactions with the New England world I understood to be alive and communicative. Such attunement to nonhuman voices comes from a willingness to be immersed in the more-than-human worlds that penetrate our own. These cross-species ties are severed by 'adult' concepts of modernity built on human exceptionalism. In my goal to restore youthful engagements with the world I am reminded of feminist philosopher Luce Irigaray's lament for the child within who becomes exiled in adulthood:

> I leave the girl in her preferred landscape with her winged and furry friends. Being thus immersed in life was her consolation, her happiness. She demanded nothing more.
> But what became of her exiled in 'adult life'? In 'society'? In the 'city'?[73]

In part I have written this book to call up my own rural childhood where it was easy to talk to a dog, to feel the will of a tree or to be swayed in the arms of a river. I do not want the place of my youth – a place which 'holds childhood motionless in its arms'[74] – to slip into oblivion. I seek to keep my New England tableland home with the magic of its stones, trees, animals, waters and skies in the world of the living – a part of the living world.

Notes

1   Judith Wright uses the term 'blood's country' in her poem 'South of My Days', about feelings of belonging in her New England tablelands home. I have adopted the term here because it captures the problematic nature of settler belonging in rural Australia, in lands stained with Aboriginal blood. Many of Judith Wright's works engage with the ambivalence of finding belonging in a country scarred by the violent dispossession of Aboriginal Australians.
2   M. Somerville, *Body/Landscape Journals* (North Melbourne: Spinifex Press, 1999), 5.
3   Deborah Bird Rose discusses the distinction between monological and dialogical ethics of engagement in *Reports from a Wild Country* (Sydney: University of New South Wales Press, 2004), 19–23.
4   Stephen Muecke asks, 'If we are passionate about what we do, then our expressions should perform or at least embody some of the passion. Why do people pull back from their natural forces in order to demonstrate a more measured objective response?' ('What the Cassowary Does Not Need To Know', *Australian Humanities Review* 39–40 (2006): www.australianhumanitiesreview.org/archive/Issue-September-2006/muecke.html. Similar concerns are raised by Karen Barad in *Meeting the Universe Halfway* (Durham and London: Duke University Press, 2007), Bruno Latour in *Pandora's Hope: Essays on the Reality of Science Studies* (Cambridge and London: Harvard University Press, 1999) and *We Have Never Been Modern* (Cambridge and London: Harvard University Press, 2001), and Thomas Nagel in 'What Is It Like to Be a Bat?', *The Philosophical Review* Vol. LXXXIII, no. 4 (October 1974), 435–450.
5   T. Nagel, 'What Is It Like', 444–445.
6   D. Rose, *Wild Country*, 22.

7   K. Gelder and J. M. Jacobs, *Uncanny Australia: Sacredness and Identity in a Postcolonial Nation* (Carlton South, Melbourne University Press, 1998), xiv. Gelder and Jacobs use the term 'uncanny' to describe this experience as part of the modern Australian condition 'where what is "ours" may also be "theirs", and vice versa'. They write: 'In an uncanny Australia, one's place is always already another's place and the issue of possession is never complete, never entirely settled' (138).

8   See Stephen Muecke's *No Road (Bitumen All the Way)* (Fremantle: Fremantle Arts Centre Press, 1997), for an extended meditation on this idea. This concept is discussed in greater detail in Part 1: Stone Country.

9   See Chapter 1 for a more in-depth discussion of these ideas.

10   A. Memmi, *The Colonizer and Colonized* (New York: Orion Press, 1965), 20.

11   A. Curthoys, 'An Uneasy Conversation: The Multicultural and the Indigenous', in *Race, Colour and Identity in Australia and New Zealand*, eds. John Docker and Gerhard Fischer (Sydney: UNSW Press, 2000), 32.

12   S. Biermann, 'Knowledge, Power and Decolonisation: Implication for Non-Indigenous Scholars, Researchers and Educators', in *Indigenous Philosophies and Critical Education*, ed. George J. Sefa Dei (New York: Peter Lang, 2011), 394.

13   R. Garbutt, S. Biermann and B. Offord, 'Into the Borderlands: Unruly Pedagogy, Tactile Theory and the Decolonising Nation', *Critical Arts* 26, no. 1 (2012): 63.

14   Ibid., 63.

15   D. Rose, *Wild Country*, 35.

16   V. Plumwood, 'Decolonising Relationships with Nature', *Philosophy, Activism, Nature* 2 (2002): 8.

17   V. Plumwood, *Environmental Culture: The Ecological Crisis of Reason* (London: Routledge, 2002), 8.

18   M. Somerville, *Body/Landscape*, 16.

19   V. Plumwood, 'Shadow Places and the Politics of Dwelling', *Australian Humanities Review* 44 (March 2008): www.australianhumanitiesreview.org/archive/Issue-March-2008/plumwood.html.

20   D. Rose and L. Robin, 'The Ecological Humanities in Action: An Invitation', *Australian Humanities Review* 31–32 (April 2004), 1: www.australianhumanitiesreview.org/archive/Issue-April-2004/rose.html.

21   W. Steffen, P. Crutzen and J. McNeill, 'The Anthropocene: Are Humans Now Overwhelming the Great Forces of Nature?' *Ambio* 36, 8 (2007): 614.

22   J. W. Moore, *Capitalism in the Web of Life: Ecology and the Accumulation of Capital* (London and New York: Verso Books, 2015).

23   G. Bateson, *Mind and Nature: A Necessary Unity* (New York: E. P. Dutton, 1979).

24   V. Despret, 'The Body We Care for: Figures of Anthropo-zoo-genesis', *Body and Society* 10, no. 2–3 (2004): 111–134.

25   G. Bateson, *Mind and Nature*.

26   See F. Mathews, *For Love of Matter: A Contemporary Panpsychism*, Chapter Four, 'The Priority of Encounter over Knowledge' (Albany: State University of New York Press, 2003), 73–88. I adopt the idea of encounter as the methodological framework for Chapter 2.

27   Liz Ferrier describes colonisation as a spatial practice, and cartography or mapmaking as a colonising activity, in 'Mapping the Space of the Other: Transformations of Space in Postcolonial Fiction and Postmodern Theory' (PhD thesis, University of Queensland, 1990).

28   Deborah Bird Rose offers the following definition of Aboriginal country: 'Country is multi-dimensional – it consists of people, animals, plants, Dreamings; underground, earth, soils, minerals and waters, surface water, and air. There is sea country and land country; in some areas people talk about sky country. Country has origins and a future; it exists both in and through time', in *Nourishing Terrains: Australian Aboriginal Views of Landscape and Wilderness* (Canberra: Australian Heritage Commission, 1996), 8.

29 K. Benterrak, S. Muecke and P. Roe, *Reading the Country: Introduction to Nomadology*, (Fremantle: Fremantle Arts Centre Press, 1984), 219.

30 S. Cooke, *Speaking the Earth's Languages: A Theory for Australian-Chilean* Postcolonial *Poetics* (Amsterdam and New York: Rodopi, 2003), 5.

31 John Ryan, personal communication, 11 July 2010. For more on Alwyn Jones, see Chapter 4.

32 Val Plumwood argues that the presentation of the world as a material terra nullius is part of the reduction of nonhuman life in sado-dispassionate rationalist thought, and part of human colonisation of the nonhuman world. For more on this see V. Plumwood, 'Journey to the Heart of Stone', in *Culture, Creativity and Environment: New Environmentalist Criticism*, eds. F. Becket and T. Gifford (Amsterdam and New York: Rodopi, 2005), 18. These ideas are discussed in greater detail in Chapter 1.

33 F. Braudel, *On History*, trans. Sarah Mathews (Chicago: University of Chicago Press, 1980), 3.

34 M. Graham, 'Some Thoughts about the Philosophical Underpinnings of Aboriginal Worldviews', *Australian Humanities Review* 45 (2008).

35 J. Oxley, *Journals of Two Expeditions into the Interior of New South Wales, by order of the British Government in the Years 1817–18*, 1820, reprint, eBooks@Adelaide, 10 November 2012, http://ebooks.adelaide.edu.au/o/oxley/john/o95j/part2.html.

36 'Double vision' is a concept introduced by J. M. Arthur in his *The Default Country: A Lexical Cartography of Twentieth-Century Australia* (Sydney: UNSW Press, 2003). Ross Gibson also describes the settler experience of Australia as 'oddly doubled' in *South of the West: Postcolonialism and the Narrative Construction of Australia* (Bloomington and Indianapolis: Indiana University Press, 1992), x.

37 J. Arthur, *Default Country*, 27.

38 S. Ryan, *The Cartographic Eye: How Explorers Saw Australia* (Cambridge: Cambridge University Press, 1996), 17.

39 'Uncanny' is a translation of Sigmund Freud's notion of the 'Unheimlich' which refers to an instance where something is familiar yet foreign at the same time – resulting in a feeling of it being uncomfortably strange. The term 'Antipodean' has been used to similar effect.

40 J. Oxley, *Journals of Two Expeditions*.

41 J. Kristeva, *Powers of Horror: An Essay on Abjection*, trans. L. S. Roudiez (New York: Columbia University Press, 1982), 2.

42 Ibid., 2.

43 J. Oxley, *Journals of Two Expeditions*, 299.

44 E. Burke, *A Philosophical Enquiry into the Origin of Our Ideas of the Sublime and Beautiful* (1757; reprint edition, Oxford: Oxford University Press, 1999), 57.

45 S. Ryan, *Cartographic Eye*, 84.

46 Ibid., 85.

47 J. Arthur, *Default Country*, 27.

48 V. Plumwood, 'Decolonising Relationships with Nature', 23.

49 D. Rose, *Wild Country*, 57.

50 V. Plumwood, 'Decolonising Relationships with Nature', 23.

51 This process is described in great detail in Chapter 1.

52 See Chapter 1 for an extended discussion of these ideas.

53 R. Garbutt, S. Biermann and B. Offord, 'Into the Borderlands', 68.

54 See Chapters 1 and 2 for an extended meditation on this idea.

55 D. Rose, *Wild Country*, 30–31.

56 For more discussion on this see Chapter 2.

57 I. McBryde, *Records of Times Past: Ethnohistorical Essays on the Culture and Ecology of the New England Tribes* (Canberra: Australian Institute of Aboriginal Studies, 1978), 7.

58   I. Campbell, *Social Backgrounds and Relations with the Aborigines*, Armidale and District Historical Society, 1971, cited in G. Blomfield, *Baal Belbora – The End of Dancing: The Agony of the British Invasion of the Ancient People of Three Rivers, the Hastings, the Manning & the Macleay, in New South Wales* (Alternative Publishing Co-Operative: Sydney, 1981).

59   I. McBryde, *Records of Times Past*, 4.

60   'Squattocracy' is a term used to describe wealthy and prestigious livestock graziers. In New England the squattocracy dominated colonial society and have had a strong historical and social impact on the pastoral region.

61   D. Rose, *Wild Country*, 21–22.

62   Ibid., 22.

63   See Chapter 1 for an extended discussion of these ideas.

64   A. Moreton-Robinson, 'I Still Call Australia Home: Indigenous Belonging and Place in a White Postcolonising Society', in *Uprootings/Regroundings: Questions of Home and Migration*, eds. S. Ahmed, C. Castañeda, A.-M. Fortier and M. Sheller (Oxford: Berg, 2003), 31.

65   B. Offord, 'Landscapes of Exile (and Narratives on the Trauma of Belonging)', in *Landscapes of Exile: Once Perilous, Now Safe*, eds. A. Haebich and B. Offord (Oxford: Peter Lang, 2008), 8.

66   B. Offord, 'Landscapes of Exile', 8.

67   G. Bateson, *Steps to an Ecology of Mind* (San Francisco: Chandler Publishing, 1972), 491.

68   M. Tredinnick, *The Blue Plateau: A Landscape Memoir* (Brisbane: University of Queensland Press, 2009), 237.

69   Ibid., 7.

70   M. Somerville, 'Towards Universities for the Twenty-First Century', *Higher Education in Europe* 16, no. 1 (1991): 79–86.

71   Jane Bennett observes that experiencing the world as enchanted is akin to 'a momentary return to childhood joie de vivre' in *The Enchantment of Modern Life: Attachments, Crossings and Ethics* (Princeton: Princeton University Press, 2001), 104. Similarly, Freya Mathews describes childhood landscapes as 'intensely animistic' and explores ways we might 're-enter the terrain of enchantment' in *For Love of Matter*, 1 and 22.

72   Val Plumwood observes that the association of an enchanted world and nonhuman intentionality with childhood (both evolutionarily and personally) 'speaks volumes about the instrumental reductionism we have normalized as adult life' (*Heart of Stone*, 22).

73   L. Irigiray, 'Animal Compassion', in *Animal Philosophy: Essential Readings in Continental Thought*, eds. M. Calarco and P. Atterton (London and New York: Continuum, 2004), 196.

74   G. Bachelard, *The Poetics of Space*, trans. Maria Jolas (Boston: Beacon Press, 1969), 8.

Part I

Stone country

Figure 1 Strata of New England, Armidale, 2016

Early on in this research project I decided that I wanted to revisit places that I remembered from childhood. Because the only feasible way to travel the stretched-out distances of New England is by car, getting to these places required a road trip. That I needed an automobile, the bitumen highways, traffic laws, petrol and everything else that accompanies the assemblage of car travel in Australia in order to visit New England places indicates that from the very outset my research was already deeply implicated in a colonial, perhaps colonising, experience of land and country.

Because I don't have a licence, my parents drove the car, so I spent long interludes reclining in the backseat in air-conditioned comfort. As a passenger I watched through dusty windows as streamlined tableland landscapes rose and fell from my vision. Film theorist Michael Atkinson argues that automobility, with its 'screen-like, Panavision-shaped lens of the windshield', determines basic experiences of reality: 'how we measure the width of continents…how we simultaneously close ourselves up within our self-made universes and gain access to every forgotten corner of the globe'.[1]

The car as a microcosm of comfortable spectatorship seems to speak volumes about settler alienation from place. On a personal level the idea of a vehicular bubble symbolises the distinctly non-Aboriginal Australian life-world I have grown up in – a circle of familiar whiteness traversing a black land. My position as a passenger also resonates with my pervasive feeling that I have been carried along by processes of violent invasion and colonisation. While I have never really seen myself as being in the driver's seat, I have certainly benefitted from my position as a white Anglo-Saxon settler in a colonised country – carried forward with the volition of the smooth and totalising movement of colonial 'development'.[2]

Even within an attempted decolonisation of a home-place, where exiting the car at significant spots focuses my full attention on issues of settlement and Indigenous sovereignty, I am bound by the criss-cross of bitumen that territorialises this country. Stephen Muecke writes that 'Australia is a country where deep Indigenous narrative lines have been confused by the imposition of another grid of lines'.[3] Confined to highways and freeways, is it possible to talk and write meaningfully about decolonisation? Is it delusional to try to address problems of settlement when the experience of being on the road means that I necessarily embody a territorialising aesthetic?

The road has been essential to the process of observing, cultivating and possessing geographic territory. Paul Virilio has noted that 'Possession of territory is not primarily about laws and contracts, but first and foremost a matter of movement and circulation'.[4] The smooth flow of rubber tyres against tar and the soothing hum of an engine seem to ease away the social and environmental destruction that these highways symbolise: the erasure of Indigenous tracks, the war against nature, a mobilised violence against people and their places.

The grids of bitumen that stretch across the vast geography of our lands have been referred to as 'Anthropocene rock'[5] – the most obvious sedimentary layer of a species whose impact on the planet is so profound as to be considered a geological event. Terrestrial mobility is often cited as the beginnings of the transition from biological species to geological agent, with James Watt's invention of the steam engine identified as the inauguration of the age of man – 'the one artifact that unlocked the potentials of fossil energy and thereby catapulted the human species to full-spectrum dominance'.[6] Our ability to accelerate the speed with which we traversed continents facilitated the 'Great Acceleration' in the human impact on the planet, leaving nuclear signatures in soils and sediments.

Hurtling through New England back country in my parents' sedan, I'm reminded that my movement through place is enabled by a fossil economy. The exhaust pipe coughs polluting streams of carbon into the atmosphere as I approach remote New England places with 'speed, noise, all those things that add up to Western productivity, to make some use of a place, to violate its "quiet fossil murmur"'.[7]

Thinking of the deposits of millennia of creaturely existence – the birth and death of countless individuals and species – that have been extracted from the deepest veins of the earth to be converted into crude oil that perpetuates a territorialising, motoring hum, I am plagued by Stephen Muecke's question:

> What kind of story do you tell on the road if you don't want to write like an imperial highway, on the road to further colonial expansion, where you engage in trade, slow down, get boring, lay out the plan for a town, create rectangles and climb into a coffin?[8]

The following two chapters offer a counter-colonial story of being on the road in a colonial country in the era of the Anthropocene. Journeying from the 'time-space compression' of a vehicle confined by a surface grid of highways,[9] into subterranean layers of granite etched with the 'deep Indigenous narrative lines'[10] of the continent, I write with New England's ancient gorge country that has carved itself into my life and mind. This is stone that is etched into my memory, and stone into which a memory of the human species is now forever consigned.

Notes

1 M. Atkinson, *Ghosts in the Machine: The Dark Heart of Pop Cinema* (New York: Proscenium Publishers, 1999), 43–44.
2 This is similar to the is/is-not-me settler condition described in the introduction, and supported by Albert Memmi's description of the colonial condition.
3 S. Muecke, *No Road*, 192.
4 P. Virilio and J. Armitage, 'The Kosovo War Took Place in Orbital Space: Paul Virilio in Conversation', trans. Patrice Riemans, *CTheory* (18 October 2000), www.ctheory. net/articles.aspx?id=132.
5 J. Zalasiewicz *et al.*, 'The New World of the Anthropocene', *Environmental Science & Technology* 44.7 (2010): 2228–2231.
6 A. Malm and A. Hornborg, 'The Geology of Mankind? A Critique of the Anthropocene Narrative', *The Anthropocene Review* (2014), 63.
7 S. Muecke, *No Road*, 134.

8   Ibid., 192.
9   Geographer David Harvey coined the term 'time-space compression' in his work
     The Condition of Postmodernity (Oxford: Blackwell Publishers, 1990). In relation
     to transport technologies, time-space compression describes the alteration of the
     relationships between time and space as high-speed mobility enables one to travel
     large distances in minimal time. I am contrasting this experience to the kinds of
     layering of time made tangible in sedentary rock formations.
10 S. Muecke, *No Road*, 192.

1 Standing stones and stratigraphic time in the Anthropocene

'Shallow roots', Ellen heard him saying. 'They haven't really taken in this place. And the soil, there's thinness in the soil. I'd say we haven't been here long enough, we don't go in deep.'

—Mr Cave, in *Eucalyptus* by Murray Bail (1998)

Our car pulls into the green picnic area by the New England highway at Glen Innes. I'm sleepy from the long drive, but wakefully intrigued by the monument we are about to view. The Australian Standing Stones were erected in 1992, when I was six years old, and while I have passed through Glen Innes many times I have never visited them.

Figure 2 The Australian Standing Stones, Glen Innes, 2010

Glen Innes has never seemed to be much more than a place for a pit stop. I remember primary school buses lined up along the main drag so all of us kids could run out to get McDonald's for lunch before continuing our long journey to the coast. It's a place that has always been on the way to somewhere else. A pastoral town with a population of less than six thousand people, Glen's main tourists are passers through. And the Standing Stones are next to the New England highway. Rushed past, they live less in geography than in the ephemeral visions of commuters. Viewed from the vantage point of accelerated automobility, the stones are morphing and indeterminate, distorted by an aesthetic of speed until they blend into the streamlined moving body of the landscape.

But this time we are parking the car just to see them. There are a few other tourist-looking types around, stretching their legs in the green surrounds. I crawl out of the air-conditioned bubble of automobility and clumsily reacquaint myself with solid ground. With the monument in full view, I am struck by its magnitude. It is almost too big to be powerful. It feels, from the side of the road, excessive and fake. As I amble down the slight incline toward the Stones I watch my eager mother stream out ahead of me and become dwarfed by the granite giants. A brief sentiment of humility in the face of these towering rocks is quickly undercut by the overpowering sensation of superficiality, unreality.

It is an experience of oscillation to wander through this tract of country. My body swings into the sublimity of the evocative granite – running fingers across them I feel the vibrations of their symbolic resonance, and stare up, open-mouthed, at towering figures of history. But then I jolt quickly back in moments of disorientation. The Stones feel false to me because they are too deliberate; they are kitsch, themed and obvious – so mimetic that they could almost be moulds of plastic.

The Australian Standing Stones were opened in 1992. They were erected with the support of the Celtic Council of Australia as part of the 1988 Bicentenary Year where monuments were built throughout Australia to mark two hundred years of European settlement. The Stones are now the site of Australia's annual Celtic Festival, and continue a nation-building rhetoric that claims colonisation as the beginning point of Australia's history.

In the tourist discourse the Australian Standing Stones are the physical manifestation of Celtic rights to the land based on a claim of first settlement. The tourist information pamphlet declares that the stones 'reflect Glen Innes' Celtic heritage, where the first settlers, largely Scots, arrived in 1838'.[1] Similarly, John Keller asserts that 'From the earliest days of white settlement, the Glen Innes area had been *claimed* by Celtic Scots'.[2]

This chapter engages with the Australian Standing Stones as a tangible chronotopic monument to colonial nationhood. Literary philosopher Mikhail Bakhtin coined the term 'chronotope' to describe the way time becomes bound to space. Bakhtin used the concept to analyse novels, but the same narrative time-knots pervade our lived landscapes, as each culture constructs its own time-space coordinates.[3] Walking through the Standing Stone array it is easy to feel the 'inseparability of time and space', the way the two have become 'fused' through the use of millennial granite carved into nation-building motifs.[4] This fashioning of time is fundamental to the development of the nation-state, its configuration becoming part of the 'common sense' social knowledge[5] of a country, a determining stylistic element in the 'imagined political community'.[6]

Benedict Anderson's sophisticated study of the development of nationalism explains that the phenomenon of the modern nation-state was first developed in the Americas and then exported to Europe in the nineteenth century. Settler colonies like Australia have adopted this imagining of invisible communal ties that bind them to their fellow colonials.[7] 'Chronotopes thus stand as monuments to the community itself, as symbols of it, as forces operating to shape its members' images of themselves.'[8] Underpinning this image of communion are shared commonplace assumptions about the nature of metaphysical reality – concepts of time and place that are both territorialising and fundamental to perception.

In this chapter I argue that the Australian Standing Stones represent the colonial construction of a temporal monoculture in order to maintain white control of indigenous space. Monoculture is a term typically used in agriculture to refer to the cultivation of a single species over a wide area of land. Monocultures are associated with homogeneity, the destruction of native biota and the monotony of mass production in a post-industrial world. I have used an agricultural term to describe a temporal praxis to draw attention to the way time is approached as a resource which is manipulated to serve human ends.[9] Expressions such as 'wasting time' indicate that time is often understood in these materialist terms – as something which can be *used* in different ways.

Since Isaac Newton conceived of absolute time, it has become common to perceive time as a universal constant which underlies all subjective experiences. Newton wrote that '[a]bsolute, true and mathematical time, of itself, and from its own nature, flows equably without regard to anything external, and by another name is called duration'.[10] Inspired by the stratigraphy of the Anthropocene, I mobilise the agency of stone to propel me into geological meanderings that challenge the empty and homogeneous linearity of the colonial chronotope, and present a stratigraphic version of time that is multiple, embedded, embodied and more-than-human.

Conflicting chronotopes

Pulitzer Prize winner John McPhee famously allegorised human history on the planet as the sliver of a fingernail, stating that if one were to stretch their arms out to represent 4.6 billion years, with 'a single stroke with a medium-grained nail file you could eradicate human history'.

These kind of allegories are often used to emphasise species humility – to prompt us to recognise that the earth does not belong to us alone, and that our human history pales into insignificance in the face of the vast evolutionary history and deep time of the planet.[11] But I think there is an internal paradox that inhabits McPhee's statement – that the fingernail actually argues against the idea that human history sits on top, or at the edge, of deep time. Time is not linear, but embodied and embedded.

Looking at my claw-like fingernails, I am reminded that my body is the result of millennia of coevolution in a creaturely world. In our fingernails – in our very flesh – is a record of our deep co-evolutionary past. We are what Deborah Bird Rose calls 'embodied knots of multispecies time'.[12]

Humans are thought to have evolved fingernails as a kind of flattened claw, when they first began using stone tools. Stone is an agent in the evolution of a biological species – a species that, in the era of the Anthropocene, will now leave its own mark recorded in an archive of stone. Our bodies are in dialogue and co-created with the crust of the earth and so our fingernails take us back to the beginnings of our planet, and remain, as I run them along the granulated surface of a stone monument, an immanent presence.

Benedict Anderson argues that the time of a nation-state is homogeneous and empty, as the nation is perceived to move steadily through history.[13] In the colonial temporal monoculture, time appears to flow in a straight and predictable line from the past to the present and then to the future. As the future draws nearer, the past recedes, like images getting smaller in a rear-view mirror. This homogeneous linear time is politically inscribed with a discourse of progress that positions indigenous people in a 'historical catch-up position'[14] in order to maintain white cultural dominance.

In the era of the Anthropocene, the empty, homogeneous and linear time of human history has become entangled with geological time. Human flesh is folded into the stratigraphy of the planet, as our species will leave an 'event layer' that is set to become geologically significant over centennial or millennial time scales. Humanity is now archived chronostratigraphically, in what is described as 'time-rock units'.[15] This chronotope is not grounded in the linearity of nationalism, but in the aeonic history of coevolution in a creaturely world.

This aeonic chronotope has not emerged through the Anthropocene, but our newfound attunement to geological time prompts its contemplation. James Hatley has observed that the Anthropocene demands 'temporal discernment', as the human confronts coincident temporal frames of the geological and the biological and situates themselves in a creaturely world. Stone country has always been a record of the vibrant becoming of the event of life; each body, season and storm embedded in the stratigraphy like a fossil. Hatley writes:

> Storms…seas and wetlands, forests and prairies, winters and summers, dry and rainy seasons have been woven, geological era upon geological era, into the underlying depths of the ground upon which our earthly footsteps now find their way and into which our earthly remains are eventually to be consigned.[16]

Gazing at the rocky strata in the gorge country of my youth, I wonder what it means to think ourselves stratigraphically. Seeing myself recorded in an archive of rock for millennia forces a shift in perspective that dizzies the daily grind, slowing it to the rhythms of deep temporal erosion, like ancient rock to be ground down by the motion of oceans and rivers. All my daily labours and plans seem to unfurl in this vast temporal plain, where the total sum of the works of any individual life is destined for fossilisation and mineral decomposition in the granulated earth. This landscape demands a different mode of temporal cognition, outside linear historical thinking. The memory traces here are so ancient, the geology so vast, to position oneself in this expanse requires a glacial imagination.

In a stratigraphic chronotope our own stories and versions of history become part of the embedded stories of the planet – an aggregate of stories, layered through the material and semiotic interfaces of the world. Thinking stratigraphically could be a way of decolonising environments in the Anthropocene, because it requires attention to the immanent presence and agency of the past, which includes the sovereignty of Indigenous peoples and our entanglement with more-than-human life.

In the following discussion I trace a productive dialogue that emerges between stratigraphic, Anthropocene time and nationalistic time – between the deep fossil rhythms of stone country and the human carving of stone into colonial motifs. Interrogating the Standing Stone monument, I chart three movements which attempt to establish a temporal monoculture in my home region of the New England tablelands. The first movement is the erasure of ecological and social history prior to settlement and the dissemination of the fiction of *terra nullius* in its place. The second movement is the installation of new memories into this 'empty land', and the construction of a nationalistic time. The final movement is the ongoing maintenance of a temporal monoculture which ensures that the present time remains empty and anonymous rather than intimate and lived. This maintenance is predicated on the active denial of multiple temporal worlds and cross-cultural synchronicity.

Ultimately, I argue that while the temporal monoculture has been established to legitimise settler indigenaeity and sovereignty in Indigenous land, other rhythms are breaking out in the interludes between the metronomic repetition of colonial history and its fabrications.

Movement one: inventing a temporal *terra nullius*

As we enter Glen Innes from the New England highway a kitsch sign carved in the shape of Stonehenge declares 'Celtic Country'. The whole town feels like it's frozen in time. The streets house over thirty heritage-listed buildings, and the claim to Celtic beginnings is emphasised to motorists with the main street signs shown in both English and Scottish Gaelic.

The Standing Stone arrangement echoes Stonehenge, and is based on the Ring of Brodgar.[17] This Celtic symbolism is grafted onto the landscape. Rooted in local soil, and made from granite collected within a fifty-kilometre radius of Glen Innes, the monoliths punctuate the landscape like the letters of a creolised language. The monument contains a stone, called Australis, dedicated to all Australians: this 'stone marking the sunrise Summer Solstice, when taken with the North, South, East and West stones forms the Southern Cross' to give 'the array its unique Australian character'.[18] The Southern Cross appears on the Australian flag, helping the monument to enact a territorialising form of mimesis as even the stars are twisted into nation-building motifs.

The use of a material from the deep time of the continent seems to confer with the ancient origins of the original Celtic stone arrangements as the crust of Australian earth becomes mirror both to the night sky and to historical events from thousands of miles away, thousands of years ago. But this intended symmetry and rhythm is dissonant. In sculptured form this crustal origin is obscured as the granite is reshaped in the image of its Antipodean cousins. The stones are emptied of original meaning and story, creating a spatio-temporal *terra nullius*.

Terra nullius was the legal fiction that enabled British colonisers to take possession of Aboriginal land. The doctrine declared that Australia was an 'empty continent' in terms of ownership; it belonged to no one prior to its colonial settlement in 1788.[19] *Terra nullius* was founded on the denial of Indigenous agency and presence in the landscape. A temporal *terra nullius* applies the logic of an empty no man's land to time, which then becomes a vessel waiting to be filled with a colonial version of history.

Under the illusion of terra nullius the name 'Glen Innes' trumps 'Kindatchy' – an Aboriginal term for the region meaning 'plenty of stones'.[20] The lands of the Ngarabal people, the first inhabitants and traditional owners of the Glen Innes region, are now best known for an annual Celtic festival and simulacra of a Northern-hemisphere Neolithic monument. Instead of celebrating the multi-species and multicultural richness of this region, the millennial granite is carved into a theme park of monoliths which make a tenuous link to dissonant Celtic history.

The tourist information pamphlet explains that the process of gathering the Standing Stones from local material was long and arduous with hours spent 'in the bush drilling massive rocks'.[21] A local alderman by the name of George Rozynski developed a method, using a powder compound, of splitting the stones off from their larger rock bodies without explosives:

> 'The compound was...poured into the drill holes,' Mr Rozynski recalled. 'When we returned the next morning the rock was cracked...' It took more than six months of further effort...using a 12 tonne forklift and other heavy equipment to load and transport the stones on a timber loader to the Centennial Parklands site.[22]

The violent digging up, carving and erecting of the granite seems like a violation of the deep 'fossil murmur'[23] of the continent, an erasure of the temporal forces which have shaped the land.

The Standing Stone monument has a 'deep crustal origin'.[24] It is made of granite that tells the story of a shared creaturely existence on this planet as continental plates are composed in a significant part of strata into which has been poured the cadavers and other traces of entities of innumerable genera and species, as well as the perennial movements over aeons of the waters and the winds.[25]

These rocks are connected to the aeonic history of the earth – to the subterranean force of terrestrial existence. New England's granite outcrops and sharply cut cliffs tell the geological creation story of the continent:

> The New England tableland consists of ancient rocks planed down to a low-relief surface and then uplifted…with the opening of the Tasman Sea from about 80 million years ago. Granitic intrusions were eventually stripped of their cover to form stark outcrops such as the Moonbi Range in the south, Mount Duval near Armidale and Bald Rock near Tenterfield. After uplift between 50–30 million years ago, the ancient surface was blanketed with outpourings of flood lava from multiple local vents. Between twenty and fourteen million years ago, parts were also covered with lava from some of the great shield volcanoes surrounding New England…This preserved part of the ancient surface…down-cutting erosion has…formed the present east-flowing river system, which rolls sluggishly over the Tableland until it meets the gorges cutting back from the escarpment.[26]

New England granite played a key role 'in deciphering such mysteries as drifting continents and globally disjunctive flora and fauna distributions'.[27] Stone Country helped to give us the 1960s plate tectonic revolution that left us with Gondwanaland – a scientific creation story of Australia's super-continental origin. This shared geographic antiquity 'links Australia to world history' through terrestrial siblings of India, New Zealand, Antarctica, Africa and South America, 'making global connections well before the expansion of Europe'.[28] And as our continental provenance grew larger, Australian Aboriginal people grew older. At the beginning of the 1960s humans had occupied the continent for at least 13,000 years; by 1965 they had been here for over 30,000. By 1980 the country had 40,000 years of antiquity. Now, '[d]ates derived from thermo luminescence and optical luminescence have…extended the human occupation of Australia to 50–60,000 years before the present'.[29] The Australian continent is storied by a people with a Pleistocene past that penetrates geological time.[30]

The 38 granite monoliths of the Australian Standing Stone monument have been stripped of their connection to the rocky strata beneath Australian soil and to all the peoples and cultures and living beings whose blood and bones over the millennia have washed into this soil. This loss of deep time creates a temporal terra nullius which denies that 'even the smallest stone represents an amazing conjunction of earth forces'.[31]

Granite exiles

As I wandered among the Australian Standing Stone monument, I found myself wondering what the stones were saying, outside the prescriptive nation-building rhetoric carved on their surface. Severed from the body of Stone Country into alienated shards of granite, the stones stand in the landscape as exiles. The Celtic spiritual history that the monument mimics has also been torn from the Northern hemisphere and implanted into the South like the Australian convicts of the late eighteenth century. These diasporas are forced to stand as monuments to an anthropocentric dream. They epitomise the modern Australian fantasy of colonial mastery over Indigenous nature, 'a vision of progress continuously wrested from this country through torture and crucifixion'.[32]

Propped up like circus freaks, they are forced to testify to the power of settlers to carve up space and time into a glorified image of themselves. I could not help but think that these stones may be angry. And why wouldn't they be? Stephen Muecke observes that places have arguments that are 'immanent to the space itself'.[33] He says that 'the anger seeps out of the rocks and the ooze of drying waterholes'.[34] Sometimes we can't hear these arguments because we are convinced that human anger is all that matters.

Figure 3 A 'granite exile' at the Australian Standing Stones, Glen Innes, 2010

John Mathew explains that the process of splitting the granite from 'parent rock' caused the intricate markings on the edge of the stones. 'They are drill marks made in the splitting of the stones,' he explains. 'They rather add to their attraction. Attempts were made to try to erase the marks, but granite rock is unforgiving.'[35]

What is the scarification on this 'unforgiving' granite rock saying? What arguments do these carvings put forward? Fragmented from familial Stone Country, from 'parent rock', I think of the deep creaturely millennial womb from which this rock was born. I also can't help hearing an echo of the colonial fragmentation of Indigenous cultures and the shameful history of stolen generations where Australian Aboriginal children were separated from their families by the state.

These rocks have been torn out of their position in Indigenous stone country, and propped up to support colonial nationalism. Historian and philosopher Paul Carter argues that that 'to found the colony...was to embrace environmental amnesia; it was actively to forget what wisdom the ground, and its people, might possess'.[36] This process of 'unknowing' allows Indigenous place to become unknown empty space.[37] The coloniser deliberately forgets that the entire Australian landscape is mapped by Aboriginal stories, and 'that there has been no resolution to the question whose land? And whose stories can be told?'[38]

Movement two: installing new memories

The Standing Stones are a site for 'the simultaneous development of memory and amnesia'.[39] They are part of Australia's nation-building rhetoric that 'installs memory' while it 'enacts forgetting'.[40]

The main plaque tells us that the Standing Stones were opened on 1 February 1992 'In recognition of the involvement of the Celtic races in building the Australian nation'. What does it mean to say that the Australian nation was *built*? There is an implication here that before building operations began, the country did not exist. In this dedication the tract of land beneath the stones, and the entire pre-settlement continent itself, is evoked as an empty construction site – what Edward Casey describes as a 'modification of space...a modification that aptly can be called "site", that is, levelled-down, monotonous space for building or other human enterprises'.[41]

A chronological fracture

This spatial levelling-down is accompanied by a temporal rupture. Jay Arthur explains that colonisation was built on the idea of a 'chronological fracture'[42] in Australian time where the coloniser appears to 'start time again'.[43] After this chronological fracture, time is only found on one side of the colonial divide. Time is a quality that appears to belong only to the colonist, and the Indigene is left with *timelessness*.[44] Temporality then becomes a monoculture, belonging only in one form to one people after a designated moment of settlement. Nonhumans do not share the luxury of time, nor do Australian Aboriginal peoples.

In his sophisticated critique of anthropology's use of time to construct its Other, Johann Fabian argues that a logic of progress uses time politically to objectify cultures. The chronological fracture of Australian modernity leads to the practice of 'allachronism' – the casting of the Other into another time.[45] Allachronism allows for the 'simultaneity of the non-simultaneous', where things can exist at the same time but appear to belong to different worlds.[46] Subaltern historian Dipesh Chakrabarty gives the example of a 'medieval object' which we could hold in our hands yet still see 'a relic of a past world that is no longer there'. He adds that 'one could, in historicism, look at peasants the same way: as survivors from a dead world'.[47]

In Australia, Aboriginal people have been conceptualised as 'living relics of the stone age'.[48] Colonising discourse has attempted to write Aboriginal people into the geological time of the continent, its prehistory. Leaving aside the blatant racism of positioning contemporary people as ancient and primitive, thinking with geological strata presents a densely sedimented and spatialised lithic temporality, where time is layered, superimposed and coincident, challenging the fundamental coordinates of a linear colonial chronotope that allows for this 'denial of coevalness'.[49]

The stone age is marked by the use of stone as tools – the same evolutionary era that is said to have produced our fingernails. When holding a stone in one's hand, one is at once holding the object of an ancient world, an evolutionary becoming, and a material in the present. Time, in this sense, is not linear, but embedded in our environments, and embodied in our flesh. Human history does not sit at the precipice of linear time, as if it were possible to shave it off with a nail file like the sliver of a fingernail. A fingernail itself is in constant dialogue with deep time, and we ourselves, like the strata of the planet, carry in our flesh an accumulation of evolutionary moments – all those stones and all those tools and all those hours spent making them – that are gathered up into an emergent becomings, like ripples shifting into waves – waves that are embedded in us all.

A stone tool restructures the world, it is a technology crafted from an ancient reservoir of creaturely time that creates a field of future possibilities. Traditionally stone circles too were memory technologies, designed to carry information through time and across generations.

Lynne Kelly's extensive study of stone arrangements across the globe, *Knowledge and Power in Prehistoric Societies*, reveals how stone circles were used as mnemonic devices to transmit cultural knowledge, including important practical information on animal behaviour, plant properties, navigation and astronomy, genealogies, laws and trade agreements. Kelly notes that 'the Stonehenge complex of monuments, and megalithic monuments all over Britain and Ireland at the same time' were constructed as 'memory spaces'.[50] 'These monuments were places where the oral and material mnemonics served to aid the knowledge elite to retain power through control of knowledge'.[51]

In this mode, stone is a technology – a technology of our evolution that is embodied in our very fingernails, and a technology that becomes part of the mind, storing cultural memories. Stones are within us, embedded in our flesh and our cognitive circuits. We are always thinking with these structures that are entangled with cultural power dynamics – apparatuses that have cosmological implication. Stone circles are not quaint monuments, but worlds enacted – an ordering of temporal and spatial coordinates that communicates what reality we are inhabiting, what relationships are important and whose histories matter.

Whitening deep time

The Australian Standing Stone monument is built to do important colonial work, silencing minoritarian voices and ordering the landscape to reproduce it as a 'white possession'.[52]

The coloniser marks their arrival as the beginning of history – the starting of the clock[53] and the building of the nation, at the same time as they reach into the temporal depths of the continent to legitimise their historical sovereignty. Because settler nations have shallow roots, like Mr Cave in Murray Bail's *Eucalyptus*, there is a perceived need to temporalise settler presence to legitimise claims of belonging and sovereignty. Denis Byrne argues that this leads settler peoples to attempt to bond 'to the exotic terrain by sending roots down into the continent's past'.[54] One way to do this is to turn the past into a temporal monoculture, enabling colonial roots to take hold in the deep time of the continent.

The grey-hued monoliths of the Australian Standing Stones represent the 'whitening' of Australian deep time. The monument derives poetic power not simply from the mimesis of stone arrangements in Europe and the United Kingdom, but from the authenticity conferred by using local granite and moulding the earth's skeleton in the shape of an Anglo-Celtic myth. Cultural theorist Rob Garbutt uses the term 'white autochthony' to describe these attempts at settler indigenisation which usurp Aboriginal autochthony.[55]

The term autochthony is derived from the Classical Greek word *autochthon* meaning 'sprung from the land itself'[56] or 'children of the land itself'.[57] In Australia, claims of autochthony involve grafting displaced social practices and myths transported from England and Europe on to Australian lands. Garbutt explains that in Australia 'white autochthony' is:

> a type of cultural autochthony that collapses Australian settler culture and nature, people and place into a complex of material and imaginary relations between people, peoples and land. In Australia it takes its particular form by articulating cultural autochthony with practices and social orders transported from England and located within the Australian context.[58]

In the case of the Australian Standing Stones this grafting is then naturalised by the use of local material, which aims to smooth over the displaced effect of having a Celtic stone arrangement in the middle of native bush. The arduous and violent process of harvesting the stones from local sources can also be likened to the early colonial pioneering work of Australia that granted legitimacy to claims of an essentialist Australian identity. The process of 'building the nation' was necessarily difficult, and shaped the unique Australian character – just as the stones were chiselled from the rock, so too white Australian faces have been carved by the harshness of the land, the toughness of their labour: 'From the mixing of sweat and soil emerged the autochthonous birth of the pioneer.'[59] In a mixing of flesh and dirt, poetic Nativism is granted to colonial migrants through the imagined autochthonous provenance 'of a seed planted, of being a child of the soil, of coming from a place as distinct from the womb'.[60] In this process Australian settlers naturalised themselves to the land and became 'unmarked: the natives born to the nation, the locals'.[61]

In this process migrant origins are not forgotten, but instead are celebrated as part of the 'building of the nation'. This monument affirms an emplaced regional identity at the same time as it evokes a diasporic longing for homelands. For example, the plaque on the stone for Cornwall reads:

> The Cornish are a proud Celtic people and have a deep sense of belonging. Even when they leave their homeland there are invisible ties that bind them. This plaque is dedicated to all the Cornish pioneers and settlers that came to Australia.

The stones are mnemonic of lands once loved, now lost. Some visitors to the stones are alleged to have been overcome with feelings of nostalgia. John Keller tells of a Cornish couple that 'spoke of being teary-eyed' on their first early morning approach to the Standing Stones and on reading the dedicated plaques. They spoke, too, of Glen Innes as 'homecoming', and of 'feeling a deep sense of belonging'. Keller claims that this is a common experience for people of 'Celtic stock' for whom the stones have captured a 'clan essence'.[62]

Rob Garbutt explains that the process of white autochthony involves a form of 'forgetting one's arrival' in order to naturalise oneself in an Australian place, as 'having always been "from here"'.[63] At the Australian Standing Stones one's 'arrival' is forgotten by a peculiar move in which Celtic country is re-established in Indigenous land. Historian Tom Griffiths has observed that the desire of 'white locals' for 'deep-rootedness' in Australia has sparked a renewed interest in family history.[64] It does not seem to delegitimise claims of localness that these explorations often 'uncover a geographical identity that always leads away from intricate rootedness confined to Australian soil towards a succession of places across oceans and towards a complex multi-sited identity based on migration'.[65] This is because the places from which settlers have migrated have been reconstructed in the Antipodes, and time and space before colonisation has been conceptually levelled out to become an empty construction site – an *unland*[66] – which did not really exist until 'Celtic stock' began to build the nation. This allows for the construction of a temporal monoculture in which colonial history dominates all other temporalities of place.[67]

White multiculturalism

Rob Garbutt's concept of white autochthony slots into a larger body of whiteness theory which interrogates the construction of whiteness as part of a racialised hierarchy. This theory posits that whiteness is not a fixed racial category, but an ongoing production of privilege, with certain groups 'qualifying' as 'white' at different times.[68]

Whiteness contains many unexpressed presumptions and exclusion clauses: must be English-speaking, must be of a certain class, must have a certain genetic background. These exclusions have functioned politically to articulate whiteness as a state of Anglo-Celtic privilege within Australian culture. The Immigration Restriction Act of 1901, widely known as the 'White Australia' policy, limited the immigration of 'non-Europeans' and 'coloured races' before World War II.[69] This Anglo-Celtic dominance continued even after the White Australia policy was dismantled, supported by an official assimilation rhetoric that insisted 'new Australians' be absorbed socially and culturally into the mainstream Anglo-Australian community.[70]

At the inauguration of the Standing Stones the governor of New South Wales, Peter Sinclair, stated:

> As we move further down the path of a diverse multi-cultural society, the Australian Celtic communities are providing a wonderful example as to how pride in cultural origins and pride in being Australian can be exercised freely together without detriment to either. The Australian Standing Stones will further that proud reputation.[71]

This claim extols cultural diversity while at the same time putting boundaries around what counts as welcome diversity. It excludes and marginalises those from non-Anglo-Celtic backgrounds.

Whiteness studies scholar David Roediger notes that whiteness is defined by the 'absence of marked culture'[72] and Rob Garbutt argues that white autochthony also has 'the unmarked form of whiteness'.[73] The Standing Stones are unusually positioned within this discourse because they celebrate Celtic ethnicity as distinct from Australian whiteness.

If, as whiteness studies theorist Anne Brewster has observed, giving up ethnic markers is part of the process of accruing whiteness, then the Standing Stones' celebration of ethnicity could be read as a decolonising move toward multiculturalism. This positive reading of the Stones is undermined, however, by the way the Stones 'Celticise' the Glen Innes region, or, one might say, 'Celt-wash' its ethnically diverse history, while ensuring that the Celticity that is celebrated affirms White Australian values.

The Chairman of the Glen Innes Celtic Foundation gave directions that the Stones were to be exclusively Christian, and would not be the location of any Pagan rituals: 'It had never been intended, and never will be, that the object of the Standing Stones project is to conduct heathen rites.'[74] The four cardinal stones of the monument are said to represent 'the Cross on which Christ died for all of us'.[75] This ambiguous, yet totalising, 'all of us' excludes other faiths and spirituality from the place. On the day of the monument's opening Malcolm Brown Q.C., Chairman of the Scottish Australian Heritage Council, said the Lord's Prayer in Gaelic and the stones were blessed by the Rev. Charles Abel, New South Wales Moderator of the Presbyterian Church,[76] ritually activating the stones to exclude marginalised spiritualities.

The colonising impact of Christianity has had a devastating effect on Aboriginal spirituality and traditions in the New England region. Anaiwan Elder Steve Widders expressed the depth of this communal and personal loss:

> In the old days the men were told they weren't allowed to talk their language, they had to start learning English and weren't allowed to go and have their ceremony. They had to go to the church, you know, the church the missionaries came and set up. They said, 'You have to learn our way'. So with that, that's a big disappointment with me, because even though I'm part of this land, I would have liked to have gone through the stages that my grandfather did. And that's where it stopped, and part of your identity's gone.[77]

The Publicity Notes for the Standing Stones adopt a legal understanding of the Aboriginal sacred which denies the impact of this loss:

> It is important to note that the Australis Stone was originally intended to be a stone for the Australian Aborigines, suitably named. The local Land Council was approached, and the matter discussed, an invitation being extended to them to be involved. After deliberations amongst themselves, they agreed, only to withdraw later. They did assure us, however, that we were not encroaching on any sacred site and wished us well.[78]

The encysting of the Aboriginal sacred to contained sites can be understood, in part, as a white hegemonic practice that spatially and temporally marginalises Aboriginal identity and sovereignty in Australia. By 'offering' to name a stone after 'the Aborigines', settler white Australians engage in a dialectic of inclusion and exclusion which ensures they remain in control of Australian space, despite the underlying, unacknowledged tension of Aboriginal sovereignty. In this sense the stones reproduce what Ghassan Hage calls a 'white national fantasy of multicultural tolerance',[79] enacting a form of 'symbolic violence in which a mode of domination is presented as a form of egalitarianism'.[80]

That the 'Australis' Stone, named after the nation-state, and not any local Aboriginal nation or language group, was intended to be 'a stone for the Australian Aborigines' demonstrates the way Aboriginality is simplified and homogenised in settler discourse. Instead of acknowledging Ngarabal people, recognising the land as being sacred to these traditional owners, and lamenting the violent processes of colonisation that have scarred the country and fragmented the culture, there is a vague statement about the presence of the generic 'Aborigine' in 'Australia: The Nation'.

It is significant that there is very little celebration of Aboriginality in Glen Innes. The local Land of Beardies Museum, for instance, has a Celtic room but no reference to Aboriginal history.[81] Cultural theorist Katrina Schlunke analyses the uneasy exclusions involved in the establishment of settler indigeneity in Australia. She writes that, within the discourse of 'being a local', a real 'born and bred' local must have connections to the colonial history of the place they claim to belong to. 'These colonial proofs exclude Aboriginal people of the area who, in a bizarre, carnivalesque manoeuvre, are too local to be "local".'[82] The whitening of deep time involves a colonisation of the past into time immemorial.

Aboriginal author Melissa Lucashenko commented that white Australian people sometimes tell her they belong 'because their family has been here, in their narrow terms, "forever"'.[83] This version of 'forever' is crucial to the colonial chronotope of the Australian nation-state, and it indicates the presence of a temporal monoculture that has attempted to whiten deep time and colonise all other temporal worlds. The more-than-human cycles of birth, death and regeneration, the millennial movements of granite, the emplaced temporalities of Aboriginal Australian nations, all succumb to a colonial version of time which privileges the white autochthon.

Movement three: preventing multi-temporal synchronicity

It is noteworthy that Indigenous Australians produced their own stone arrangements constructed from local granite throughout the New England tableland region. In 1963 local archaeologist Isabel McBryde reported on a series of stone arrangements discovered near the Serpentine River in the Ebor district. She argued that 'the systematic arrangement of stones, either in cairns, mounds, or in ordered patterned lines' is an accepted aspect of Aboriginal culture and 'part of the living traditions of the tribes concerned'.[84] These sites were often sacred 'Bora grounds or initiation grounds'.[85]

These local Indigenous stone arrangements are not mentioned anywhere in the tourist dialogue surrounding the Standing Stones, and that conspicuous absence can be understood in light of the granite's indoctrination into amnesiac colonial history. Katrina Schlunke writes on the way colonial culture disciplines material in order to control and limit its mnemonic resonance, practising 'tactics of isolation and separation from the people and place of which it remains a part'.[86]

Stratigraphic resurgence

Recent research into Aboriginal astronomy has uncovered stone arrangements in New South Wales that align to approximate cardinal directions, with evidence that these cardinal points were found by Indigenous Australian people by using the positions of astronomical bodies.[87] Aboriginal Australian people, too, were using stone to mirror the night sky, but this astronomical stone to sky cosmology was not grounded in nationalism, in the ritual celebration of the Southern Cross constellation that sings up the Australian flag, but instead functioned as a cultural technology to pass on vital information gathered over tens of thousands of years of habitation on the continent. It has recently been revealed that significant parts of Australia's highway network trace Aboriginal star maps that were used as memory technologies for navigation before colonisation. Robert Fuller explains:

> The pattern of the stars showed the 'waypoints' on the route. These way-points were usually waterholes or turning places on the landscape. These waypoints were used in a very similar way to navigating with a GPS, where waypoints are also used as stopping or turning points... These directions would no doubt reflect the easiest routes to traverse, and these were probably routes already established as songlines. Drovers and settlers coming into the region would have used the same routes, and eventually these became tracks and finally highways.[88]

Ghassan Hage has observed that 'Western modernity's greatest "achievement" has been to make us monorealists', but he notes that minor realities 'continuously make an incursion into our modern world, giving us a hint – sometimes more than a hint – of their presence'.[89] On the road in stone country, I find it incredible to think that even the territorialising infrastructure and motions of automobility trace the 'deep narrative lines' of Indigenous cultures. Gilles Deleuze writes that 'the world is made up of superimposed surfaces, archives or strata'[90], and notes that in '*stratigraphic* time... "before" and "after" indicate only an order of superimpositions'.[91] Aboriginal knowledges are embedded in stone country, not as 'stone age' – a past receding; but as 'stone agent' – a past resurfacing; as if it were ancient strata that can be uplifted by seismic shifts of consciousness. Gilles Deleuze and Felix Guattari write:

> Mental landscapes do not change haphazardly through the ages: a mountain had to rise here or a river to flow by there again recently for the ground, now dry and flat, to have a particular appearance and texture. It is true that very old strata can rise to the surface again, can cut a path through the formations that covered them and surface directly on the current stratum to which they impart a new curvature...[92]

Claire Colebrook, building on Deleuze's concept of stratigraphic time, observes that the linear time of history 'presupposes a time in which the past is *only actual* – a set of archived and stored events that have occurred and been completed – rather than a permanently pregnant (*virtual*) past that harbours potentials that may be seized upon in each present, and that never arrive at absolute fulfilment'.[93] Positioning ourselves stratigraphically acknowledges the past as an agential and ongoing presence, a past that 'may harbor potentials to which we are not yet attuned'.[94]

Widders paddock and Cohen's paddock

In the totalising movements which construct the temporal monoculture, the stratigraphic, synchronous presence of Aboriginal culture and the agency of Aboriginal peoples disappear. New England poet Judith Wright lamented the impact of colonisation in her poem 'Bora Ring':

> The song is gone; the dance
> is secret with the dancers in the earth,
> the ritual useless, and the tribal story
> lost in an alien tale.

Poet and critic Stuart Cooke notes that Wright's poem concerns the '[buried] prehistory of the nation-state'.[95] It is not about 'terrestrial' people who share our place and time, but about 'subterranean people' who 'rise up from the bowels of the earth', and then return to their archaeological home.[96] Wright's 'Bora Ring' perpetuates the illusion of a temporal monoculture by conceptually removing Aboriginal people from the landscape and encysting Aboriginal culture into a timeless prehistory. This linear vision of destruction and replacement ignores the active and ongoing presence of Aboriginal people. In fact, Wright's New England life-world was densely populated by Aboriginal people, who were by no means subterranean. And nor were they strangers; all the New England Elders I spoke with held Wright's Wollomombi pastoral family in high regard.

Aboriginal Elder and former New England councillor Margaret Walford spoke of the extensive farmland where Wright grew up as a place where she felt a close connection because her grandfather spent many years living and working as a stockman with the Wrights.

> Grandfather Jack Cohen worked out at Wongwibinda – he worked out there from the 1890s, and he had many, many years there. He was part of the Wright family – the rich Wrights. He lived with them and helped rear their kids and all that. So to me that's very special. Every time I go to the coast and go past that way, I say, 'Oh fancy my grandfather rode his own white horse all over that country over there' – and huge it is. So it's very special to me because he was working and living there as one of the family…he was there with all the Wright kids. So that place out there is very special, and Mum always talked about it, about Grandfather working there.

The depth of Margaret's feeling of attachment to this piece of pastoral land is demonstrated by her efforts to memorialise her grandfather's presence in the area:

> I am negotiating with the council to get a recognition of him and put a big plaque down at Georges Creek, and a photo of him on his white horse, and

then all the information about how he worked at Wongwibinda, and he travelled down to Georges Creek, and he had his little shack there, and then he used to ride up the mountain to Kunderang station in the hills...

Grandfather Jack Cohen's active movement through this colonial settler landscape mounts a serious challenge to the vision of Aboriginal identity as prehistoric. His collaborative engagement with the Wright family is an example of the lived presence and synchronous experiences of Aboriginal Australians and English settlers in the region.

New England Elder and Anaiwan-descendent Steve Widders also spoke of Wollomombi as a personal place of belonging and connection to land. He explained that while he hasn't been there himself he feels connected by historical ties between his Aboriginal family and the Wrights: 'I can connect with the place because the old fellas used to live there, and they had a long association with that family down at Kunderang there, with the Cohens and the Widders.'

The collaborative engagement between the families was shaped by colonisation – the Wrights employed the Aboriginal people as workers, but the relationship was mutualistic and respectful. Steve explained that:

The Wright elders had a strong connection with the Aboriginal people, always made sure they had their land right, that they practiced their traditions and everything on the land. They allowed them to do that and, in later years, employed a lot of them. My grandfather's brothers – they practically lived out there because they were allowed to.

Steve emphasised to me that his family was very special to the Wright people. This is reflected in the naming of two paddocks – one is named Widders Paddock, and one is named Cohen Paddock.

The idea of paddocks of pastoral land being named after Aboriginal workers from the early twentieth century offers a timely and welcome reminder that the colonial temporal monoculture is only part of the story. As Baden Offord observes, contemporary Australians occupy two distinct sociocultural environments. One is 'monoculturally bound and historically and contextually institutionalised' while the other is 'the everyday reality of a multicultural environment where alterity frames ongoing encounters'.[97]

Colonial narratives of progress misrepresent the actual lives of people in New England as monocultural. Aboriginal people are part of the colonial history of the region, moving in synchrony with settlers, not only as victims, but as active participants. Illusions of a dying race, the mantle of Autochthony being passed, dissipate in this polychronic sharing of time in place.

What these paddocks also demonstrate is that there was nothing natural or inevitable about the destruction of Aboriginal Australian culture. Deborah Bird Rose has observed that social Darwinism popular in late nineteenth and early twentieth century thought posited a telos of human progress and civilisation which saw the disappearance of cultures as part of 'the inevitable (natural) tide of history', and envisioned an 'end of history' where the world would be populated by a 'human monoculture'.[98] The human monoculture, like the temporal monoculture, is an illusion based on the colonisation of time in the past, present and future. In colonial Australian discourse Aboriginal people were positioned 'at the bottom of the evolutionary or developmental rung', understood to be at 'the dawn or childhood of humanity'.[99] Rose explains that this enabled colonisers to feel that the deaths they inflicted on Aboriginal people were an inevitable reality of progress and civilisation, and that whatever cultural destruction 'they did not complete, nature or history would complete for them'.[100] And yet, the paddocks are there. The Widders and Cohen descendants are there. The Elders spoke to me of their continuing presence in the land as the continuation of culture, and linked their lives and deaths to the land as an ancestral home.

PAT COHEN: I think it's the land, it's our home, and a lot of our loved ones are buried here that have passed on. And I feel, I wasn't born here, I was born about fifty k's down the road a bit, but...

LORNA HAGUE: But your people walked upon the land, didn't they, everywhere. All of our people did.

PAT COHEN: I want to die here. I want to be buried here.

CHRISTINA KIM: And I've been here ever since, and I'll die here.

STEVE WIDDERS: It's my place. It's my home. And like Aunty Chrissy, this will be my last resting place as well. It's always been home.

Time is embodied and embedded as an immanent presence in the earth as individuals connect their lives and deaths to deep aeonic ancestral rhythms.

At the official opening ceremony for the Standing Stones, New South Wales Governor Peter Sinclair made an intriguing observation. He said:

> I wonder as I see these New England granite stones, whether people visiting the site in two to three thousand years' time will understand their origins – or whether the same mystery will surround them as it does with Stonehenge and the Ring of Brodgar. And are these stones likely to outlive all other evidence of our civilisation in centuries to come, as have other Standing Stones of previous centuries?[101]

The projected future indecipherability of the Stones is a great instance of metonymy in the construction of histories and futures; here the Stones are given the job of anchoring in granite a vision of the transience of cultures based in linear time. Sinclair's evocation of the inevitable tide of history wearing down the Standing Stones, like Shelley's Ozymandias, fails to recognise that the destruction of Neolithic civilisations in Europe was not inevitable, but the outcome of invasion and colonisation. Transience is not a natural flow of time, but a mode of conquest. The mystery that enshrouds the Standing Stones of Europe also enshrouds Aboriginal stone arrangements in New England, for many of the same reasons.

Looking at the layered marking on the side of the stones, a scarification from their violent separation from 'parent rock', I cannot help but think of the way humans are now recorded as a chronotopic event in the stratigraphy of the Anthropocene. As humans increasingly think themselves with the fossilised crust of the planet, another discourse could form around the stones – like a shifting constellation around a star. If the Anthropocene prompts attention to the deeper rhythms of a creaturely world, rather than narcissistic histories built on hyper-separation, the Standing Stones may start to rhyme with deep co-evolutionary time, a poem composed with the cadence not of colonial seasons of conquest, but with epochs and aeons.

The coordinates of knowledge/power embodied in this material memory technology are not fixed, but shifting, in response to alternative temporal models that attune us to different modes of dwelling in time. Katrina Schlunke notes that material 'can emerge as a particular kind of disruption to a colonial culture that has used material artefacts to mark other strict divides between the Indigenous and the modern, past and present, and between indigenous ownership and white possession'.[102]

With the glacial imagination prompted by the emergence of the Anthropocene chronotope, encounter with a historical monument becomes an encounter with the stone within – the stone that is an agent for our evolution – the stone that helped carve our fingernails and social systems – the stone as a mnemonic technology that is part of our ecology of mind – and the stone into which a memory of our species is forever consigned.

Just as the fingernail inhabits Joseph McPhee's deep time allegory like a parasitical paradox – a Trojan horse attack against linear temporality – so too the stones inhabit the monument as an inherent argument against it. In constellations of deep time awoken by the Anthropocene, where mirroring the stars is not mirroring a nationalistic Southern Cross, but the vast cosmological order of a universe held in an aggregate of stories, the stones slip from their confinement in territorialising symbols. Embodying deep multispecies, multinatural time, the stones make different arguments, tell different tales and keep different minutes.

Conclusion: uninhabited time

As I look now at a photograph of my mother dwarfed by the Standing Stone array I recognise an irrevocable sadness in the Standing Stone monument and its landscaped surrounds. I keep looking at the grass and not the stones – that levelled-out, sprinkler-watered ground where all Indigenous and creaturely stories have been razed for the construction of a temporal monoculture.

The temporal monoculture of settler Australia is built on a regime of progress which devalues the lived experience of the present. Within this empty linear time, we live in what Deborah Bird Rose has termed the 'disjunctive moment':

Figure 4 Mum at the Australian Standing Stones, Glen Innes, 2010

> The present becomes a place in which we are estranged from the actual conditions of our lives, where agency is alienated, responsibility cast elsewhere, and morality subjected to a double deflection as it aims towards a future which will, in due course, become the past.[103]

From within this temporal monoculture it is impossible to actually inhabit time, just as one cannot truly inhabit an airport. Time is always on the move to somewhere else, and the present moment is not a site of 'lived' or 'liveable' time. Settler alienation is not only a detachment from place, but also a condition of living out of time, disconnected from the rhythms of a multi-temporal world. Being connected to history and place by displaced symbols, more than by lived and embodied experience, is the condition of a people unable to inhabit the present, living lives as passengers, always passing through, trapped on the surface, never quite tapping into the deeper rhythms.

Sitting in Crofters Cottage, a cramped café by the Standing Stones, I'm surrounded by tartan and waiting for a pastie. My Irish partner and my Mum are poking through souvenirs. In the discourse of white autochthony and Celtic genealogy, mass-produced tea-towels become genetic markers, evidence of belonging to a prestigious bloodline that founded the nation. *No thanks, Mum, I don't want one.*

As our car pulls away from the stones, I fumble in my bag to find the map from the visitor information centre. The ink-printed road is colour-dotted with more sites to see. We follow the highway as it curls up ahead through the tableland, unaware that we are tracing an ancient map recorded in the stars.

Notes

1 Glen Innes Tourism, 'Australian Standing Stones Brochure', Glen Innes and Severn Shire Tourist Association, www.gleninnestourism.com/pages/australian-standing-stones/, accessed 15 November, 2012.
2 J. Keller, 'The Celticising of Glen Innes', *Australian Folklore* 16 (2001), 203. My emphasis.
3 See D. Rose, *Wild Country*, 37. These ideas are further developed in relation to seasonality in New England in Chapter 4.
4 M. Bakhtin, *The Dialogic Imagination* (Austin: University of Texas Press, 1981), 84.
5 D. Rose, *Wild Country*, 37.
6 B. Anderson, *Imagined Communities* (London & New York: Verso, 1991), 6.
7 Ibid., 6.
8 Bakhtin, *Dialogic Imagination*, 7.
9 For more on the agricultural implications of monocultures see Chapter 3.
10 I. Newton, Scholium to the Definitions in *Philosophiae Naturalis Principia Mathematica*, Bk. 1 (1689), trans. A. Motte and rev. F. Cajori (Berkeley: University of California Press, 1934), 6–12, http://plato.stanford.edu/entries/newton-stm/scholium.html.
11 In a similar vein, astrophysicist Carl Sagan famously condensed cosmic history into a solar year, with the big bang on the first day of January, the Milky Way arriving 1 May, earth's oldest rocks 2 October and dinosaurs thundering across the continents on Christmas Eve, departing four days later. Modern humans make their belated appearance on New Year's Eve, with mere minutes separating the Crusades (all of them) from the first manned flight to the moon.
12 D. Rose, 'Multispecies Knots of Ethical Time', *Environmental Philosophy* 9, no. 1 (2012): 127–140.
13 B. Anderson, *Imagined Communities*, 25.
14 S. Muecke, *Ancient and Modern: Time, Culture and Indigenous Philosophy* (Sydney: University of New South Wales Press, 2004), 8.
15 J. Zalasiewiczi et al. 'Stratigraphy of the Anthropocene', *Philosophical Transactions of the Royal Society* 369 (2011): 1038.
16 J. Hatley, 'The Virtue of Temporal Discernment: Rethinking the Extent and Coherence of the Good in a Time of Mass Species Extinction', *Environmental Philosophy* 9, no. 1 (2012) 1.
17 The Ring of Brodgar is a Neolithic stone circle on the Mainland, the largest island of Orkney, Scotland. It is listed as a UNESCO World Heritage Site.
18 J. Ryan and J. S. Tregurtha, 'Standing at the Array: A Celtic Tradition Re-enacted at Glen Innes, New South Wales', *Australian Folklore* 7 (1992): 73.
19 The silencing of Indigenous rights and sovereignty enabled the myth of settler Australians as 'first possessors' to be consummated. The doctrine of *terra nullius* was overturned in law following the Mabo decision of 1992. In the High Court case of *Mabo and Others v The State of Queensland*, Indigenous people of the Murray Islands were determined to retain title to their land that had been annexed to the colony of Queensland in 1879. This established native title in common law (see B. David, M. Langton & I. McNiven, 'Re-inventing the Wheel', *Philosophy, Activism, Nature* 2 (2002): 35). Despite this, overhangs of the *terra nullius* doctrine persist in Australian society and the denial of Indigenous sovereignty is ongoing.
20 B. Kennedy, *Australian Place Names* (Sydney: ABC Books, 2006), 111.
21 Glen Innes Tourism, 'Australian Standing Stones Brochure'.
22 Ibid.

23 J. Baudrillard, *America* (London and New York: Verso, 2010), 6.
24 W. Pitcher, *The Nature and Origin of Granite* (London: Chapman and Hall, 1993), 341.
25 J. Hatley, 'Temporal Discernment'.
26 R. Haworth, 'The Rocks Beneath', in *High Lean Country: Land, People and Memory in New England*, edited by A. Atkinson, J. S. Ryan, I. Davidson and A. Piper (Crows Nest: Allen and Unwin, 2006), 24–25.
27 Ibid., 27.
28 T. Griffiths, 'Deep Time and Australian History', *History Today* 51, no. 11 (2001): 25.
29 Ibid., 21.
30 Ibid., 25.
31 V. Plumwood, 'Heart of Stone', 20.
32 D. Rose, *Wild Country*, 65.
33 S. Muecke, 'Can You Argue with the Honeysuckle?' in *Halfway House: The Poetics of Australian Spaces*, edited by J. Rutherford and B. Holloway (Crawley: UWA Publishing, 2010), 34.
34 Ibid., 34–35.
35 J. H. Mathew D Ua, *The History of the Australian Standing Stones* (Glen Innes: The Australian Standing Stones Management Board, 2012), 21.
36 P. Carter, *The Lie of the Land* (London and Boston: Faber and Faber, 1996), 6. Carter conceptualises the white invasion and territorialisation of Australia as a form of 'spatial writing' which erased earlier Indigenous meanings. He argues that from within this erasure settlement 'became a question of giving back to a desolated, because depopulated, land a lost significance' (Carter, *The Road to Botany Bay: An Essay in Spatial History* (London: Faber and Faber, 1987), 165).
37 J. Arthur, *Default Country*, 54.
38 M. Somerville, *Body/Landscape*, 5.
39 R. Garbutt, S. Biermann and B. Offord, 'Into the Borderlands', 64.
40 Ibid., 73.
41 E. Casey, *The Fate of Place: A Philosophical History* (Berkeley: University of California Press, 1997), x.
42 J. Arthur, *Default Country*, 46.
43 Ibid., 44.
44 Ibid., 46.
45 J. Fabian, *Time and the Other: How Anthropology Makes its Object* (New York & Sussex: Columbia University Press, 2002), xii
46 D. Chakrabarty, 'The Time of History and the Times of Gods', in *The Politics of Culture in the Shadow of Capital*, eds. L. Lowe and D. Lloyd (Durham: Duke University Press, 1997), 29.
47 Ibid., 49.
48 K. Gelder and M. Jacobs, *Uncanny Australia*, 71.
49 J. Fabian, *Time and the Other*.
50 L. Kelly, *Knowledge and Power in Prehistoric Societies: Orality, Memory and the Transition of Culture* (Cambridge University Press: New York 2015), 233.
51 Ibid.
52 A. Moreton-Robinson, 'Introduction', in *Sovereign Subjects: Indigenous Sovereignty Matters*, ed. A. Moreton-Robinson (Crows Nest: Allen and Unwin, 2007), 2.
53 J. Arthur, *Default Country*, 52.
54 D. Byrne, '*Deep Nation*: Australia's Acquisition of an Indigenous Past', *Aboriginal History* 20 (1996): 82.
55 R. Garbutt, 'White "Autochthony"', ACRAWSA e-journal 2, no. 1 (2006): 3, www.acrawsa.org.au/files/ejournalfiles/88RobGarbutt.pdf.
56 A. Delbridge cited in R. Garbutt, 'White "Autochthony"', 2.
57 Isocrates cited in R. Garbutt, 'White "Autochthony", 2.

58 R. Garbutt, 'White "Autochthony"', 9.
59 Ibid., 10.
60 R. Garbutt, 'Local Order', M/C Journal of Media and Culture 7, no. 6 (2005): http:// journal.media-culture.org.au/0501/08-garbutt.php.
61 R. Garbutt, 'White "Autochthony"', 6.
62 J. Keller, 'The Celticising of Glen Innes', 207.
63 R. Garbutt, 'The Locals: A Critical Survey of the Idea in Recent Australian Scholarly Writing', *Australian Folklore* 21 (2006): 174.
64 T. Griffiths, *Hunters and Collectors: The Antiquarian Imagination in Australia* (Melbourne: Cambridge University Press, 1996), 224.
65 Garbutt, 'The Locals', 178.
66 J. Arthur, *Default Country*, 85.
67 Rob Garbutt has observed that settler Australians have no language for perceiving their arrival as migration. The migrant is always the Other that came after from somewhere else ('Towards an Ethics of Location', in *Landscapes of Exile*, eds. A. Haebich and B. Offord (Bern: Peter Lang, 2008), 179). The similarities between 'boat people' of now and 'boat people' that settled in the late eighteenth century are vehemently denied in Australian cultural discourse. Cultural theorist Katrina Schlunke claims that this is because the migrant possesses a threatening 'sameness' that could decentre the white subject of normative multiculturalism and destabilise a supposedly 'settled' post-invasion Australia. The refugee is a spectre that activates white settler anxiety, a reminder that 'others can become Australians by arriving and staying' ('Sovereign Hospitalities?', *Borderlands* 1, no. 2 (2002): www.borderlands. net.au/vol1no2_2002/schlunke_hospitalities.html).
68 Australian Critical Race and Whiteness Studies Editorial Committee, 'About', on ACRAWSA's website (January 2012), www.acrawsa.org.au/about/.
69 J. Stratton and I. Ang. 'Multicultural Imagined Communities: Cultural Difference and National Identity in Australia and the USA', *Continuum: The Australian Journal of Media and Culture*, 8, no. 2 (1994): wwwmcc.murdoch.edu.au/ReadingRoom/8.2/ Stratton.html.
70 C. Simpson, R. Murawska and A. Lambert, 'Introduction: Rethinking Diasporas – Australian Cinema, History and Society', in *Diasporas of Australian Cinema*, eds. C. Simpson, R. Murawska and A. Lambert (Bristol & Chicago: Intellect, 2009), 18.
71 P. Sinclair, cited in J. Ryan & J. Tregurtha, 'Standing at the Array', 76.
72 D. Roediger, *Towards the Abolition of Whiteness: Essays on Race, Politics and Working Class History* (London & New York: Verso, 1994), 196.
73 R. Garbutt, 'White "Autochthony"', 6.
74 J. Connell and B. Rugendyke, 'Creating an Authentic Site? The Australian Standing Stones, Glen Innes', *Australian Geographer* 41, no. 1 (2010): 92.
75 J. Tregurtha, cited in J. Ryan and J. Tregurtha, 'Standing at the Array', 74.
76 J. Ryan and J. Tregurtha, 'Standing at the Array', 74–75.
77 Elder Pat Cohen told me that the last traditional initiation ceremonies in the New England tableland area were held in 1932 in Bellbrook.
78 Cited in J. Ryan & J. Tregurtha, 'Standing at the Array', 72.
79 G. Hage, *White Nation: Fantasies of White Supremacy in a Multicultural Society* (Pluto Press: Annandale, 1998), 101.
80 G. Hage, *White Nation*, 87.
81 J. Connell and B. Rugendyke, 'Creating an Authentic Tourist Site?', 99.
82 K. Schlunke, *Bluff Rock: Autobiography of a Massacre* (Fremantle: Curtin University Books, 2005), 43.
83 M. Lucashenko, 'All My Relations: Being and Belonging in Byron Shire', in *Landscapes of Exile*, eds. A. Haebich and B. Offord (Bern: Peter Lang AG, International Academic Publishers, 2008), 65.

84 I. McBryde, *Aboriginal Prehistory in New England: An Archaeological Survey of Northeastern New South Wales* (Sydney: Sydney University Press, 1974), 137.

85 Ibid., 138.

86 K. Schlunke, 'One Strange Colonial Thing: Materian Remembering and the Bark Shield of Botany Bay', *Continuum: Journal of Media & Cultural Studies* 27, no. 1 (2013).

87 D.W. Hamacher, R.S. Fuller and R.P. Norris, 'Orientations of Linear Stone Arrangements in New South Wales', *Australian Archaeology* 75 (2012): 46–54.

88 R. Fuller, 'How Ancient Aboriginal Star Maps have Shaped Australia's Highway Network', *The Conversation* 2016: https://theconversation.com/how-ancient-aboriginal-star-maps-have-shaped-australias-highway-network-55952.

89 G. Hage, *Alter-Politics: Critical Anthropology and the Radical Imagination* (Melbourne: Melbourne University Press, 2015), 47.

90 G. Deleuze, *Foucault*, trans. and ed. Seán Hand (New York & London: Continuum, 2006), 98.

91 G. Deleuze and F. Guattari, *What is Philosophy?* (Verso: London & New York, 1994).

92 Ibid.

93 C. Colebrook, 'Stratigraphic Time, Women's Time', *Australian Feminist Studies* 25, no. 59 (2009): 12.

94 Ibid., 12.

95 S. Cooke, 'Speaking the Earth's Languages', 41.

96 S. Cooke, 'Speaking the Earth's Languages', 41, citing G. Deleuze and F. Guattari, *A Thousand Plateaus*, 375.

97 B. Offord, 'Landscapes of Exile', 10.

98 D. Rose, 'Aboriginal Life and Death in Australian Settler Nationhood', *Aboriginal History* 25 (2001): 152.

99 B. David, M. Langton and I. McNiven, 'Re-Inventing the Wheel', 37.

100 D. Rose, 'Aboriginal Life and Death', 152.

101 Cited in J. Ryan and J. Tregurtha, 'Standing at the Array', 76.

102 K. Schlunke, 'One Strange Thing', 19.

103 D. Rose, *Wild Country*, 18.

2 Encounters – a road trip through stone country

Like many colonial descended people across the globe, my places of intimate habitation are scarred by a genocidal and ecocidal past. The little block of land where I grew to understand myself and the world was stolen from a people who were targeted for annihilation. This deeply uncomfortable awareness calls upon me to engage in what Deborah Bird Rose terms 'recuperative work',[1] as an act of place fidelity – to be true to the original storying of the place where my own stories were born. In the following pages I work towards understanding how my own stories are entangled with Indigenous Australian stories, including the tragic stories of colonisation. Mark Tredinick writes:

> our true names, the only proper way to describe ourselves, are all the storylines we carry, of places and peoples, of histories, cultural and natural…To know ourselves we're going to need a literacy that is ebbing: words and songs for landforms and lifeforms, for clouds and watercourses, for family history and places on maps, for love and grief.[2]

The following pages chart a decolonising journey through New England's stone country where I trace myself in landscapes that I have to keep learning and unlearning and relearning again, as subaltern counter-colonial histories shake and rattle what was once firm and familiar home ground. If the coordinates of identity can be found in the places we know and love, then an unravelling of home is an unravelling of self. Thinking with stone, in dialogue with its deep co-evolutionary stories, is thinking in a decolonising mode. As I weave my life in and out of this confronting stone country, centripetal and centrifugal forces of self gather and scatter me through tablelands at once warmly familiar, and disturbingly unknown.

In the following pages I place myself in close proximity to the agency of Indigenous people and Indigenous country to engage with an embodied storying 'in the dialogical terms of encounter'.[3] Encounter is necessarily dialogical, rather than monological. Dialogue is essential to the decolonising project as it allows space for vulnerability and the unsettling experience of acknowledging traumatic and violent histories.[4]

This chapter is written on the road as I visit three rock formations in the New England tablelands. It is composed with the rhythms of automobility, 'the road and the interruption of travel...not just movement towards or away from...also a rhythm, that of the storyteller, stopping and starting'.[5] Looking out the window from the backseat of my parents' car as it rattles through the unsealed roads of New England backcountry, I am moved by the endurance of the granite boulders – ancients which carry hundreds of thousands of years of story, and an incomprehensibly vast geological history. I am gazing at the veins on my arm: the lifeblood, the mortal, the truth of my existence and its unavoidable end – the all-too-human. Could it be the rocks that are making me feel transient? Do these enduring ecological bodies shake the travelling spirit and unsettle prosaic, earthly thoughts? As the granite-studded horizon rises and falls from the dusty car window, I wonder whether human stories can seep into the earth, whether places can absorb them like rainwater.

Myall Creek Massacre Memorial: a healing stone

Figure 5 The site of the Myall Creek massacre, Bingara, 2010

A lot of massacres happened around here…And that will be forever a memory for everybody, all of us. Because that's part of our ancestry…Whether we come from the Anaiwan, the Dhunghutti, the Kamilaroi, or the Gumbaynggirr.

– Steve Widders

Our collective consciousness should include all the past; if Gallipoli is 'ours', so should be the relations with Indigenous people.

– Peter Read

Here, in this place, on a late afternoon in June 1838, 28 unarmed women, children and old men were murdered by a group of twelve armed stockmen on horseback. Some were shot, but most were 'hacked up' with knives and swords.[6] Their bodies were left on the sloped ridge until, two days later, the murderers returned to burn them.

To get here we drove to Inverell first, then through the wide flat red plains of Bingara. When we finally got to the memorial site I was struck by the intense red colour of the gravel – a raw affective power of sharply hued stones beneath my feet.

There was a dead fox on the red road. It was a hot, still day. No one else was visiting. It was not windy and the air felt gentle and still. It is a quiet place. You can hear lizards rustling in the long dry grass. It is pretty here, with no tell-tale signs of fear, hatred or violence.

The Myall Creek Massacre Memorial was opened in 2000, 162 years after the massacre took place. An initiative of the Myall Creek Memorial Committee, led by Kamilaroi Elder Lyall Munro Senior and Dr John Brown of the Uniting Church, the memorial brings together Indigenous and non-Indigenous community members, including direct descendants of the perpetrators, the victims and the survivors.[7]

The memorial begins with a winding, gravel path. A sign says *This path will take you through a dreadful story to a place that made Australian history.*

Along the path are remembrance stones with silver plaques attached telling the tale in chronological order. It is told in Gamiliraay (Kamilaroi) language, and translated to English, with small illustrations. At the top of each plaque, in bold black lettering, it says *We Remember Them*. I am most familiar with the phrase 'we remember them' from Anzac Day, but this memorial is a monument to the bloody violence of the colonial war against Australia's Indigenous people.

The ANZAC myth is a white-washed masculine vision of Australian nationhood that commemorates the landing of Australian and New Zealand soldiers on Gallipolli's shores in 1915. Australia's nation-wide commemorations, held on 25 April each year, are a focal point for World War I commemorations oriented toward Anglo-Australian nationalistic motifs that obscure cultural diversity. Despite the fact that hundreds, possibly thousands, of Indigenous Australian men joined the Australian Imperial Force between 1914 and 1918, World War I ceremonies and monuments remain conspicuously silent about the Indigenous experience. In contrast to the Anglo-oriented Anzac remembrance, there are very few monuments to commemorate the frontier wars of Colonial Australia.

Maria Tumarkin makes the point that, given the 'intensive involvement with the material settings of the nation's historical milestones' – for instance, the pilgrimage to Gallipolli – 'the disregard towards the places marked by histories of colonial violence and loss should be seen as profoundly significant'.[8]

'We remember them' is a contested statement in a country that practises mass amnesia. The re-contextualisation of the words at the Myall Creek Memorial to a remembrance of victims of a colonial massacre twists them into new shapes. Who is We? Who is Them? What modes of remembrance are appropriate here? Whose collective understanding of history defines the accepted ontology of this place? Whose thoughts and experiences are made real in this cultural landscape of loss?

Standing at the memorial stones, before the familiar, yet newly strange words – *We Remember Them* – I felt myself in movement: joining another 'We' and becoming re-selved in relation to this newly recognised 'Them'. The Myall Creek Massacre memorial changes my ceremony of the past and makes my subject position as a non-Aboriginal settler-descended white Australian a more problematic and uncomfortable one.

As I walked along the winding gravel path I experienced the passing of time on multiple levels: time's passage in the present and the flow of historical time. The path itself seems to embody history. This is a past that we cannot take back, and from which one might wish to flee. And yet, to turn around and return to the car before reaching the path's end would be a bodily violation of truth. The red gravel road represents a tragic timeline, and I followed it until the story could no longer be contained by language and rock. I looked out beyond the memorial stone to the ridge where the people were beheaded and burnt, and I trembled.

Dylan Trigg has argued that places of trauma cause a sense of spatio-temporal displacement. Inhabiting the stillness and silence of the present, one stands in contrast to the past – a past that we cannot access yet remains 'intensely fused with the environment'.[9]

Are the place and the crime inextricably bound together? I stand in alienating stillness, and can find no coherence between the gentle rolling paddocks and the violence of the murders. After cultural theorist and New England expatriate Katrina Schlunke visited the Myall Creek Memorial, she wrote a paper about her visceral response to an environmentally embodied trauma.[10] She quoted the German poet Rilke to describe the feeling of being 'dumbstruck' in the face of unknowable suffering. 'Our feelings grow mute in shy perplexity. Everything in us withdraws, a stillness comes, and the new, which no-one knows, stands in the midst of it and is silent.'[11] Like Schlunke, I was confronted by the weakness of my words here. I stood trying to make sense of horrific violence. *How does any of this fit? It is impossible.*

The suffering produced here is invisible and unknowable. There is no distant cry, no scarred country, to bring it closer in mind. The only sign of the life that was viciously taken is the memorial stone that carries the presence of absence. We stutter and go blank in the elliptical faces of the innocent, faces that cannot be called to light, that have vanished from view and memory. The weight of these unmarked dead is the burden of a civilisation that once had no use for the living, and treated life itself with impunity.

Deborah Bird Rose observes that national definitions of the dead, of whose deaths matter, are often monological, and that excluding certain deaths from commemoration is a political tactic that aligns with monological narratives of nationhood.[12] 'Dialogue,' writes Rose, 'works to counter monological separatism' and 'requires a "we" who share a time and space of attentiveness'.[13]

At the opening ceremony of the memorial, Beulah Adams and Des Blake, descendants of the murderers, spoke together:

> We are descendants of and represent all those who carried out murder and mayhem on the slopes below.

One Aboriginal descendant, Sue Blacklock, then spoke:

> We are descendants of all those who survived the massacre.

All spoke together:

> We acknowledge this our shared history, we seek reconciliation between our peoples and the healing of the wounds of the past.[14]

Family history is mobilised here in a mode of decolonisation. The descendants are representatives of postcolonial citizens who recognise the way their lives have been shaped by historical events. By taking responsibility for the actions of their forebears, these descendants enable others to enter this story of the past and create possibilities for a nonviolent future.

The shared remembrance at the Myall Creek Massacre Memorial is a politically important act, one that involves the re-experience of self and community. It's about 'good remembering' which involves 'getting something right about the significance of the past as judged from the standpoint of the present'.[15] Rather than a colonial narrative which 'installs memory as it enacts forgetting', the Myall Creek Massacre Memorial rejects silence and repression.[16] This progressive relational memory is, according to Sue Campbell, 'politically vital' because 'relations of greater political equality require our capacity and willingness to re-experience the actions and events of our personal and communal pasts, often conceiving their significance as quite different from what we do at present'.[17]

Instead of a narrative of progress where the annihilation of people and culture appears as an inevitable outcome of history, the remembrance of Myall Creek laments a tragic loss of life as the outcome of unnecessary and cruel violence. There is no chronological fracture to remove this atrocity from settler history, and the emplaced stones remind us of its irrevocability.

Elder Steve Widders spoke to me of the genealogical and geographical proximity of the Myall Creek violence, emphasising how close the horrors are to us in time and place:

Many of the people who live in this area, and more out west, Bingara, Warialda, Moree, around that area, they'd have connection with those people from Myall Creek... There were Aboriginal people all along the way there, all along the rivers, and people from the coast would migrate out there, so they would have had to have connection with the innocent people that were killed... My mother's ancestors were there. She thought one of her grandparents was one of the kids that survived that.

Many scholars have conceptualised Australia as a post-traumatic society.[18] Post-traumatic stress is characterised by an intense experience of past horrors which inspires a series of avoidant behaviour patterns to deny or suppress the past. Ross Gibson observes that responses to past trauma in colonial nations leads to mal-adjusted responses in the community, noting that '[t]he histories of most nations founded on violence suggests that an inability or refusal to acknowledge the past will produce evermore confusing and distressing symptoms in the body politic'.[19]

An important method in treating post-traumatic stress is to attempt to integrate the past with the present by remembering and mourning. The past needs to be brought into lived experience, not to be re-experienced, but to be accepted so that healing processes can begin. The Myall Creek Massacre Memorial performs recuperative memory work which 'aims toward engagement and disclosure' of a traumatic history which has been suppressed.[20]

Gibson writes that because the 'dead persist in stories which the living use to represent existence to themselves', the dead need to be heard and felt in storytelling and ritual, else the past haunts the present, and leads to contemporary paralysis.[21] Remembrance at Myall Creek is, in part, about situating the self in a community of ancestors – victim or perpetrator – to understand familial and communal responsibilities in the present.

A descendant of an Aboriginal survivor of the massacre, Sue Blacklock, commented to her child on the way to the Myall Creek Massacre Memorial opening commemoration: 'You know what this means to me, coming here we're coming to a funeral'.[22] At Myall Creek the sharing of grief brings 'death into the world of life'.[23]

The Nobel Peace Prize-winning author Elie Wiesel argues that memory is a reconciliatory force:

[M]emory is a blessing: it creates bonds rather than destroys them. Bonds between present and past, between individuals and groups. It is because I remember our common beginning that I move closer to my fellow human beings. It is because I refuse to forget that their future is as important as my own.[24]

The memorial stone is a participant in the remembrance process – a mnemonic structure that marks and protects a wounded site.[25] As the memorial stone creates new lights and shadows with its granite form it becomes an active part of the memory, a physical barrier to that tide of finitude which would wash away the past and make it unliveable, and so unhealable.

Figure 6 The main commemorative stone at the Myall Creek Massacre Memorial, Bingara, 2010

Yet, the grief and suffering produced by the Myall Creek Massacre is 'too great a burden for the grave, or site of death, or object, or artefact, or ritual, or place alone to carry. No single tree is able to bear such a profound charge of mourning. No inspirited site'.[26] But does the rock hold the voices of the dead? Does it breathe the story into the landscape? While it cannot contain the story, it can help in its telling. In this sense the rock is the continuing presence of the dead in the living world.

When I visited the memorial I placed a small round stone on a growing pile of stones and leaves and feathers in front of the larger memorial rock. Picking up and placing a stone, while a very small gesture, was a response that I, and many others, made to the call to remember. This is part of acknowledging the truth of colonial history through the process of decolonisation. My small gesture signalled that *I remember*. In this crossover communication between life and death, placing a stone on to a pile marks my responsibility to place myself in this story of my homeland, and to work to keep that story alive.

Bluff Rock: a badland

About two hours' drive East of the Myall Creek Massacre Memorial is Bluff Rock. A ghostly grey looming cliff, Bluff Rock is a site where Aboriginal people were allegedly thrown from the top to their deaths in 1844.

Figure 7 Bluff Rock viewed from the 'viewing area', 2010

Bluff Rock is located north of Glen Innes, on the same New England highway as the Australian Standing Stones. Separated from the Bluff by screaming trucks and bitumen, I am standing at a makeshift 'viewing area' that resembles a bus stop more than a memorial. Near some highway-side toilets there is a shelter which contains a collage of laminated newspaper clippings about the rock. There's no access to the cliff itself because it is on somebody's private land.

As I look at the cliff from a distance, cars stream past and cut the Bluff off from my present. The highway is like a slice in time – a punctuation mark separating then from now. The bitumen creates a line of sound – the rumble of automotive Modernity.

I can only really see the Bluff through a windscreen. I certainly can't see it without having to peer over the intrusive highway. I'm entirely trapped by the road, by laws of property, by colonial cartographies that cut up the country into squares and rectangles. Bluff Rock is wedged between the present and the past, and unable to affect either. And me, well, I'm just passing through.

In her extensive work *Bluff Rock: Autobiography of a Massacre*, Katrina Schlunke claims that the tourist dialogue surrounding the Bluff superficially acknowledges Aboriginal massacre while simultaneously disavowing its ramifications:

How useful and how 'practical' to believe that *that* is where it all happened. And if we do not think of the cottages and the paddocks and the neatly organised cattle, we will never remember the cars and the roads and the reservations and the barristers and the cities which made the systematic dispossession and dispersal of Aboriginal people possible. That is far away.[27]

The Bluff temporally and spatially concentrates Australia's brutal history, draining knowledge of violence into one place and blending stories from many places into one story. It is a version of what Ross Gibson terms 'a badland' – a haunted place where the wild violence of colonisation can be concentrated so that the illusion of tame society can continue. Gibson explains that badlands exist in every society, but that they are 'especially compelling within *colonial* societies'.[28] Badlands enable the spaces of the present to be cleaned of a savage past. Murder happened 'over there', and death is contained in the rock, incarcerated in the abrasive surface of a granite ancient.

A huge granite cliff face is a useful landform to have as a poetic metaphor of contained concentration of time and place. The Visitors' Information Sheet tells us '[t]he Truth will be forever in the bosom of one of the most impressive landmarks along the New England highway', and evokes the endurance of the rock:

> Bluff Rock stands above the surrounding area because it has been more resistant to erosion, probably due to having fewer cracks along which water can penetrate and accelerate the erosion process.[29]

History and geology rhyme as the narrative 'presumes a fossilised past, a past that cannot change, a past that we cannot change'.[30] The past is removed from the present, rendered static and archival, just as the rock is rhetorically removed from the living landscape. The Bluff is not only a geological landform, it is also a home for animals and plants, absorbing heat in the day and exuding it at night, creating shadows. It is constantly interacting and engaging with the surrounding environment – an active part of the living world. But as a badland it becomes a closed system, locked in the past.

This containment of memory contrasts sharply with the Myall Creek Massacre Memorial, where interaction with the stone is encouraged. In the contact zone between flesh and granite, a counter-colonial space of healing forms. As Bluff Rock incarcerates the past it prevents this form of healing by holding the dead apart from the living world.

The discourse of the massacre at Bluff Rock is a familiar colonial one of Aboriginal extinction which seeks to remove Aboriginal people from the landscapes of the present – what Schlunke terms 'a fable of annihilation'.[31] Bluff Rock, as a badland, produces passivity. The dead do not call out to the living to remember and to work toward non-violence and healing in the future. The call to responsibility is muted by encysting the dead in distance and in history. But Ross Gibson reminds us that the perimeters of badlands are rarely secure. The land surrounding the Bluff is shrouded in darkness, and, as every child knows, darkness and haunting go hand in hand. The violence of the past cannot be temporally and spatially contained so easily because 'forgetting simply does not work'.[32] Just outside the glare of our headlights,[33] memory endures, disturbing the soul.[34]

Mount Yarrowyck rock art: learning stories

Down south from the Bluff, past Glen Innes and nearing Armidale, my parents and I are heading toward an Aboriginal rock-art site in the traditional territory of the Anaiwan people, just outside the Uralla township. The site was recorded in the 1960s and is estimated to have been produced between 150 and 500 years ago. This means that it could predate settler Australians by centuries or it could be contemporary with settlement.[35]

We leave the station wagon in an empty car park and begin a relaxed stroll along a cleared track, surrounded by blossoming white wildflowers. After about twenty minutes of walking we reach the site, and there is a sense of palpable frustration in the air as we look blankly at an indecipherable granite face coated in symbols we cannot understand.

Mount Yarrowyck is an uncomfortable reminder of unacknowledged, silenced local histories. The enduring red ochre seems to testify that the colonial cartographies of New England are by no means incontestable or settled. That the art may be so recent intensifies this unsettling affect. A nearby sign erected by National Parks and Wildlife explains to visitors: 'The tracks, circles, short lines and dots may remind you of birds' feet, people, lizards and even bird eggs. You may be right, you may be wrong. Unfortunately we will never know the true meaning of the site.'

On the walk back to the car there is little conversation because there's not much to say. There are more stories in this region than I know, more than I can ever learn. As our car eases over the bald contours of the tablelands I watch the familiar lean country stream by. The outlines of flat, treeless plains sketch out a bothersome question: can I really claim to know this place at all?

When I met with New England Elders I expressed my distress at my own ignorance of their culture. It felt like there had been massive gaps in my education. While I did learn about corroborees and the meaning of the colours on the Aboriginal flag, this knowledge was not linked to my home-place in any meaningful way – I had never heard of Mount Yarrowyck.

My ignorance of Aboriginal places within my homeland made me feel displaced. The forced displacement of Aboriginal people from these lands intensified this feeling. When I spoke with the Elders I gained a rich sense of stories, multiple and layered throughout the New England tablelands. This was unsettling, transformative conversation for me as my colonial inheritance of place came 'physically into an uneasy and simultaneous relationship with the "always theirs" of Indigenous belonging' in the region.[36]

The entire Australian continent is mapped by story and songlines. Indigenous philosophy emerges from an epistemic web, where thoughts and meaning arise from the land, and in dialogue with ancestral connections to that land – an 'ecology of mind' sustained by human-nonhuman place-based feedback loops. Knowledge cannot be separated from place because it is held in complex relational more-than-human networks that are nourished and protected by story.

The Mount Yarrowyck Rock Art sits within an intimate cartography of storied places. But is it even possible for me, a settler descended Australian, to immerse myself in these webs of meaning, to hear and understand songlines – lines of becoming, lines of flight – that forge the way into an entirely different territory, one mapped not by detached cartographic measurements, but by the rhythms of a well told story?

Stephen Muecke observes that 'movement is more important to Aboriginal modes of being than territoriality and lines (or pathways of movement) more than boundaries'.[37] Moving out of the car, with its climate control and the familiar criss-cross coordinates of a bitumen grid, and on to a dirt track heading toward the Rock Art site in the heat of the day, I enter another pattern: not a structure made of rectangles and right-angles, but an entangled multidimensional web – a rhizomatic multispecies ecology.

This place is noisy with grasshoppers, birds, bees and cicadas. A nearby lizard camouflages itself into a stone crevice, carrying in its flesh a record of co-evolutional becoming-with place: of how, over millennia, a reptile has come to embody an aesthetic pattern perfectly matched to a particular texture of granite. Is it possible for me to slip into a living web of place, to camouflage myself in its multispecies song? Does my story even belong here?

Henri Bergson noted that the intellect 'is intended to secure the perfect fitting of our body to its environment', but that 'our concepts have been formed on the model of solids' and fail to adapt to the dynamic movement and becoming of the living world.[38] Every time I place pen to paper I am plagued by the thought that my colonial and anthropocentric language and its tools undermine my own attempts at decolonising thought. How can this 'writing' – the marking of English letters and symbols in ink on to paper extracted from forests and transported across the planet – how can such a process possibly translate or even touch upon ochre, centuries old, painted onto stone? This rock and the ochre and I, do we even share shards of the same language?

Ochre itself is made of rock – ground-down rock fragments mixed with water – which fingers scoop up and layer in patterns onto stone: this painting is *of* the body, and *of* the earth. The art emerges from the ground: there is no remove – all immanent, all touching – in this intimate performative ecology that makes place meaningful, that gives it its rhythms.

There is evidence that the rock art at Yarrowyck was part of an ongoing, ritual process. Prominent archaeologist of the New England region and its Indigenous history, Isabel McBryde, notes that:

> The differences in colour observed in these figures, and their superimpositions, suggest two periods of painting at this site, the earlier represented by the light figures, the later by those in a rich dark red … Towards the southern end

of the rock face, at the base of the group, there are some very faint bird tracks in a pale red colour which may represent traces of a third, and even earlier, period of painting.[39]

Here art is becoming, not static. But now the process has stopped. The cave is protected by a wooden post, and a plastic-coated sign next to the art reads:

> Silicone drip lines have been placed above the art to divert any moisture. Every effort has been made to protect this site while allowing visitors to enjoy it. Please help by keeping behind the barrier at all times. Please do not touch the art.

Silicone shields the ochre and visitors are spectators. We are removed by rope and silicone from the ceremony, and positioned as if visitors at an art gallery. Yet, while the rock might initially appear as a static canvas, it is only a second before a spider drops down in front of the paintings from the overhanging cave and begins to wrap up an insect entangled in its web, and human eyes become alive to the movements of lizards across lichen-covered granite. Here, story and art are alive on a living canvas, weathered by wind and sun, and home to a myriad of species. The art is made of pieces of the earth, and it is more-than-human.

Martin Heidegger wrote that 'stone is worldless', arguing that material objects were impoverished by a complete lack of agential and perceptive qualities.[40] On the contrary, I want to suggest that this stone creates a world. It is generative because it helps to produce a complex codified matrix sustained by relational connections between art, Country, ceremony and the multispecies community this stone nourishes. This ecosystem of knowledge is materialised in story, and enunciated in the oral testimony of Elders who hold on to its cultural resonance.

But what happens when a story is lost or broken? What happens when storytelling stops and the narrative no longer moves dynamically through generations? What happens when story is taken away from its people, and those people taken away from the Country that holds and protects their stories? James Hatley observes that 'Genocide is a practice that focuses not only on the bodies of those to be annihilated but also on their stories'.[41]

Standing by the Mount Yarrowyck Art is a sign erected by New South Wales Parks and Wildlife. It contains selected quotes from essays written by Aboriginal high-school students reflecting on a visit to the site. One comment in particular drew my attention:

> I had a feeling of sadness when I looked at the rock paintings because I could not understand them.
>
> – Ernest Lovelock

I told Elder Steve Widders that I had been moved by these words, that reading them made me feel very sad. He explained to me that this sense of cultural loss was not unique to youth.

Aboriginal people have had a tradition of oral history, and of putting their stories on landmarks...rock art tells a lot of stories. There's probably quite a bit of that around here, but I think most people would be like that young kid's comments there – sad because he doesn't understand it. That would apply to so many people. I'm an adult and I've never been taught what it is. I've never been taught the meanings of the paintings at Mount Yarrowyck because I've never met anybody that knows. And Mount Yarrowyck's only one [of those places].

Steve later spoke of many deeply personal sorrows that have been caused by colonial devastation of Aboriginal culture. He regretted not asking his father more about the stories before he passed away, and shared in the pain of the community at the loss of stories – 'pain that they've forgotten it, they don't know it. Like me, it's never been told'.

The mass violence of colonisation ruptured stories that connect vast temporal and spatial matrices and so damaged the link between Aboriginal people, their Country and their ancestors. Steve explained that because he is unable to practise traditional initiations he has lost an important tie to culture and land. He said:

I've been to ceremonial ground but I've never been there for ceremony. I wish I knew more about that...It could be more powerful if I understood the meaning of it. Like that young bloke at Yarrowyck you know, it would be more powerful to him if he could understand the story.

Each of the Elders I spoke to expressed an urgent need to 'rekindle and reclaim'[42] their connection with Country. They explained that the loss of language, tradition and story is a loss of continuity with ricochet effects on social stability, self-respect, cultural determination, and health and wellbeing:

STEVE WIDDERS: Once you start losing the connection with culture you lose...
PAT COHEN: Lose respect.
STEVE WIDDERS: You lose order and respect.
LORNA HAGUE: I would say respect before culture because if you're not taught to respect your Elders then you don't respect your culture either, which is what's happening at the moment actually.
STEVE WIDDERS: Part of the culture is respect.
ME: Do you think that translates to respect for land and respect for environments as well?
CHRISTINA KIM: The land is very sacred.
STEVE WIDDERS: Yeah, the connection with land is very much part of culture.
MARGARET WALFORD: It's very important.
STEVE WIDDERS: I think we've lost a little bit over the past fifty years of so because...
PAT COHEN: No one's sitting down talking.
STEVE WIDDERS: That's it, no one is passing it on. And when an older person dies so does part of the culture. Because if the language is not passed on then the stories are not passed on.

The young man at Yarrowyck was sad because he wanted to know more than he could. The ochre marks on the granite face call out to him and make him want to know more, just as they probably have done for hundreds of years. The terrible sadness is that there is no one for him to ask, no one left who knows the story. As Steve Widders imparted to me, 'There's so many gaps here, Kate. This land here – so many stories have gone, so much culture lost'.

Yet the power of the art to provoke curiosity suggests that while the story might be forgotten, the site still speaks and invokes. The cultural loss has not been totalising, and the impetus to 'rekindle and reclaim' is made strong by the palpable connections of people to places and their stories. The stories have gaps and silences, some of them remain untold, and yet their very wounded quality offers evidence of connections. Despite all the damage and violence, the presence of story remains, like a lizard in hibernation, waiting to be awoken.

Joseph Pugliese writes that 'stone and other material entities bespeak histories – geological, climatic, historical, political, cultural and social – that are simultaneously autonomous *and* indissociable from the human subjects whose lives they touch and enable'.[43] Both Elders and places are knowledge-holders. In an epigenetic relationship, stories come alive and are activated by long ancestral connections of people to this particular stone and this song of place. A song that sings of how peoples have learned, over tens of thousands of years, to fit their bodies and lives into this pocket of the world.

The affective connectivity of this storying process remains 'immanence-as-resistance' in a 'geography of dispossession'[44] that refuses to allow colonial warfare to unleash a tide of oblivion.

Uncle Steve Widders explained:

> Well, I feel very sad and very unfortunate that I don't have the connection that I would like to have. But the older I get, the more urgency I have to try and understand it a little bit so I can pass it down to my kids. And they can learn it with me as well, and then pass it down to their kids.

Through my dialogue with Elders and the encounter with the Rock Art site, I found an ongoing process of storying the land. There is a story of loss, of the devastation of colonisation – its assault on culture. This story of severed ties is accompanied by a story of continuity, of connections which have remained and connections which are being actively repaired. In the shadows of loss there is the will to rekindle the flame – a story of a cultural survival. Then there is my story, of hearing these stories, and the ethics of listening. Bindi MacGill et al. explain that the process of a settler learning Indigenous stories in a decolonising mode involves reciprocity between listener and storyteller. The story is a gift, but it is an uncomfortable and unsettling one, and there is a responsibility on receipt of this difficult gift to continue to carry the story.[45]

The painted rock face at Mount Yarrowyck holds the dead in the living world, not by memorial or active remembrance, but by traces that invoke stories that reverberate down through generations. As someone outside the story it is difficult to know my responsibility, to position myself ethically to the unknown and unknowable. Deborah Bird Rose observes that 'The demands of witnessing are demands of memory', and 'if the purpose of violence was to extinguish certain people, knowledges, and perspectives, then memory continues to resist that violence'.[46] Situating my own stories in these entangled histories of loss and revival is a form of recuperative memory work that refuses to participate in the ongoing violence that is sustained by the disconnection of people from their stories.

In the space of decolonising encounter (both being at the stone and speaking with the Elders), I was prompted to move beyond the tangible ochre etched on granite into the space of 'what has been displaced, ruptured, altered, preserved or lost'.[47]

As the dead seem to resonate in the living world through the ochre marks in a granite cave, I carry a story of community survival, and the way that survival bears witness to suffering and loss. This is a cultural resistance marked not by continuity, but by rupture, by witness and by an ethical call. The Elders' urgent appeal to rekindle and reclaim culture in the face of colonial fragmentation speaks of a desire to reinhabit a place where many stories have been lost, but where the presence of story is vivid and alive.

Notes

1 D. Rose, *Wild Country*.
2 M. Tredinnick, *The Blue Plateau*, 115.
3 V. Plumwood, 'Heart of Stone', 23.
4 The reasons for this are outlined in the Introduction to this book.
5 S. Muecke, *No Road*, 59.
6 R. Ward, 'Massacre at Myall Creek', *The Good Weekend, Sydney Morning Herald*, 5 November 1977.
7 Parliament of New South Wales, 'Full Day Hansard Transcript', Legislative Assembly (8 June 2000), www.parliament.nsw.gov.au/prod/parlment/hanstrans.nsf/V3ByKey/LA20000608?Open&refNavID.
8 M. Tumarkin, 'Secret Life of Wounded Spaces: Traumascapes in the Contemporary Australian Landscape' (PhD Thesis, University of Melbourne, 2002), 36.
9 D. Trigg, 'The Place of Trauma: Memory, Hauntings, and the Temporality of Ruins', *Memory Studies* 2, no. 1 (2009): 98.
10 K. Schlunke, 'Dumb Places', Balayi: Culture, *Law and Colonialism* 6 (2004): 72–81.
11 Ibid, 72.
12 D. Rose, *Wild Country*, 29.
13 Ibid., 30.
14 J. Collins, '"Caring for Country" in NSW: Connection, Identity, Belonging' (PhD thesis, Southern Cross University, 2006), 322.
15 S. Campbell, 'Our Faithfulness to the Past: Reconstructing Memory Value', *Philosophical Psychology* 19, no. 3 (2006): 362.
16 R. Garbutt, S. Biermann and B. Offord, 'Into the Borderlands', 73.
17 S. Campbell, 'The Second Voice', *Memory Studies* 1, no. 1 (January 2008): 45.
18 Ross Gibson deals with this notion in his work *Seven Versions of an Australian Badland* (St. Lucia: University of Queensland Press, 2002) and Maria Tumarkin in her PhD thesis 'Secret Life of Wounded Spaces'.
19 R. Gibson, *Badland*, 158–159.

20 D. Rose, *Wild Country*, 24.
21 R. Gibson, *Badland*, 20.
22 J. Collins, '"Caring for Country"', 325.
23 D. Rose, *Wild Dog Dreaming: Love and Extinction* (Charlottesville and London: University of Virginia Press, 2011), 74.
24 E. Wiesel, *From the Kingdom of Memory* (New York: Summit Books, 1990), 10.
25 Val Plumwood argues that '[s]tone can help mark and protect a wounded area' when it is used in a way that does not affirm transcendence from the earth, but instead continuation of life and the dissolution of the individual body into an 'ecological body' ('The Cemetery Wars: Cemeteries, Biodiversity and the Sacred', *Local/Global: Identity, Security, Community* 3 (2007), 59).
26 P. Read, *Haunted Earth* (Sydney: University of New South Wales Press, 2003), 75.
27 K. Schlunke, *Bluff Rock*, 122.
28 R. Gibson, *Badland*, 15.
29 Tenterfield and District Visitors' Association, *Bluff Rock: Location and History* (Tenterfield: Tenterfield and District Visitors' Association, no date).
30 K. Schlunke, *Bluff Rock*, 35.
31 Ibid., 244.
32 R. Gibson, *Badland*, 179.
33 Ibid., 2.
34 Gibson writes '[d]isturbance in the soul is perhaps more prosaically understood as persistence in the memory' (Ibid., 92).
35 New South Wales National Parks and Wildlife Service, *Heritage Walk: Mount Yarrowyck Nature Reserve Rock Art Site* (Information Pamphlet: NSW National Parks and Wildlife, no date).
36 R. Garbutt, S. Biermann and B. Offord, 'Into the Borderlands', 69.
37 S. Muecke, *Ancient and Modern*, 16.
38 H. Bergson, *Creative Evolution*, trans. A. Mitchell (New York: Henry Holt and Company, 1911), ix.
39 I. McBryde, *Aboriginal Prehistory*, 107.
40 M. Heidegger, 'The Question Concerning Technology', in *The Question Concerning Technology and Other Essays*, ed. M. Heidegger (New York: Harper and Row, 1977).
41 J. Hatley, 'Naming Coyote in Hebrew: A Memoir', *TEXT Special Issue 20: Writing Creates Ecology and Ecology Creates Writing*, eds. M. Harrison, D.Rose, L. Shannon and K. Satchell (2013): 8.
42 Steve Widders, personal communication, 23 December 2011 at Caffiends café, Armidale.
43 J. Pugliese, 'Forensic Ecologies of Occupied Zones and Geographies of Dispossession: Gaza and Occupied East Jerusalem', *Borderlands* 14, no. 1 (2015): 1–37.
44 J. Pugliese, 'Forensic Ecologies', 19.
45 B. MacGill et al., 'Ecology, Ontology and Pedagogy at Camp Coorong', *M/C Journal of Media and Culture* 15, no. 3 (2012), http://journal.media-culture.org.au/index.php/mcjournal/article/viewArticle/499.
46 D. Rose, *Wild Country*, 31.
47 R. Garbutt, S. Biermann and B. Offord, 'Into the Borderlands', 65.

Part II
Trees

Figure 8 Deciduous tree in Armidale, Autumn 2016

When I was in high school my older brother, Ben, asked me to draw a picture of time. He had been studying philosophy at university, and often came home with these kinds of metaphysical challenges. I was about fourteen years old, and I can't remember what I drew, but I do remember that he found it unsatisfactory.

'No!' he declared, before giving me a profound reason why my picture was utterly wrong.

This failing must have stayed with me, because I have often thought about it since, and wondered at different moments – what would I draw now? What kind of symbol or picture could represent this creature I am perpetually getting to know, but that always remains beyond my knowing: *Time?*

If time were an animal, what kind of animal would it be? I can imagine it as a bird that flits in and out of vision, just as time flits in and out of our thoughts. It migrates with the seasons, and is whisked away on the cusp of the wind. But it always returns, singing in the dawn.

Or would it be mammalian – a creature bound to the Earth and its orbital rotations that give us our metered hours?

Or is it impossible for time to be embodied in this way? Is it far too abstract a concept to ascribe an animal form? I know that one obvious image of time would be a straight line, in that familiar old narrative of progress and development. But then others would see time as a circle, perhaps mirroring the quotidian hours of the clock on the wall, or as some sort of mythic snake devouring its own tail.

In this section of my book I explore the way time is woven into place through trees. I am handing to my brother (and other readers of this work) an image of time as a botanical body that reaches up from the belly of the Earth into blue horizons. My vision of botanically shaped time is not limited to the tree alone, but composed of all the relationships which form around it – the symbiotic relationships with birds that disperse its seeds, with soil organisms that ensure its growth; and the less direct relationships of trees to a community of beings who share their place, including the human.

Natasha Myers has argued that our current era should be called the Planthropocene, because we are radically dependent on botanical life, and yet oblivious to our 'interimplication', to the fact that 'these green beings have made this planet liveable and breathable for animals like us'.[1] In the following pages I attempt to write with botanical collaborators, to undertake a 'planthropology', and to infuse my words and scholarship with the scent of a local pine forest and the hues of a deciduous autumn to honour these life-sustaining kin. Contemplating what it means to live among colonial treescapes in an era of deforestation, I raise the problematic postcolonial question: How are we to live ethically in places which are both damaged and beloved?

Note

1   N. Myers. 'Photosynthesis', Theorizing the Contemporary, *Cultural Anthropology* website, 21 January 2016. https://culanth.org/fieldsights/790-photosynthesis.

3   A beloved shadow place

When I walk the wide dirt roads of the Armidale Pine Forest, I feel as though I'm strolling through my past. The conifer forms that texture this pocket of Australian land preserve some of my earliest memories. The pines hold the shape of all the years I spent living beside them – from an early childhood searching for pine cones with my mother, to hazy teenage years of booze and boyfriends, these trees, despite their exotic origins, have been intimately familiar throughout my life.

Time spent in a place fills it up so that it becomes charged with the force of the past. Edward S. Casey has argued that place contains memory, and that remembering is not so much a temporal journey but an act of re-emplacement as

Figure 9 The Armidale Pine Forest, Armidale, 2009

we return to the environments that hold significant moments of our lives.[1] Our most intimate memories are embodied in tangible earthly forms, shared between mind and world in a way that unsettles any simplistic division between the two.

The Armidale Pine Forest is a poly-chronic patchwork where time gathers together in pleats and folds. Social time rubs up against the time of ecology as individual human lives, tree growth and reproduction, a rhizomatic underworld of roots and earth, a developing community and commercial timber harvest all come together like sundials throwing a criss-cross of shadows across the trees.

Journeying into this beloved multitemporal childhood forest I hope to develop a greater understanding of how 'beings and places are at stake in each other'[2] when transnational commodity flows and the exploitation of more-than-human labour can make deforestation appear to be an invisible and distant issue. Through the lens of an eco-mental model of trauma where attachments of mind and memory are brought into dialogue with taxonomies of nativism and worth, I argue that risky attachments to production landscapes in the Anthropocene may help us to develop a situated botanical ethics that responds to questions of how to live, think and work well in an era of global environmental devastation.

Inheriting damaged places

The land on which the Pine Forest grows is Aboriginal land, with Armidale being home to the Anaiwan people for tens of thousands of years. The area was set aside as a commons in 1866 – a form of public land ownership which was enabled by violent processes of dispossession and deforestation. The 'commons' in early twentieth-century Australia was most often land that had already been deforested but was not suitable for agriculture, defined as 'land belonging to a community, esp. unenclosed waste land'.[3]

The Pine Forest's most recent management plan was produced by Forests NSW, a Public Trading Enterprise tasked with managing public native forests and plantation timber. It states that the report by consulting archaeologist Suzanne R. Hudson notes 'no significant findings of Aboriginal cultural significance' in the area.[4] As with the definition of sacred sites at the Australian Standing Stones, Aboriginal presence in the landscape is confined to places of cultural significance. This demarcation of Aboriginal sovereignty prevents the unsettling recognition that the entire region is Aboriginal land, and, as Fabienne Bayet-Charlton reminds us, that '[t]he whole of Australia is an Aboriginal artefact'.[5] That the pre-settlement period of the Pine Forest's history remains largely unrecognised in official discourse highlights that the past is contested territory, implying that emplaced memories and personal narratives are also contested.[6]

The Australian landscape is a massive crime scene. Almost every place is stained with the social and ecological violence and trauma of colonial invasion. The aftershocks ripple through relational multispecies landscapes, producing what Joseph Pugliese has called 'ecologies of suffering'.[7] As I set out on the journey of decolonising a homeland, I must tackle the question of how to value sites of trauma and dispossession which are also personally beloved. At heart, this is a question central to living well in the Anthropocene: a question of 'how to inherit'. Donna Haraway notes that the notion of inheritance is entangled with notions of accountability.[8] Inheritance recognises that we are deeply implicated, personally, politically, and intellectually, in the conditions of our world.[9]

From within the 'harshly situated presence'[10] of being a settler-descended Australian, my memories are preserved in the colonising forms of introduced pine trees which dominate native lives and obscure other memories. In the following pages I encounter and embrace the immanent affective ecology of my personal and autobiographical relation to the Pine Forest as a way of 'staying with the trouble'[11] of living in a colonised country in the era of the Anthropocene.

In the Pine Forest I find solace and intimacy, having spent many years becoming-with[12] its vibrant multispecies community of living selves.[13] That the area is a site of colonial trauma and amnesia unsettles my ease in the landscape, but does not lessen the intensity of my feelings of intimacy in place.

The Pine Forest of my youth is both a beloved place of dwelling and also a space where I am forced to encounter the devastating impact of capitalism and colonialism on more-than-human life. This plantation is a complicated version of what Val Plumwood termed a 'shadow place'. Plumwood explains that shadow places in colonised lands are 'all those places that produce or are affected by the commodities you consume, places consumers don't know about, don't want to know about, and in a commodity regime don't ever need to know about or take responsibility for'.[14]

The Pine Forest intervenes into this capitalist framework of distance and con-cealment[15], as it is a both a community forest *and* a timber plantation, combining a commodity market and capitalist extractivism with human attachment in a place of multispecies connectivity. This is an atypical situation because in the logic of global markets, beloved places are usually kept separate from places that bear our ecological footprint.[16] This presents an opportunity for exploring what happens when people directly encounter the consequences of the material support for human society on an idealised home-place.

100 years of risky attachment

The Pine Forest has a long and convoluted history. In 1910, 246 hectares of colonially usurped land that had been designated a 'commons' became the Armidale Afforestation Station, one of the earliest pine plantations in New South Wales.[17] Plantings and sporadic timber harvest continued in the area now known as the Pine Forest until 1936, when a state-wide review of pine plantations concluded that the area was not suited to pines. At this time plantings ceased, and it was proposed that the forest be disposed of as private farmland. However, in 1947 the local State Member of Parliament, David Drummond, halted this process, arguing strongly in favour of the local benefit of the area as a children's forest, a place for recreation and a community asset. Limited planting resumed in the mid-1960s and continued until 2001.[18]

In 2000, State Forests decided to undertake clear-felling and 20 hectares of pines were destroyed. This sparked community outcry, leading to the formation of the 'Friends of the Pine Forest' advocacy group who proposed to maintain the area as a reserve and appoint a trust to preserve the forest's 'scientific, historical and recreational values'.[19] Despite this advocacy of the forest as of more-than-timber value, its commercial identity was again given dominance in May 2007 when a further 35 hectares of the plantation were clear-felled by State Forests. This felling was particularly upsetting for the community because it occurred in a dedicated historical and recreational zone of the forest, 17 hectares of which were close to the entrance and clearly visible from the nearby road. The justification by Forests NSW for this action was that the pines were in a dangerous condition after being damaged by a severe hailstorm in December 2006. However, many claim that a lot of the pines were not badly affected by the storm (maritime and loblolly varieties remaining in relative health) and that Forests NSW indiscriminately clear-felled all the trees in that particular zone.[20]

In September 2009 a public meeting was held with the local council, concerned community members and other stakeholders to discuss the future of the forest. Following this meeting a Pine Forest Committee was established, with a new management plan which recommended an unprecedented level of 'formal community involvement in management of the area'.[21] Since this time, volunteers have planted 10,000 native trees in place of the felled pines and Forests NSW have constructed a series of colour-coded walking tracks fostering emplaced connections between the community and the timber plantation.

The community outrage at the Pine Forest's destruction highlights that the conifer plantation has become a site of 'risky attachment,' where people have developed an intimacy with one of 'the sacrificed spaces of production landscapes'.[22] Unlike community gardens that keep food and goods production within the community, the Pine Forest connects with the commodity form of the global economy. In a dance of shadow and light these beloved conifers demand a conception of ecological justice which stretches beyond the local. Encounter with the forest is an encounter that evokes alternate forms of 'place accountability'[23] connected to transnational networks of exchange and consumption. In other words, the dilapidated pines call out to us, 'Hey! You know your paper has to come from somewhere!'

The colonising plant

Conifer plantations are part of a vast array of biological invasions into Indigenous Australia. Introduced invasive flora and fauna has caused the ecocide of native environments, implicating exotic nonhuman species in colonial violence. Colonialism was sustained by 'ecological imperialism' and the 'biological expansion of Europe' throughout the world.[24] Colonial transformation of the natural world also helped to usher in the Anthropocene, and the name 'plantationocene' has been coined to describe the transformation of small-scale

Figure 10 The Armidale Pine Forest, Armidale, 2009

agriculture into extractive and enclosed plantations, a significant turning point that paved the way for the emergence of our new geological era.[25]

With their ties to a legacy of botanical colonisation and environmental devastation, it is not surprising that the conifer is regarded as a 'colonising plant' that threatens autochthonous life. Australia is a major cultivator of pine, with almost one million hectares growing across the country.[26] Plantations like the Armidale State Forest are often established on cleared native land, leaving a pocket of alien exotics in the middle of native bush. This can lead to conifer invasion of surrounding areas[27] via the dispersal of winged pine seed by wind and birds, which has, in fact, altered native ecosystems across the country by acidifying the soil, and changing basic ecological processes such as water flow and fire intensity.[28]

Plantations are also condemned as stand-alone forests for lacking in resources for native flora and fauna.[29] The widespread notion that conifer plantations are 'biological deserts' has come under significant attack, however, with recent studies demonstrating that plantations do produce a range of important conservation and protection services for native inhabitants.[30]

It is difficult to draw any definitive conclusions as to whether pine plantations are valuable or hazardous to native life, as they are more than likely both. What is significant here is the rhetorical division drawn between the native and the introduced. This dualism is the subject of sustained critique in environmental philosophy because it depends on a disjunctive temporal division drawn at the point of European settlement – 1788. Environmental philosopher Thom van Dooren points out that the native/introduced divide is 'fundamentally premised on the reification of a specific historical moment that ignores the changing and dynamic nature of ecologies'.[31] The fundamentalism of the divide is challenged by recent ecological theory which emphasises ongoing change, rather than stability, as the norm for ecological communities.

Matthew K. Chew and Andrew L. Hamilton argue that '[b]iotic nativeness is theoretically weak and internally inconsistent, allowing familiar human desires and expectations to be misconstrued as essential *belonging* relationships between biota, places and eras'.[32] Essentially, nativism confers a degree of scientific legitimacy to a moralised relationship between a being and a place.

The native/introduced division in Australia also perpetuates the 'chrono-logical fracture' of colonial time described in Chapter 1. Because colonisers perceived themselves as 'agents of disjunction' and appeared to 'start time again',[33] pre-settlement life is marked as radically different and discontinuous to the post-settlement environment. Jay Arthur explains:

> Australia is constructed as a place marked by the knowledge that 'once' this place was different. The colonised space is differentiated from the indigenous space by the loss of aspects of indigenousness. The vocabulary of loss renders Australia as a place where 'once' there was an indigenous regime, where there was 'once' a different range of animals and plants ... This loss occurs in time, creating a mark in the chronology ...[34]

This disjunctive temporality diminishes perceptions of ecological continuity, instead focusing on absence, and positioning the impact of colonial settlement as totalising change. While it is true that colonisation across the globe has been a huge 'planting and displanting enterprise', and the violent temporal fracture of settlement is not merely an abstraction, but the creation of a colonial state[35], continued emphasis on native/introduced dichotomies can perpetuate problematic definitions of the 'passive native'.

In the Australian context, 'authentic Australian nature' is temporally contained as pre-colonial vegetation and wildlife, recasting Indigenous Australian environments as virgin wilderness. That 'Aboriginal Australians shaped the reproductive mechanisms of the forest' is conveniently ignored in the construction of natural-Indigenous/anthropogenic-alien dichotomies.[36] Leading Australian Aboriginal scholar Marcia Langton argues that the denial of the ecological agency of Indigenous Australian people is politically motivated. Because this denial conceptually removes Australia's first inhabitants from the landscape, it colludes with the doctrine of *terra nullius*.[37] Plumwood also notes that this is an important component of the hyper-separation of the coloniser and the Indigene, as 'the heroic agency of white pioneers in "discovering", clearing and transforming the land' is stressed while Australian Aboriginal labour embodied in the land is positioned as 'nature' or 'wilderness'.[38]

The term 'native' is entangled with emotionally and culturally loaded concepts of timelessness, passivity and purity of origin, which are transposed from cultural contexts on to the biological world. While it is undeniable that New England's conifers are implicated in the colonial remaking of relations between people, plants and place and the associated dispossession and traumas, it is vital we interrogate the historically and culturally contingent classifications of invasive and native ecologies because these eco-political designations have life and death consequences for the more-than-human world. 'Native' and 'invasive' are classifications in which the stakes couldn't be higher – they are part of a taxonomy of worth that determines which plants and animals are valuable and which are expendable, with real world impacts on which lives humans decide to kill, to harvest or to conserve.

A multispecies collaboration

With its extensive history of human intervention, it is easy to look upon the Pine Forest as one might look at a piece of industrial infrastructure. Past human relations to the plantation are predictably anthropocentric, obscuring the nonhuman agency involved in the forest's growth and development. The illusion of human mastery over a passive nonhuman world within the forest is sustained by the dominance of a linear time-frame which focuses on teleologies of progress and rationalist development, while neglecting the agential capacities of nonhuman life.

The assumption that nonhuman life is non-autonomous and lacking agency is particularly tenacious in the case of plantation forests. Yet humans are only one player in a 'participative co-evolution' between the pine tree and other species.[39] The vision of millions of pine seeds flying through the air in the stomachs of birds serves to humble the anthropocentric spirit, not to mention the invisible 'underground world of roots, microbes, fungi, minerals, and other nutrients known as the rhizosphere' that keeps the pines alive.[40] Beneath the feet of State Forest workers and Pine Forest walkers is a buzzing ecology of soil organisms making the clear-felling and plantation operations in the topsoil look far less totalising.

Recent research into plant cognition and biology reminds us that while plantation pine seeds may be dispersed by human hands this is a relatively small part of a forest's complex coevolution. Plants are demonstrably intelligent and intentional, as individual botanies seek to continue their own life, and the life of future generations, through adaptive responses to the environment.[41] Contrary to popular perception of plant behaviour as automated and stimulus driven, plants demonstrate trial-and-error learning capabilities as they integrate external information with internal knowledge; that is, plants possess memory capacities that are vital to their survival. These plantation pines have borne children and established lines of kin through generations.[42] The Armidale conifers' individual and genealogical memory stretches the temporal boundaries of a supposedly human-dominated plantation forest.

A traumatised land and its people

Despite being firmly embedded in an official paradigm of exotic plantation timber and its temporal monoculture, the Pine Forest has become a place of ecological and social connectivity for humans too. The former State Member for the Northern Tablelands, Richard Torbay, a vocal activist for the protection and restoration of the conifers, has argued that the Pine Forest's historical status as an environment for communal gathering and recreation means that it 'has had a special place in the hearts of the people of Armidale over a long period of time'.[43] He emphasises the 'crucial role that the adjacent community plays in the welfare of the forest, especially the Rural Fire Service, which has already "saved" the forest several times from bushfire'.[44] Here, the valuation of the Pine Forest as a beloved community place is grounded in time-depth and shared experience over generations.

The 2000 and 2007 clear-fells were market-driven operations that neglected the forest's relational value and reduced it to commercial interest alone. These operations were conducted without community consultation, as if the community's concerns were meaningless, or did not exist. This is a violent assault on connections between people and place that have been forming for over a century.

Torbay, like many Armidale citizens, reacted with great distress at the two clear-fell operations, which, he argued, turned a 'magic place' into 'a wasteland'.[45] Clear-felling is an ugly process. Where there were once high, green pines, it leaves blackened, charred tree carcasses and torn-up denuded earth. At the local council meeting on the future of the Pine Forest, community members complained about the 'lack of respect' in this process, arguing that 'responsibility seems to belong to no one' with the forest left in such an unsightly mess.[46] It seemed as if the bodies of the trees had been discarded without appropriate burial, or the forest was serving as nothing more than a rubbish tip for the discarded off-cuts of the State Forest enterprise.

The communal distress felt at the Pine Forest's partial destruction is an experience of ecological trauma. Existing work into ecological trauma demonstrates that this experience is widespread and expected to grow in the Anthropocene, as we are faced with a 'pandemic of earth-related distress that will only get worse'.[47] Considering the Armidale Pine Forest as a site which preserves individual and communal memory enables a relational definition of ecological trauma that helps to develop a framework for understanding damage in dynamic environments. In places where change is ongoing, alterations to place cannot be regarded as traumatic events. I contend that the cause of ecological trauma is not flux but massive environmental destruction that severs connections formed to and in place, including memories and other deep emotional attachments. Understanding ecological trauma as a breakdown of connectivities makes sense of the personal anguish that often accompanies environmental devastation and redefines ecological damage as a multispecies experience that is psychological as well as biological.

Figure 11 'Your forests are in safe hands': State Forests sign at the Armidale Pine Forest after clear-fell, 2009

Conceptualising memory as 'place-oriented' and 'place-supported' positions environmental damage as attacks on emplaced experiences which are maintained in environmental forms. This is significant because it acknowledges that the past is not a static moment in history, but something that is ongoing, lived and performed. Beloved places are not merely generic environments from which we just happen to derive solace, but rather are sites of intimate worldly engagements formed across time and space and sustained by memory. Vital to this conception of ecological trauma is the notion that it is not only an individual human's memory that comes under assault when beloved places are destroyed, but waves of memory shared across many species and cultures over vast spans of time.

Val Plumwood has argued that contemporary capitalist societies operate according to a pervasive mind/body split that 'permeates the global economy, and is inseparable from our concepts of identity, economy and place'.[48] At the Pine Forest we witness the psychological consequences of dematerialisation, where humans are forced to confront the collapse of a 'singular, elevated, conscious "dwelling" place' into one of earth's 'multiple disregarded places of economic support'.[49] Situating this experience within our non-innocent entanglement in the conditions of the Anthropocene is a way of understanding how we ourselves are at stake in the global environmental devastation of the Anthropocene.

Disremembering

One important implication of an eco-mental model of ecological trauma is the idea that suffering can occur, regardless of individual proximity to the environmental damage. It is not necessary to be physically close to a site of trauma to be emotionally affected by it, because we carry places with us even after we leave them, and those places help to protect our memories and shelter our pasts.

When I returned to the Armidale Pine Forest in 2009, before restoration by volunteer groups had begun, I was surprised at my own grief despite my geographic distance from the destruction. No longer part of the Armidale community, I could claim no offence at an interruption to my everyday lifestyle, but I did feel distress at an interruption to my memories, to the parts of my narrative self that took the forest as their setting. This all-too-common experience of the industrial devastation of environments and the associated feeling of alienation demonstrates place as fundamental to our sense of self-through-time, a continuous narrative carved across earth, rock and tree. I felt an unexpected loss at the realisation that place-based memories cannot survive very well in ruins. Out of the charred earth came nothing.

This experience suggests that large parts of my memory, and therefore my identity, were stored, environmentally, in the Pine Forest. Cognitive philosopher Mark Rowlands explains that we have actually evolved to remember with the world: 'Our memory capacities have been shaped and forged by the information in the world around us and, accordingly, we cannot separate off…our ability to remember from our ability to exploit this ambient information'.[50]

After the clear-fells of the Pine Forest, my 'environmentally embodied'[51] memories of childhood stored in the trees were no longer accessible to me in the same manner. This external part of my mind was corrupted so that I could not remember in the same way that I had grown used to. This is not the destruction of an idealised 'nature' place, but the destruction of part of one's self.[52]

The reliance on the Pine Forest for access to a part of my past was surprising to me, perhaps because humans, particularly in the West, are so used to thinking of themselves as independent cognising beings. Yet, as Edward Casey has argued, place is essential to the preservation of memory: 'As much as body or brain, mind or language, place is a keeper of memories – one of the main ways by which the past comes to be secured in the present, held in things before us and around us'.[53]

We cannot, in other words, separate mind from world. It is no wonder then that losing a childhood forest left me feeling winded. The sensation of a memory that had been taken out of me makes sense if 'the biological brain is itself incomplete'.[54] The dismembered trees became a kind of 'disremembering'; my past was cut off from me, severed in a way that was disconcerting and beyond my control.

Film theorist Janet Walker uses the term 'disremembering' in her analysis of documentary films portraying traumatic events. With a focus on the intersection between memory and history, Walker interrogates a form of non-veridical traumatic recall, where the past is not forgotten but is 'dismembered, cut up and off, and not re-membered'.[55] Disremembering fails to restore presence in the mind's eye like remembering does, and so makes absence 'exquisitely tangible'.[56] Walker's term 'disremembering' resonates with the traumatic loss of memorial places, not least for its phonetic qualities. If memories are environmentally embodied, when a place is destroyed those memories become disremembered from the mind, in the same way an arm might be dismembered from the body. Though no longer accessible, the limb's lack of presence is starkly apparent, 'exquisitely tangible'. As State Forests dismembered the conifers, they also dismembered an eco-mental system, cutting off environmentally embodied memories and releasing the confused trauma of disremembering into the bleak yet visceral emptiness where the pines once stood.

There is a fleshly poetics to the process of disremembering. It evokes an inter-corporeality that is viscerally worldly at the same time as being cognitive. Rowlands emphasises the ultimate permeability of human thought, arguing that: '[t]he skin has no relevance to understanding cognition. Cognition is not just something we do in our head. Cognition is fundamentally something we do in the world'.[57]

Human synapses are intimately entwined with the roots and limbs of plants and trees in nature-culture assemblages, where human bodies help to create, and continue to shape, the morphology of forest ecologies, and where botanical organisms inhabit the most intimate human memories and ecologies of self. Because memory traces are shared across botanical and human worlds, disremembering is an experience situated within relational ecologies, where the human is not the sole thinker or rememberer, and memory is a dynamic multispecies and relational project.

Trees and forests too, experience relational ecological trauma that can be understood as a form of disremembering. There is evidence that ecological devastation in the Anthropocene is inducing a form of systemic environmental amnesia. Josef Keulartz explains:

> loss and fragmentation of natural habitats caused by agriculture, forestry, urbanization, construction of infrastructure and tourism often affect the large-scale and slower systems that foster the 'memory' of small-scale and fast systems. Such a loss of memory makes it difficult or impossible for systems to recover after shock or surprise and to replicate earlier adaptive cycles.[58]

Emergent research into plant neurobiology has demonstrated that individual botanical organisms possess the capacity for both short-term and long-term memory.[59] This cutting-edge research undermines the notion that the isolated brain is the only site of memory, locating the capacity to remember in non-neural networks:

> It is now known that many non-neural cells are capable of processing information via ion flows generated by ion channels/pumps and propagated by cell: cell junctions [e.g. cardiac tissue (Chakravarty and Ghosh 1997); bone cells (Turner et al. 2002)]. Simulating neural network-like dynamics, stable bioelectrical gradients among non-excitable cells could store information, memories and exhibit many other properties usually reserved

for brains (Tseng and Levin 2013). Plants are no exception, especially when we consider that they have, in fact, well-developed pathways for the effective transmission of information via electrical signals (Volkov et al. 2008)…the process of remembering may not require the conventional neural networks and pathways of animals; brains and neurons are just one possible, undeniably sophisticated solution, but they may not be a necessary requirement for learning.[60]

In response to these discoveries, evolutionary biologist Monica Gagliano advocates an expanded approach to cognition that moves beyond anthropocentric tendencies to a wider biological perspective. Drawing on Chilean biologist Humberto Maturana's conceptualisation of cognition, Gagliano proposes an understanding of cognition not as 'a fixed "property" of an organism but rather a dynamic "process" of interactions in the organism-environment system'.[61]

Michael Marder develops a similar understanding of cognition in his philosophical meditation on 'plant-thinking', writing of a mode of thought that 'takes place in the interconnections between the nodes, in the lines of flight across which differences are communicated and shared, the lines leading these nodal points out of themselves, beyond the fictitious enclosure of reified and self-sufficient identity'.[62] Just as with Gregory Bateson's ecology of mind, Marder's vision of thought is not an internal process of isolated reason, but a dynamic and multispecies assemblage, fundamentally contextualised and embedded in place. In this context of radical exposure and multiciplicity, 'The question is not who or what thinks, but "when and where does thinking happen?"'[63]

This ecological and pluralistic notion of thought pushes us to think not only from the perspective of plants, but to recognise our own thinking as already implicated in botanical worlds. Isabelle Stengers advocates 'collective thinking in the presence of others' to produce a 'common account' of the world.[64] If thought is already distributed across multiple bodies in an organism-environment system, thinking-with the world to produce a cosmopolitics is about expanding our understanding of cognition in connection with the ecological communities we arise from, are nourished by and return to, and understanding that this nourishment stretches across the mind/body dualism.

Marder writes that 'plants are the first material mediations between the concrete universality of the earth and the purely abstract ideal being of light', and where 'humans remember whatever has phenomenally appeared in the light, plants keep the memory of light itself'.[65] Plants teach us about the connections between thoughts and materiality, between the world of appearances and the ecological pulse of organic life on the planet. Botanical bodies hold the memory of light as photons soak into their chlorophyl pigment just as images soak into the emulsion of film. Memory is a materiality folded into their being, intimately connected to processes of photosynthesis. Light and life cannot be separated, and what phenomenally appears circulates through networks of more-than-human meaning.

Figure 12 Tree stump at the Armidale Pine Forest, 2015

Photographing a felled tree in the pine forest, I thought of the way plants hold memory in their flesh: an index of weather, an archive of growth and becoming, sequence and synchrony, carved into the material world. This 'material remembering'[66] carries the 'pattern that connects',[67] and reminds us that time is not abstract linearity, but a visceral, worldly and granulated thing that flows through our bodies and lives.

Rings of growth extend outward, as if ripples in a pond. These are broken apart by blocks of becoming etched into the wood, as the tree trunk collapses inward, expands and begins to fall apart when exposed to heat, and dry and rains. Centripetal and centrifugal forces of an individual life in the world, of organism- and-environment, create an exquisite artwork. This timber flesh is intricately moulded in the shape of all it has experienced – a material memory of organic life on earth.

Rings of growth in trees are accentuated by difference – etched deeper and sharper when the contrast between seasons is stronger. The 'difference that makes a difference'[68] is carved inside the living woods of the world. Time is carried in the body, patterns of seasons and weather scribbled across flesh and bark. Astrida Neimanis and Stephanie Walker call this 'thick time'. Thick time 'understands that matter has a memory of the past, and this memory swells as it creates and unmakes possible futures'.[69]

Contemplating the trauma of disremembering captured in my photograph of a severed tree trunk prompts me to ask difficult questions about living and working well in the Anthropocene. Whose memories am I erasing as I write this chapter? I am so anxious about my story erasing Indigenous stories, but have given little thought to the material memories I am excavating and writing over by the use of this very paper. Our thoughts and scholarship arise in a culture of demateriali- sation, where representations of place may be deliberately counter-colonial and inclusive, open to the voices of more-than-human others; but the materials those representations are made of – the real, living world, stuff of scholarship – seems to disappear, along with the memories and thick time held enduring in the tangible matter of the world. The mind/body dualism is insidious, and paper is anonymous, infused not with the scent of a beloved pine forest, but embodying the mass-produced invisibility of global trade.

Non-innocent love

Deforestation is a major, and catastrophic, marker of the Anthropocene. Each year, 16 million hectares of forest disappear, and half the forests that once covered the Earth are now gone. In the Anthropocene, rainforests are being cleared at a rate of 1.5 acres per second.[70] Forests are intimately linked to the carbon cycle, and deforestation is contributing to climate change. Scientists estimate that forests sequester around 40 per cent of anthropogenic carbon emissions annually,[71] absorbing 8.8 billion tonnes of carbon dioxide through photosynthesis.[72] Forests also release carbon when deforested, from soils and decaying plant matter.[73] This means that deforestation and forest degradation globally contributes about 17 per cent to Earth's carbon dioxide emissions – more than transportation related green- house gas emissions annually.[74] Loss of forest is also a major cause of extinction, with habitat destruction contributing to the world's sixth mass extinction event.[75]

Val Plumwood observes that while love of environment is vital for developing an ecological consciousness, under the exploitative conditions of capitalism and colonialism in the Anthropocene, individual love for a specific place is 'unlikely to be innocent, may register false consciousness and be exercised at the expense of other places'.[76] As I print my intimate autobiographical accounts of a beloved pine forest on paper shipped to me from an anonymous plantation somewhere in the world, it occurs to me that the repositioning of the Armidale Pine Forest as primarily a community forest where timber production is minor raises the problematic question of where the timber once supplied from the plantation will now be harvested from. Plantation forests help prevent deforestation, with fast-growing trees like Radiata Pine providing an alternative to logging of the world's ancient ecologies, like the Amazon. Forests NSW, the trading enterprise that manages the Armidale Pine Forest, is the largest producer of plantation-grown Radiata Pine timber in Australia, selling enough timber to construct approximately a quarter of the houses built in Australia each year.[77] The valuation of the forest as a protected community site is not without consequence, and it could result in the destruction of native forest.

Val Plumwood argues that, in the name of ecological justice, we need to consider power relationships within celebrations of love and sense of place, and to ask 'whose place is made better, whose worse', in order to discern patterns of beloved and sacrificial shadow places that are based on power and privilege.[78]

Australia has one of the largest carbon footprints on Earth. Our citizens live lifestyles that would require three or more planets if they were replicated globally. Given this affluence, perhaps the burden of living among sacrificed shadow places and forming risky attachments to the production landscapes of commodity capitalism, such as Radiata Pine plantations, is ours to bear, especially if it mitigates against the destruction of ancient forests.

Living in a world dominated by capitalist modes of consumption, where distance and concealment perpetuate environmental damage and injustice in far away shadow places, Plumwood suggests that we heed some advice from Indigenous Australian Elder Bill Neidjie who says, 'You got to hang onto this story because the earth, this ground, earth where you brought up, this earth he grow you',[79] 'This piece of ground he grow you'.[80]

Remembering that our lives are the product of more-than-human labours, that the earth that grows us is the same earth we are intimately attached to, an earth that nurtures and protects our memories, reminds us that we are indebted to a more-than-human creaturely world, and that growing 'is a 'process in which the energy of others is actively invested'.[81] In Chapter 1 I wrote of the way our flesh is inscribed with patterns held in deep reservoirs of creaturely time. The pine forest reminds me that our embodiment of ecological patterns of connectivity is not confined to cellular or genetic inheritance. We continue, throughout our lives, to inherit place and the geopolitical forces that make it, and to carry the becomings of our world, like the rings of a tree, inside our bodies and our minds.

Understanding that our most intimate cognitive experiences are interwoven with the pasts and futures of the more-than-human world has profound implications for how we live in an era of deforestation, extinction and environmental tipping points. If distance and concealment perpetuate global devastation, then we need to bring the Anthropocene home, and connect the global to the local. And what could be more local than the intensely personal coordinates of memory and thought in a homeplace?

The permeability of the human mind to the more-than-human world has also implications for our understandings of how our ecological ethics can be directed toward decolonisation. Deborah Bird Rose has argued that within an ecological body there is space for cross-cultural and cross-species dialogue. Applying Bakhtin's study of the grotesque body as the exposure of human beings to the world, Rose argues that permeability to environments 'opens us to dialogue not only with place, but with the history of the place'.[82] She writes:

> The country that gets into people's blood invariably contains the blood and sweat of Aboriginal people as well as settlers. It may contain convict blood, and the remains of the dead. It will contain the blood of childbirth, and the blood and bones of massacres. It will contain the remains of animals, of extinct species, perhaps…the same soil gets into our blood, the same waters quench our thirst, the sweat of us all resides in the ground.[83]

The country that gets under the skin and into the blood is the same country that holds memories. The emplaced interconnection of beings, past and present, human and nonhuman, has huge implications for how we think about the past. One essential question that arises from the 'harshly situated presence' of a settler descendant is: what does it mean to rely on a place to remember, when that place contains the memories of so many others? At sites of dispossession, trauma, massacre, what happens to our environmentally embodied memories? If the mind is permeable to place, does remembering involve a transformative porosity where wounded places get under our skin, into our bodies and lives?

A politics of possibilities for the Anthropocene

Recognising the radical intercorporeality of human lives, bodies and thoughts with the more-than-human world is a political act. It is an ethic of knowing and being that reimagines the way we are intra-actively composed with our earth others, and this can open up possibilities for change. Karan Barad writes that what is needed in our current political and environmental moment is 'a politics of possibilities: ways of responsibly imagining and intervening in the configurations of power, that is, intra-actively reconfiguring spacetimemattter'.[84]

Such a politics is not, and cannot, be about starting again and remaking the future, because that would continue colonial erasures of Indigenous presence, and deny the irrevocable damage that has already been done to people and their places. Instead this politics of possibility can begin what Donna Haraway terms 'modest' and 'partial' recuperations in the Anthropocene. This involves the 'mourning of irreversible losses'[85] alongside 'the activation of the chthonic powers which are within our grasp, as we collect up the trash of the Anthropocene and the exterminism of the Capitolocene to something that might possibly have a chance of ongoing'.[86]

In the Armidale Pine Forest, volunteers have initiated a process of fostering resilience and life in the charred ruins of a production landscape. From mid October, 2009, people started to devote their weekends and weekday afternoons to recuperative efforts that enacted what Eben Kirksey has termed 'biocultural hope': modest acts of care that encourage the flourishing of life in severely compromised states.[87]

The goal was to plant 'an open woodland of native trees' that 'will be of great value to future generations'.[88] Since that time over 10,000 native trees have been planted, including angophoras, peppermint gums, apple box, stringy bark, red gum and snow gum.[89]

The planting of native flora does not affirm a native/introduced dualism because the existing conifers are not devalued in the new management discourse. The Forest Management Plan states that '[t]he part of the old forest that was not cleared has significant historical value' and 'all efforts should be maintained to preserve this area'.[90]

Acknowledging the heritage value of the pines to the community while simultaneously recognising the importance of restoring native life in the area positions the Pine Forest as a multi-temporal site rich with diverse memories. This decolonising approach avoids the construction of a monological historical narrative which would simplify the site's history and create a temporal monoculture. Instead humans and nonhumans are working together to convene 'new publics on the planet'.[91] This is a form of botanical decolonisation, where humans work alongside more-than-human agents to intervene in capitalist and colonial geographies of power.

Environmental justice and love

Val Plumwood argues powerfully for environmental justice to frame love and protection of idealised places. This is an 'injunction to cherish and care for [special and beloved] places, but without in the process destroying or degrading any other places, where "other places" includes other human places, but also other species' places'.[92] This requires us to ask difficult questions, like how does loving and protecting a pine forest create a shadow place? How does this paper, that I write on to celebrate this place, contribute to deforestation of ancient forest? Who is winning in this recuperation, who is losing?

Asking these questions is not about presenting a cynical barrier to recuperative endeavours of biocultural hope in the Anthropocene, nor is it about undermining people's genuine love and attachment for cherished homeplaces. On the contrary, it is about expanding that love through the complex entanglements of life in the Anthropocene – the often disturbing flows of material, energy and information through global networks that constitute our lived world. This radically inclusive approach to loving damaged places collapses the mind/body dualism, and in doing so, illuminates the shadow places that sustain our lives. Val Plumwood writes:

Think what it would mean to acknowledge and honour all the places that support you, at all levels of reconceptualisation, from spiritual to economic, and to honour not just this more fully-conceived 'own place' but the places of others too. Such a program is politically radical, in that it is incompatible with an economy of privileged places thriving at the expense of exploited places. Production, whether from other or self-place, cannot take the form of a place-degrading process, but requires a philosophy and economy of mutual recognition.[93]

At the Pine Forest we witness the beginnings of a politics of possibilities in the Anthropocene – a recuperative effort to live ethically within a production landscape. This experiment in inhabiting and inheriting damage has grown from the collision between materiality and memory, between the places we think of as emotionally and cognitively significant, and the devalued places that provide material nourishment.

Bringing the experience of personal loss to bear on questions of place value does not lead us to any simple answers about how to restructure our environmental classifications and relationships. In many ways, it is precisely this lack of simplicity that is fundamental in developing an inclusive ethic of environmental care. Determining which organisms should live and which should die should not be an easy process because life is complex and connected. Conceptual systems that make these decisions easy, such as native/introduced dualisms, often rest on the oversimplification of place and the denial of the legitimacy of certain ways of valuing it. An eco-mental paradigm challenges this denial by highlighting the complex entanglements between minds and the world which make all land multi-temporal and multi-vocal.

The question of how to inherit a radically transformed colonial ecology in the Anthropocene is central to how we think about living well in a period of rapid environmental transformation. By advancing a dynamic understanding of ecology, an eco-mental paradigm of place and memory approaches time as something that collects within an environment forming rich temporal topographies. This undermines the seemingly obvious hierarchical taxonomies of native/introduced which are based on the disjunctive moment of European settlement. It also refuses the reduction of multi-species landscapes to resources for extraction by celebrating nonhuman agency and ecological connectivity.

In fostering diversity through planting native trees at the Armidale Pine Forest, the community is engaged in a type of 'resilience facilitation', which actively resuscitates a devastated eco-mental system and encourages new connectivities to form. Rose argues that resilience facilitation is essentially counter-modern because it embraces the agency of the nonhuman world by acknowledging 'the force, or desire, of living things to flourish, to be in connection, to find their mutually beneficial patterns'.[94] This form of environmental healing is part of a more-than-human decolonisation as it reactivates an ecological system's own desire for growth and connection.

Richard Torbay, commenting on the reforesting project, said that 'new life is being breathed into the devastated Armidale Pine Forest'.[95] As these trees outgrow the protective milk carton coverings that have been carefully installed by community volunteers, connections between earth and growth, death and life, human and nonhuman will continue to thrive. Through tree planting, humans insert themselves into the forest life cycle, becoming active agents in cultivating resilience. Like pollinators or soil organisms, humans become vital to a shared multispecies future, as they literally *breathe* life into the more-than-human atmospherics of a forest ecology.

Lynn Margulis and Dorion Sagan observe that '[l]ife is an extension of being into the next generation, the next species'.[96] When visualising the vitality of life, beyond the boundary of the skin of the individual organism, we can grasp an understanding of memory and time that is both intimate and worldly.

My childhood past held in the arms of those ancient conifers is reborn and evolving in the newly seeded soil. This past does not belong solely to me, but links me to all beings that share memory and life in New England's blood country. Such memory is deeply personal but it is also ecologically permeable. This has immense implications for how we approach more-than-human decolonisation and the recuperation of damaged places in the Anthropocene.

Considering memory as an ecologically involved process connects mind to body and local to global in a way that is personally affective and embraces commitment to change and decolonisation. That my memories are environmentally embodied in a land that holds the memories of others, including Indigenous Australians and the more-than-human world, tells me that I am already connected and therefore responsible for this place and its many lives. As Peter Read observes, 'those places which we loved, lost, and grieved for were wrested from the Indigenous people who loved them, lost them and grieve for them still'.[97] This is a moral claim personal enough to inspire direct action.

As the Armidale people continue to restore their forest of memory, they connect lives along lines of shared earth and experience. Such recuperative work involves an engagement with the past which is multicultural and multinatural.[98] This small pocket of healing in a post-colonial country, traumatised by ecological and social damage, offers hope for a future of responsibility, remembrance and love.

Notes

1   E. Casey, *Remembering: A Phenomenological Study*, Second Edition (Bloomington: Indiana University Press, 2000), 201.
2   T. Van Dooren, *Flight Ways: Life and Loss at the Edge of Extinction* (Columbia University Press: New York & Sussex, 2014), 82.
3   H. W. Fowler & F. G. Fowler, *The Concise Oxford Dictionary of Current English*, Fifth Edition (London: Oxford University Press, 1964), 243.
4   Armidale Dumaresq Council, 'Supplementary Management Plan: Armidale State Forest 2009'.
5   F. Bayet-Charlton, 'Overturning the Doctrine: Indigenous People and Wilderness – Being Aboriginal in the Environmental Movement', in *Blacklines: Contemporary*

Critical Writing by Indigenous Australians, ed. M. Grossman (Carlton: Melbourne University Press, 2003), 174.

6   D. Rose, *Wild Country*, 11.

7   Pugliese has written on the way nonhuman entities, like conifers planted in the middle of deforested native land, bespeak histories of dispossession, loss and trauma in 'Forensic Ecologies', 1–37.

8   N. Gane, 'When we Have Never Been Human, What is to be Done?: Interview with Donna Haraway', *Theory Culture Society* 23 (2006): 145.

9   L. Instone & A. Taylor, 'Thinking about Inheritance Through the Figure of the Anthropocene, from the Antipodes and In the Presence of Others', *Environmental Humanities* 7 (2015): 140.

10 D. Rose, *Wild Country*, 22.

11 D. Haraway, 'Staying with the Trouble: Sympoiesis, String Figures, Multispecies Muddle', Lecture, University of Alberta, 25 March, 2014, accessed 5 June 2014, www.new.livesteam.com/aict/DonnaHaraway.

12 I use the term becoming-with in keeping with Donna Haraway's understanding of becoming as a multispecies collaborative and emergent event (*When Species Meet* (Minneapolis and London: University of Minnesota Press, 2008), 244). For more discussion on this see K. Wright, 'Becoming-With', *Living Lexicon for the Environmental Humanities*, 5 (2014): 277–281.

13 Eduardo Kohn describes a forest as a community of living selves in his *How Forests Think: Towards an Anthropology Beyond the Human* (London: University of California Press, 2013).

14 V. Plumwood, 'Shadow Places'.

15 For more on distance and concealment in capitalist societies, see R. Nixon, *Slow Violence and the Environmentalism of the Poor* (Cambridge: Harvard University Press, 2011).

16 V. Plumwood, 'Shadow Places'.

17 The first commercial conifer plantation project was initiated at Tuncurry, near Taree. The Armidale State Forest is the site of the First Forest Experimentation Station (R. Horne, 'The Philosophy and Practice of *P. Radiata* Plantation Silviculture in New South Wales', School of Forestry, Melbourne University, Beecroft: Forestry Commission of New South Wales, 1986, www.dpi.nsw.gov.au/__data/assets/pdf_file/0009/389925/The-Philosophy-and-Practice-of-P-Radiata-Plantation-Silviculture-in-NSW.pdf.

18 R. Torbay, 'Armidale Pine Forest' (2004).

19 R. Torbay, 'Armidale Pine Forest'. Private member's statement, 22 October 2008, www.richardtorbay.com.au/parliamentary/armidale-pine-forest.php.

20 Ibid.

21 Armidale Dumeresq Council, 'Supplementary Management Plan'.

22 L. Instone & A. Taylor, 'Thinking about Inheritance', 147.

23 V. Plumwood, 'Shadow Places'.

24 A. Crosby, *Ecological Imperialism: The Biological Expansion of Europe, 900–1900*. Second Edition (Cambridge: Cambridge University Press, 2004).

25 D. Haraway, 'Anthropocene, Capitalocene, Plantationocene, Chthulucene: Making Kin', *Environmental Humanities*, 6 (2015): 162.

26 M. Williams and G. Wardle, '*Pinus Radiata* Invasion in Australia: Identifying Key Knowledge Gaps and Research Directions', *Austral Ecology* 32, no. 7 (2007): 721.

27 Ibid., 722.

28 M. Williams and G. Wardle, '*Pinus Radiata* Invasion in New South Wales: The Extent of Spread', *Plant Protection Quarterly* 24, no. 4 (2009), 146.

29 D. Lindenmayer, M. McCarthy, K. Parris and M. Pope, 'Habitat Fragmentation, Landscape Context, and Mammalian Assemblages in Southeastern Australia', *Journal of Mammalogy* 81, no. 3 (2000); J. Smith, *Further Ecological Comparisons Between Pine*

Plantations and Native Forests, Clouds Creek, NSW (Armidale: University of New England, 1997).

30 C. O'Loughlin, 'Environmental Services Provided by Plantations', Guest Editorial, *New Zealand Journal of Forestry* 49, no. 4 (2005): 2.

31 T. van Dooren, 'Invasive Species in Penguin Worlds: An Ethical Taxonomy of Killing for Conservation', *Conservation and Society* 9, no. 4, (2011): 289.

32 M. Chew & A. Hamilton, 'The Rise and Fall of Biotic Nativeness: A Historical Perspective', in *Fifty Years of Invasion Ecology: The Legacy of Charles Elton*, First Edition, ed. D. Richardson (Oxford: Blackwell Publishing, 2011), 36.

33 J. Arthur, *Default Country*, 44.

34 Ibid., 152.

35 T. Mastnak, J. Elyachar & T. Boellstorff, 'Botanical Decolonization: Rethinking Native Plants', *Environment and Planning D: Society and Space* 32 (2014): 374.

36 M. Langton, 'What Do We Mean by Wilderness? Wilderness and *Terra Nullius* in Australian Art', *The Sydney Papers* 8, no. 1 (1996): 31.

37 Ibid., 20.

38 V. Plumwood, 'Decolonising Relationships with Nature', 13.

39 M. Hall, 'Plant Autonomy and Human-Plant Ethics', *Environmental Ethics* 31, no. 2 (2009): 172.

40 Ibid., 174.

41 Ibid., 176.

42 Ibid., 172.

43 R. Torbay, 'Armidale Pine Forest' (2004).

44 Ibid.

45 R. Torbay, 'Armidale Pine Forest' (2008).

46 Armidale Dumaresq Council, 'Pine Forest Stakeholder Analysis' (2009).

47 G. Albrecht, 'The Age of Solastalgia', *The Conversation* (7 August 2012), https://theconversation.com/the-age-of-solastalgia-8337.

48 V. Plumwood, 'Shadow Places'.

49 Ibid.

50 M. Rowlands, *Externalism: Putting Mind and World Back Together Again* (Chesham: Acumen Publishing, 2003), 177.

51 M. Rowlands, 'Environmental Epistemology', *Ethics and the Environment* 10, no. 2 (2005): 5–27.

52 Peter Read describes numerous cases of this loss in *Returning to Nothing* (Cambridge, New York & Melbourne: Cambridge University Press, 1996) where he documents personal experiences of eco-mental distress in a variety of circumstances.

53 E. Casey, *Remembering*, 213.

54 J. Sutton, 'Remembering', in *The Cambridge Handbook of Situated Cognition*, eds. P. Robbins and M. Aydede (Cambridge: Cambridge University Press, 2009), 230.

55 J. Walker, *Trauma Cinema: Documenting Incest and the Holocaust* (Berkeley & Los Angeles: University of California Press, 2005), 17.

56 Ibid., 18.

57 M. Rowlands, 'Environmental Epistemology', 24.

58 J. Keulartz, 'The Emergence of Enlightened Anthropocentrism in Ecological Restoration', *Nature and Culture*, 7, no. 1 (2012): 60.

59 M. Gagliano, M. Renton, M. Depczynsky and S. Mancuso, 'Experience Teaches Plants to Learn Faster and Forget Slower in Environments Where It Matters', *Oecologia* 175: 63–72.

60 Ibid.

61 Gagliano explains 'Viewed through this lens, cognition does not equate with the presence of a nervous system; the nervous system may expand an organism's range of potential actions and interactions but does not in itself generate cognition. With a nervous system or not, the presence of cognition and the array of cognitive

capacities in living organisms may be understood as the workings of a continuous process of evolution by natural selection, hence advocating a paradigm capable of unifying a great diversity of expressions of the raw cognitive foundation common to all living systems.' 'In a Green Frame of Mind: Perspectives on the Behavioural Ecology and Cognitive Nature of Plants', *AoB Plants* (2015), http://aobpla.oxford journals.org/content/7/plu075.

62   M. Marder, *Plant-Thinking: A Philosophy of Vegetal Life* (Columbia University Press, New York, 2013), 169.
63   M. Marder, *Plant Thinking*, 169.
64   I. Stengers, 'The Cosmopolitical Proposal', in *Making Things Public*, eds. B. Latour and P. Weibel (Cambridge: MIT Press, 2005), 2002.
65   M. Marder, *Plant-Thinking*, 156.
66   K. Schlunke, 'One Strange Colonial Thing'.
67   G. Bateson, *Mind and Nature*.
68   G. Bateson, *Ecology of Mind*, 459.
69   A. Neimanis & S. Walker, 'Weathering: Climate Change and the "Thick Time" of Transcorporeality', *Hypatia* 29, no. 3 (2013): 571.
70   V. Gaia, *Adventures in the Anthropocene: A Journey to the Heart of the Planet We Made* (Minneapolis: Milkweed Editions, 2014), 267.
71   D. Bengton and M. J. Dockry, 'Forest Futures in the Anthropocene: Can Trees and Humans Survive Together', *The Futurist* 48, no. 4 (2014): 34–39.
72   G. Vince, *Adventures in the Anthropocene*, 264.
73   Ibid., 265.
74   D. Bengton and M. J. Dockry, 'Forest Futures in the Anthropocene'.
75   E. Kolbert, 'Enter the Anthropocene – Age of Man', *National Geographic* (2011): http://ngm.nationalgeographic.com/2011/03/age-of-man/kolbert-text/2.
76   V. Plumwood, 'Shadow Places'.
77   Forests NSW, 'The Pine Plantation Rotation', www.forestrycorporation.com.au/__ data/assets/pdf_file/0009/238473/pine-plantation-rotation.pdf.
78   V. Plumwood, 'Shadow Places'.
79   Bill Neidjie, *Story about Feeling* (Broome: Magabala Books, 1989), 166.
80   Ibid., 61.
81   V. Plumwood, 'Shadow Places'.
82   D. Rose, 'Dialogue with Place: Toward an Ecological Body', *Journal of Narrative Theory* 32, no. 3 (2002): 321.
83   Ibid., 321–322.
84   Ibid.
85   D. Haraway, 'Anthropocene, Capitalocene, Plantationocene, Chthulucene: Making Kin', 160.
86   D. Haraway, 'Anthropocene, Capitalacone, Chthulucene: Staying with the Trouble', *Anthropocene: Arts of Living on a Damaged Planet* (2015): http://opentranscripts.org/transcript/anthropocene-capitalocene-chthulucene/.
87   S. Eben Kirksey, N. Shapiro and M. Brodine, 'Hope in Blasted Landscapes', *Social Science Information* 52, no. 2 (2013): 228–256.
88   Armidale Dumaresq Council, 'Supplementary Management Plan'.
89   R. Torbay, 'Volunteers Helping to Bring Armidale Pine Forest Back to Life' (2009).
90   Armidale Dumaresq Council, 'Supplementary Management Plan'.
91   J. K. Gibson-Graham, 'A Feminist Project of Belonging for the Anthropocene', *Gender, Place, and Culture* 18, no. 1 (2011): 1-21.
92   V. Plumwood, 'Shadow Places'.
93   Ibid.
94   D. Rose, *Wild Country*, 49.
95   R. Torbay, 'Volunteers Helping'.

96 L. Margulis and D. Sagan, *What is Life?* (Berkeley and Los Angeles: University of California Press, 1995), 144.

97 P. Read, *Belonging: Australians, Place and Aboriginal Ownership* (Cambridge: Cambridge University Press, 2003), 2.

98 Bruno Latour uses the term 'multinaturalism' to challenge the notion that there is a singular nature. Instead Latour argues that 'nature is *plural*. Just like cultures' (S. Muecke, 'Cassowary').

4 Autumnal becomings

Last autumn, Armidale, 2015

My friend is very sick – she has terminal cancer. She lives in Sydney, and she's 35 years old. I'm lying on my back on the green grass at the edge of a football field, camera-in-hand, to make her a video of autumn leaves. Underneath a maple tree, the sky is a pattern of red and yellow falling out of blue. My still, silent body is carried away by wind and light, as leaves scatter my thoughts across time and place.

My friend loves the brilliant colours of autumn in this town where she spent her teenage years, and she told me that she longs to come back to see them but with all the treatments it is not possible for her to leave the city. Her body is tormented by growing tumours and cracking bones, by chemotherapy and radiation, but her mind is returning to a childhood season – to trails of yellow, orange and red stretched out across the green fields of youth.

She died in the last month of spring, before she could get a chance to see another autumn. Sometimes I imagine her thin pale body stretched out on white hospital sheets, with her mind wrapped up in the falling colours of the world.

This autumn, Armidale, 2016

I am five months pregnant with my first child. I can feel the baby kicking and nudging me from inside at regular intervals throughout the day, a rhythmic reminder that my body is entangled in evolutionary time – in the creative emergence of multispecies births and deaths patterned across the flesh of the world.

Gregory Bateson asks 'what is the pattern that connects all living things?' 'This is an aesthetic question', he says.[1]

A spider's web
Rings on a tree
A bird's nest
The ripples of fireflies on the water like rain
The pregnant body
The wrinkled hand
The ripened fruit
The falling leaves of autumn

I long to welcome my little baby into a world painted with patterns that connect, to watch his tiny body grow beyond my own – as life extends itself outward – unfolding from the shared flesh of the world to the sun.

Seasons provide a rhythm for terrestrial life. Changes in the temperature and hue of quotidian existence remind us of the nonhuman life that surrounds and envelops us: cycles of growth, death and birth that permeate all living creatures. To contemplate the pattern of fallen orange autumn leaves is one way to ponder the ongoing dance of earthly life and death.

The aesthetics of deciduous seasonal change are borne of connectivity and the complex interactions of botanies with their environment. Summer is green with chlorophyll – that generative pigment that takes the rays of the sun and turns them into food. As hours of light in the day become fewer and the air cools with autumn winds, the veins of each leaf begin to close, and chlorophyll degrades. Beneath the deep green of a summer leaf are hidden colours – yellow xanthophylls[2] and orange beta-carotenes[3] – that reveal themselves in autumn skies. Accompanying these yellows and oranges are reds and purples – anthocyanins[4] – produced in late summer through a combination of bright summer light and each tree's own aging process. Autumn colour comes from within and without, and acts as a signal to insects, birds and a variety of mammals to hail an oncoming winter.

The colourful change of seasons is an example of Mikhail Bakhtin's 'chronotope' that expresses 'the inseparability of space and time'.[5] The year is a metamorphosis from green, soft leaves, to loud crackling reds and yellows that fall into piles of crumbling cellophane-like colour in parks and fields so that, finally, all that is left is a bare skeleton of bark and tree bones silhouetted in the winter grey. Then, in spring, the branches flower. All this visceral, tangible change 'thickens time' so that time 'takes on flesh, becomes artistically visible' and 'space becomes charged and responsive to the movements of time'.[6]

In seasons, the passage of time is witnessed through changing states, that is, through transformation. Bakhtin describes the temporal sequence of metamorphosis as a 'line with "knots" in it'.[7] These time-knots portray the entire life of a being through distinctive moments. Rather than the mundane tick-tock of linear time, the seasons show 'sharply differing images' of the one tree, the one place. Time is 'not merely technical, not a mere distribution of days, hours, moments that are reversible, transposable, unlimited internally, along a straight line'. Instead time is integrated and whole. The passage of time is made clear through moments of crisis and rebirth[8] – through tangible earthly change. This is the fullness of the chronotope.

The human experience of time is also one of transformation and embodied stages. Time is felt through differing states of corporeal existence, and it is only when we notice discrepancies between these states that we infer the passage of time, for example, in 'getting older'. Time 'in our bodies' and 'in our bones' does not flow as a linear sequence, but is an experience of metamorphosis that resonates with the rhythms of the seasons.[9]

Seasonal change materialises cycles of life that are shared across human and nonhuman bodies. Bakhtin writes of stages that apply to individual life and to 'the life of nature': states of pregnancy, ripening, old age and death, all of which are 'profoundly chronotopic'.[10] Human and nonhuman, individual organism and earth, are bound together through the metamorphosis of space through time. In these intimate corporeal connections, time 'is sunk deeply in the earth, implanted in it and ripening in it... fleshed out, irreversible'.[11]

The resonances between seasonal transformation and embodied stages of human existence are taken up by American nature writer Henry Thoreau in his essay on a different New England autumn – the deciduous Fall of the northeastern United States. This New England autumn was a native one, and, according to Thoreau, too much ignored by a utilitarian city-dwelling culture. Thoreau implored American citizens to recognise the metamorphosis that grips the countryside in October, believing deciduous trees are teachers of vital multispecies lessons in earthly life and graceful death, lessons that are open to all who are willing to see and hear them, as 'all children alike can revel in this golden harvest'.[12]

But these ecological lessons take on a different tone in Armidale, Australia, where the autumnal becomings of red, gold and orange leaves are not native, but part of the problematic legacy of botanical colonisation. Introduced deciduous trees produce a chronotopic version of what Jay Arthur describes as colonial 'double vision' that perpetuates a disconnection from Indigenous ecologies and privileges imported aesthetics of time and transformation.[13] This disconnection is significant because the way time is measured and perceived determines 'what counts as change and for whom'.[14] Émile Durkheim argued that the way cultures measure time is neither objective nor arbitrary, but instead reflects what is most relevant to a particular group, corresponding 'to the periodical recurrence of rites, feasts, and public ceremonies'.[15] In Armidale, the bonding experience of sharing time is synchronised to the Eurocentric aesthetic of four annual seasons, meaning that the relationships that come to matter are connections to a colonial homeland.

In the following pages I embark on a journey into the beautiful autumnal trees of my hometown to explore alternatives to the colonial 'ecology of mind' that emerges when patterns of time and change have become displaced from the conditions of the native environment. In dialogue with Thoreau, I immerse myself in the rhizomatic multispecies ecology of a diasporic treescape to argue that in the relational becomings of this constructed autumn there are other rhythms breaking out, against the stultifying metronomic beat of a predictable four seasons.

Seasons as the pattern that connects

'We love to see any redness in the vegetation of the temperate zone', wrote Thoreau. 'It is the colour of colours. This plant speaks to our blood.'[16] Thoreau's writings trace a series of intimate encounters with patterns of nonhuman life and death. In his work we witness the affective power of sensuous connection to the more-than-human world. He writes of walking over beds of 'fresh, crisp, and rustling leaves' in a New England autumn, and says that these fallen leaves 'teach us how to die', as they 'decay at the foot of the tree, and afford nourishment to new generations...One wonders if the time will ever come when men, with their boasted faith in immortality, will lie down as gracefully and as ripe'.[17] For Thoreau, trees are teachers that can offer us moral lessons that get to the heart of what it means to be mortal in an ecological community.

> The trees are now repaying the earth with interest what they have taken from it...to add a leaf's thickness to the depth of the soil...We are all the richer for their decay...The ground is all partly-colored with them. But they still live in the soil...and in the forests that spring from it.[18]

Life flows through our shared places and our shared bodies. It is a multispecies achievement,[19] enabled by the deaths and births of all of Earth's inhabitants. The 'thick time'[20] of autumnal becoming is a time where the visceral process of decay is made beautiful by colour, and where life transforms itself into new generations and new species.

Autumn brings a colour and contrast to temporal patterns, aesthetically sensitising us to change. Thoreau writes:

> October is the month for painted leaves...As fruits and leaves and the day itself acquire a bright tint just before they fall, so the year nears its setting. October is its sunset sky; November the later twilight.[21]

Gregory Bateson used the notion of the pattern that connects to understand the formative principles that course through living bodies and systems on Earth. Perhaps our own entanglement with these patterns is why the biological pulse is attuned to the pulse of seasons, why 'hundreds of eyes are steadily drinking in this color'.[22] Bateson argued that the patterns that connect are not fixed, but in motion, like music or dance. A season patterns itself across a landscape. An autumn wind blows leaves at your feet and places you inside the pattern that connects. The pattern is a 'deeper symmetry in formal relations'; it is a 'meta-pattern, a pattern of patterns'.[23]

Autumn, Armidale, 2016

Stretched out on a blanket of red and yellow autumn leaves I am wrapped in living time. Beneath the bough of a tree, I watch as the wind, the breath of the world, makes the leaves above me quiver and tremble in sunlight. I think of Thoreau. 'Stand under this tree and see how finely its leaves are cut against the sky', he writes. 'There they dance, arm in arm with the light – tripping it on fantastic points, fit partners in those aerial halls. So intimately mingled are they with it, that...you can hardly tell at last what in the dance is leaf and what is light'.[24]

Flitting in and out of sun, elliptical leaves tease my eyes that long to hold them still. The only way to watch is to succumb to the pattern, to seek not the leaf nor the light, but the dance between them, the dance of being and non-being, the dance of presence and absence. I am, with this sun and this leaf and this light, immersed in a block of becoming, in a world made of states of change.

Armidale's imported autumn

A season is a rhizome. The autumnal trees of my youth are not arborescent and ordered, they are rhizomatic and relational. The neural pathways that hold my memories are interwoven with the intricate pattern of veins on a leaf. I think *with* these trees, I remember *with* this place. Deleuze and Guattari write, 'The wisdom of the plants: even when they have roots, there is always an outside where they form a rhizome with something else – with the wind, an animal, human beings...'[25]

But what happens when the rhizomatic ecology of a season is colonised by an anthropocentric structure? If seasons pulse with ecological patterns of connection, what happens when that seasonal pulse is manipulated to serve human ends?

In Armidale, autumn was imported. It is a season created by the displanting of native trees, and the plantation of imported deciduous trees. A fabrication of the late twentieth century, Armidale's autumn brings colour to a colonial fantasy of tame nature, predictable seasons and Eurocentric aesthetics of change and time.

Growing up in Armidale in the 1990s, I formed memories and attachments within a legacy of botanical colonisation that I was barely aware of. The fiery oranges, reds and yellows that painted my childhood always seemed endemic to the land, I never really thought twice about the exotic provenance of the trees, and it was only in my late twenties that I discovered Armidale's autumn has only existed since the 1950s, and grew from the abstract designs of a single man. On a research trip to the University of New England in 2011, Professor John Ryan informed me that it was Alwyn Jones – a local accountant – who coloured the landscape in its vibrant autumnal hues. Over five decades, Jones initiated the planting of 9000 diasporic trees throughout the city. The town is now filled with an incredibly diverse global range of botanical species, trafficked in from around the globe. American sweetgums (*Liquidambar styraciflua*) native to eastern North America, Mexico and Central America; Chinese pistachios (*Pistacia chinensis*) native to central and western China; claret ash trees (*Fraxinus angustifolia* subsp. *oxycarpa*) native to South Australia; European ash trees (*Fraxinus excelsior*) native to most of Europe; and almond trees (*Prunus dulcis*) native to the Middle East and South Asia, line the streets and parks.

Looking now, at their brilliant colour, I try to picture the autumnless Armidale of the 1940s, and it feels as though I am trying to remember a scene from a black and white film. Trying to picture Armidale pre-colonisation and settlement is even more difficult.

I live, like many Australians and colonial-descended peoples across the world, in the 'colonial present' – perpetually immersed in the rhythm of ongoing colonial ecologies. In my hometown, botanical colonisation, which involved the colonisation of both place *and* time, is a process that is so complete it is no longer noticed.[26] With its tourist catchcry of 'The City of Four Seasons', an annual 'Autumn Festival', and the circulation of public relations imagery of red and yellow foliage, Armidale has embraced a chromatic European autumn as its image of seasonality. This colonial aesthetic of time as four antipodean seasons is now so utterly congealed with the environment through the physical transformation of the land and treescape that it seems as natural as the sun rising and setting.

Being aware of the ways the landscapes of the present are built on the actions of the past is essential for the process of decolonising a home-place. The celebration of Armidale's chromatic autumn fails to acknowledge the many human and nonhuman agents who have patterned the streets and parks into the coloured shapes we have come to know, and ignores the specific and contingent choices which have determined the rhythms of this 'temporal environment'.[27]

That Alwyn Jones is largely a forgotten figure in Armidale is central to colonial possession and domination – an active forgetting of processes of spatial and temporal erasure. With the environment remade by a colonial planting enterprise, chronotopic temporality has been twisted into Western calendrical shapes.

A temporal grid

The four season model of change is based on an evenly spaced calendar of seasons that each last three months. These calendrical seasons are measured in abstract linear time – little boxes of congealed space-time-matter that are symmetrical, and similar to the visual representation of temporality through days on a calendar in even square spaces. Australia has a climate that is extremely diverse, and includes ecological zones of monsoon tropics, desert, savannah, alpine and temperate regions. Using a rigid calendrical model of transformation to cover seasonal change across the Australian continent is an abusively simplistic homogenisation of place and time, and the rhizomatic exchange that constitutes a season. It is as if a table of four even seasons has been placed over the passage of time in much the same way that grids of bitumen lines were laid over the 'deep Indigenous narrative lines' of country.[28] This colonisation of time mirrors processes of colonial territorialisation and its 'construction of Australia as a blank space to be drawn on'.[29]

Michelle Bastian has written on the way time is generative and socially produced. Time, argues Bastian, is not 'a quantative measurement, but…a powerful social tool for producing, managing and/or undermining various understandings of who or what is in relation with other things or beings'.

When Armidale's autumn trees begin to change colour, they signal something emergent and profound, a multispecies transformation deeply resonant with patterns of change that are at the heart of ecological life on Earth. Humans seem tuned in to this transformative ecology, noticing it, drinking it in, 'reveling in the golden harvest'. But in Armidale, this moment of shared becoming is corrupted by a colonial temporal and spatial ideology.

The problem of disconnection lies not so much in the imposition of *four* seasons in particular, but in imposing a calendrical map of seasons which occludes relational seasonal knowledge that is built on the synchronicity between beings. Calendar seasons are mono-temporal – measuring time in one way, and manipulating temporal environments to fit that measurement.

'Let us have Willows for spring', writes Thoreau, 'Elms for summer, Maples and Walnuts and Tupeloes for autumn, Evergreens for winter, and Oaks for all seasons'.[30] There is something vitalistic about measuring temporality and change through the bodies of our botanical kin. But Thoreau's celebration of his own New England seasons is radically different from Armidale's imported autumn. For Thoreau, attentiveness to seasonal change is deeply situated and responsive to the native environment. Patterns of more-than-human transformation in a place he has come to know intimately reveal a beautiful process of metamorphosis, which, he argues, is in *every* place, and visible in *every* plant.

> These bright leaves which I have mentioned are not the exception, but the rule; for I believe that all leaves, even grasses and mosses, acquire brighter colors just before their fall. When you come to observe faithfully the changes of each humblest plant, you find that each has, sooner or later, its peculiar autumnal tint.[31]

In Thoreau's autumnal journey through his own New England treescape, he is practising, and promoting, what Anna Tsing calls 'arts of noticing'. An 'art of noticing' is cultivated through attunement to the rich complexity of nonhuman life and patterns of interaction. Tsing argues that through 'passionate immersion' in the lives of nonhumans, humans can learn to notice and perceive subtle differences in hidden ecologies that surround them. This could enable us to become more aware of 'differences that make a difference',[32] and more alive to the pattern that connects.[33] Central to this attunement is an acceptance of the 'indeterminacy' of nature and a resistance to human attempts to control and shape it.[34]

Armidale's chromatic autumn is a manifestation of human attempts to manipulate the nonhuman world to serve human ends. Alwyn Jones formed the Armidale Progress Association and the Armidale Improvement and Beautification Committee in the early 1940s, after he arrived in the town and was disappointed at the lack of foliage, having 'experienced the beauty of the trees in Bathurst and Orange, two cities on the central tablelands with a climate similar to Armidale'.[35] To Jones' dismay Armidale had 'virtually no street trees' and 'practically no autumn colour'.[36] Believing that 'something needed to be done'[37] to improve the drab country town, Jones lobbied the City Council to begin a tree-planting and street beautification program that would import a variety of trees, particularly species with deciduous colour, into the town. Jones emphasised the importance of autumnal aesthetics in developing civic pride[38] as well as promoting tourism, noting that both Bathurst and Orange had visitors that came to see the colours of the towns' trees in spring and autumn.[39]

The tree-planting throughout Armidale can be viewed as a kind of large-scale civic gardening, where certain plants have been cultivated to 'improve' the aesthetics of the township and align them with colonial values. In a relational ecology, reshaping the trees to perform a particular seasonal pattern colonises not only the aesthetics of the landscape, but the aesthetics of environmental change; in essence, it determines what differences are noticed and, so, what environmental information is perceived and responded to. And this could be incredibly dangerous.

Michelle Bastian warns that by '[u]sing the wrong time scale in the wrong context, we risk tricking ourselves into thinking we are aware of, and thus able to coordinate with, those other beings or things that are most crucial, when in fact we may be falling further and further behind'.[40] The manipulation of temporality in Armidale's imported autumn makes time, weather and climate appear cyclic and predictable through a repetitive four movement passage of seasonal change each year. But we live in a time of radically unpredictable weather, a time when seasonal patterns are shifting and unstable. Armidale's metronomic seasonal beat runs the risk of terribly damaging humans' arts of noticing, leaving us out of step with the seasonal rhythms of the more-than-human natures that surround us. If the passage of time appears in a manicured and predictable relationship to the Earth, this fosters arts of expectation and arts of routine behaviour, instead of arts of the noticing that are vital for organisms' survival in dynamic environments.

When 'arts of noticing' are damaged, long shadows fall across places and times. In this darkness lie neglected beings, often indigenous creatures who are disregarded in favour of the beloved and domesticated critters who light up lives, homes, gardens and parks. It is telling that when Alwyn Jones began his beautification program, the New England region was suffering from a period of severe 'dieback', a disease that affects native trees. Eucalypts suffering from dieback die slowly, from the tips of the branches downward, and as they shed their leaves their bodies become dry corpses that reach up into the sky with twisted bare wooden arms and fingers.

Dieback is caused by the environmental devastations of colonisation, with land clearing and grazing implicated in this particular phenomenon of 'slow violence'[41] played out on the bodies of indigenous trees.[42] New England poet Judith Wright reflected on the dieback from a natureculture perspective, seeing in the skeletons of eucalypt trees the ghosts of a dispossessed people:

> Though it took the trees longer to react to what had happened to the land, they may have given up trying to return and are dying, or dying back, as we call it. We have begun to search out reasons for what we call New England Dieback. But I think I felt them myself, when as a small child I believed I saw those dark bearded faces moving among the trees, dispossessed and silent.[43]

Colonialism unleashed terrible violence on the indigenous world. This violence spread through multispecies relational networks, and continues to infect native ecologies with toxicity and incremental violence. Jones' desire to colour

Armidale's urban centre may well have been a response to the colourless grey of a dilapidated rural landscape, where trees lose all seasons and time, and become motionless sculptures. But Armidale's autumnal streetscape does not allow for the kind of recuperative healing work witnessed at the Armidale Pine Forest. Instead it suppresses the past, and follows a logic of progress and development as it ignores the suffering of the surrounding bush and paints the town centre in celebratory colour.

When Jones embarked on his 'improvement' and 'beautification' schemes, he paid little attention to the possible environmental impacts of the imported trees on the surrounding ecosystem. The Chinese pistachio (*Pistacia chinensis*) which Jones made popular in home gardening has since been implicated in problematic biological invasions of surrounding bushland. The plant is rapidly establishing a large, wild population[44] that threatens the regional distinctiveness of local biotas with consequences for biodiversity, and ecological and human health.[45]

Armidale citizens are passionate about their imported autumnal plants, and the removal of trees from public places has repeatedly provoked citizen outcry.[46] While it is certainly positive that the Armidale people have developed strong emotional connections to the nonhumans who share the town, when this care is forged at the expense of surrounding ecosystems it disavows indigenous presence, and colludes with the doctrine of *terra nullius*. Paul Robbins observes that 'It is not species, but sociobiological networks that are invasive'.[47] The discursive privileging of colonial aesthetics provides the conditions for botanical invasion into indigenous ecological territories, and lays the groundwork for continuing slow violence.

An indigenous ecology of mind

In contrast to colonial seasons measured in abstract time, Aboriginal Australian seasonal knowledge responded to a world composed of communicative entities that collaboratively created emergent events. This world is now known by the term '*Country*'. For Aboriginal people living on Country, seasons were announced through a multispecies semiotic ecology that emerges through patterns of relation that human beings respond to, what Deborah Bird Rose, following poet Peter Boyle, calls 'creature languages'.

> The sight and smell of flowers, the pain of the march fly bite and the sensation of blood running down the leg, the sight of swifts in the sky or flower petals drifting in the river, fireflies winking and the interminable racket of cicadas: these are multi-faceted creature languages, and smart creatures take notice. Humans enhance their intelligence not by stepping out of the system and trying to control it, but by enmeshing themselves ever more knowledgeably into the creature-languages of Country.[48]

Empirically observed behavioural changes in multiple species, such as sharks breeding or wattle flowering, communicated to Aboriginal Australian peoples a shift in season. Aboriginal seasons were not symmetrical in duration, like the even three-month European seasons, but ranged from a few weeks to a number of months; and were situated in considerably longer-term weather patterns like the Mudong, or life cycle, which covers 11 or 12 years, for example.

This seasonality was not externally imposed, but emerged from Nature's becoming. Deborah Bird Rose explains that, in Aboriginal seasonal patterns, 'events are ordered by connections: sequence and co-occurrence (simultaneity) are of the first importance. When the march flies start biting, the crocodiles are laying their eggs'.[49] Because temporality and transition is understood relationally in Aboriginal worldviews, seasons are a celebration of multispecies interaction. In the Yarralin area of the Northern Territory, for example, if flying foxes are moving from the inland bush to the rivers and nesting in the pandanus palm trees the onset of rains is imminent.[50] In the Sydney area koala fighting signals that the weather will soon be extremely hot: 'the bigger the fights, the bigger the noise, the hotter the weather'.[51] Aboriginal seasonality also includes observation of celestial movements which are associated with the ripening of particular fruits or the visitation of certain animals.[52] Time is bound to a multispecies ecology that pulses through the rhythms of night and day, through the movement of the bodies of earthly kin, and through the wandering of stars against a crow-black sky.

Rose explains that while some seasonal knowledge is dispersed widely, most is localised. Many of the signs of concurrence vary from place to place, so that one really only knows what is happening in the places where one has the knowledge of what concurrences exist and what they mean.[53] This encourages humility in response to the complex agencies of the more-than-human world:

> People know there is a system here, and when they go beyond the bounds of their knowledge, they know that they are in the presence of a system they do not understand. The system is widespread, the content is local.[54]

Situated knowledge and the humility of a locally-bound worldview are important elements for living ethically in a radically changing world. We learn empirically about the world through our bodies and through our connections to our earth others. The same winds blow through us, the same rains saturate and enliven us. Alphonso Lingis writes:

> our movements are not spontaneous initiatives launched against masses of inertia: we move in an environment of air currents, rustling trees, and animate bodies. Our movements are stirred by the coursing of our blood, the pulse of the wind, the reedy rhythms of the cicadas in the autumn trees...[55]

Aboriginal Australian author Melissa Lucashenko argues that relationships across human and nonhuman lives are circular, and that intimate belonging in place requires us to recognise shared patterns of connection and our own porosity to changing patterns:

How does your home look and feel in summer? In the cool months? In the rain? In the dry? How does each tree in your yard express these differences? How do the birds and the animals? How do the ocean and rivers change with the months? How do you?[56]

Being able to answer these questions requires long stretches of intergenerational time, as people 'grow into place', and come to know relational cycles that seem to flow like clockwork. But then, Lucashenko writes:

> *something else happens.* The tree that has always burst into blossom in September decides to dry up and stay barren. The ocean brings a torrent of dead muttonbirds to South Golden Beach for the first time in six years...We learn that the natural world is infinitely variable, and that we can *never be wholly sure* of our knowledge. There is always room for error and doubt...In short, with enough time, we do learn the country, but with an even longer time we also learn to be humble about what it is possible to know.[57]

Lucashenko is speaking of wonder – that inspiring mix of surprise and curiosity at mysterious happenings beyond our knowledge. Deborah Bird Rose has argued that mystery is a necessary property of any holistic system. This is because it is impossible to remove oneself from the system one is a part of, ensuring that the system in its entirety remains perpetually beyond our comprehension. One interesting outcome of this is that, if conceptualised accurately, mystery is a cause for celebration because it indicates the integrity of larger systems. In contrast, predictability signals crisis because it indicates a loss of connectivity.[58]

In order to experience wonder we must be open to being surprised by the world. We need arts of noticing that will allow us to dispel with the illusion of predictable and tame temporal environments. When Gregory Bateson asked 'what is the pattern that connects', he did not intend there to be a singular answer, because patterns of ecological connectivity are always changing.[59] Nora Bateson, his daughter, explains that 'the goal is not to crack the code, but rather to catch the rhythm'.[60] In a climate changing world we need the flexibility to be able to respond to radically shifting seasonal patterns.

Sunrise, Armidale, 2016

A spider web emerges in the first rays of the day as if a thought (it is a thought) brought to my awareness. Particles of dew collected on strands of the web in the night are reflected by particles of light at sunrise. Materiality reveals temporality, and the thoughts of the world direct my thoughts.

What is a spider web but a refrain, each delicate thread a line in the song of home?

I crawl too close while trying to take a photograph and accidentally sever a strand. The spider loses context and connection, her web blowing wildly in an unforgiving breeze. On the edge of disappearance, she weaves quickly, creating another pattern to keep her in the world.

An ecology of living thoughts

Eduardo Kohn observes that 'life is inherently semiotic',[61] and that the 'biological world is constituted by the ways in which myriad beings – human and nonhuman – perceive and represent their surroundings'.[62] The world is a cacophonous conversation of multisensorial, more-than-human languages. Aboriginal understandings of seasonality responded to this immanent semiotic ecology, as human minds become part of an immanent system of ecological thought.

Gregory Bateson differentiated the living world (creatura) from the world of forces (pleroma), noting that in the living world *difference* is a cause, rather than forces and impacts. The 'difference that makes a difference'[63] is the information that is transcribed on the map of reality that we draw – the distinctions that each creature deems important. Deborah Bird Rose notes that in Aboriginal seasonal knowledges, 'difference is regularly…acknowledged, not erased, because many differences are of an order that makes a difference: they are information'.[64]

'*Ngumpin* going by trees, what the trees doing, and what pretty flower. When he get dry, we know October,' Yarralin Elder Old Jimmy explains.[65]

In an affective ecology, trees can communicate a great deal of environmental information that is vital for survival. Plants are incredibly adept at communicating difference because they are immersed in, and responsive to, their ecological milieu. 'Plants', write Carla Hustak and Natasha Myers, 'are difference generators,'[66] with keenly attuned anatomies that enable them to 'discern subtle differences in their worlds'.[67] Changes in temperature, 'the slightest brush of the wing of a passing insect', and differences in herbivores detected through distinct substances in their saliva, are all responded to by plants, whose 'roots and rhizomes form a network of connections as complex as an animal's nervous system'.[68]

Eduardo Kohn explains the way multispecies assemblages amplify the differences that make a difference through what he calls 'semiotic density'.[69] In a relational ecology of selves, differences in soil are translated into differences in plants, and from those plants difference extends outward through rhizomatic networks of encounter and exchange, coming to make a difference to a diverse range of living beings. Kohn argues that within this communicative relational ecology, selves can actually be understood as *living thoughts* in a biosemiotic system.[70]

Understanding thought, language, exchange as properties of organism-plus-environment system, we can see how people's seasonal knowledge situates human minds in an ecology of living thoughts. Perception is 'produced differential intensity'.[71] 'Changes in the environment are transformed into changes in the neurons, which are then transformed into changes in the firings of complexes of neurons'.[72] Seasons, weather, winds, atmosphere, float through minds and bodies that are thinking with the living thoughts of the world.

Gregory Bateson observed that 'in no system which shows mental characteristics can any part have unilateral control over the whole. In other words, the mental characteristics of the system are immanent, not in some part, but in the system as a whole'.[73] Moving beyond the neural and symbolic limits of cognition to look at other processes of differentiation, dynamism and relationality, we can understand thought as immanent, collective, affective, circulating through bodies in contact with one another.

The fissures between the firing synapses are the spaces between the insect and the pollen. The air is thick with propositions[74] deeply scented by the erotic aromas that beckon bees and butterflies to flowers. Beneath the soils a rhizomatic underworld of roots and microorganisms buzzes with life. If you follow ants into their tunnels you might find yourself entering this subterranean world from a newly formed neural pathway. Follow the ants in this vision of thought. Enter the rhizome through another passage. Come across the pattern that connects – the aesthetic logic of relations.[75]

Autumn, Armidale, 1997

My Labrador is a blur of golden exuberance rolling among red and yellow leaves that have gathered in piles in this town park. Immersed in intensities, she moves like a wind, whipping the world up into a dance of colour and motion.

The texture of the dried crackling leaves is inseparable from the feel of my dog's fur in this far away moment brought close by embodied remembering. My emotion – an exuberant joy shared with a furry friend – is woven through the autumnal trees just as a melody is woven through a song.

Living in patterns of connection our most intimate memories are entangled with branches and leaves and parks, with clouds and sun, with humidity, sideways rain and winds at dusk; significant moments are carried into our life on the cry of a currawong, or on the elegant propositions of a single autumn leaf as it floats an unknowable path from the sky to the ground.

Autumnal becomings

The imported autumnal becomings of my hometown are deeply entwined with my life – with my memories and with my experiences of change and transformation. I love Armidale's autumn because it connects me to my childhood dog, to my relationships with friends who share a love of autumnal tints, and to the beauty of the place I grew up – the place I was first surprised and delighted by the more-than-human world. The seasonal colour is like a refrain that repeats each year, alerting me to the changes that have happened in me, and in the world, while reminding me that I am wrapped up in a pattern of seasons, a pattern that is woven around me – a nest of life and time.

How am I to reconcile the solace and connectivity I experience when wrapped up in the colours of this season, with the knowledge that it is this same season that marks the displacement and dispossession of Indigenous life? Armidale's imported autumn reminds me that it is not only places that are damaged and beloved. Time too can be damaged, twisted by anthropogenic desires and perverted into colonial rhythms. Beyond the exquisite colour that binds me to significant moments and relationships in my life are tones and hues that escape my attention, colours that may illuminate shadow places and shadow times outside the colonial present.

Thoreau wrote that 'there is no power to see in the eye itself, no more than any other jelly'.[76] For Thoreau, beauty and transformation was deeply subjective, the result of arts of noticing. He wrote 'Objects are concealed from our view, not so much because they are out of the course of our visual ray as because we do not bring our minds and eyes to bear on them'.[77] Neurological research reveals that human perceptions of colour are fundamentally subjective, the result of subconscious perceptual decisions that are conditioned by culture and language. As we grow and learn we develop our own unique and emergent principles of colour, transforming refracted light into defined hues that become 'differences that make a difference'. We weave the light of the world into meaningful patterns to help us make sense of our environment.

In an Indigenous ecology of mind, seasonal patterns were awoken by multispecies relationships. This art of noticing thrived on deep immersion in a living system where 'the whole cosmos is alive and communicating'.[78] Seasonal tints were made not of colour alone, but of song and movement, of creature languages spread across Country like the delicate threads of a spider's web, a pattern of meaning woven through time and place.

A picture of time

What is an hour but a place in which to gather? A fullness, a potential, a series of divergent lines of flight. The hours of my life unfurl before and behind me like a red carpet made of autumn leaves. Each leaf that falls in my shadow carries memories and forgettings and regrets and intimacies and losses and lives touched: some lingering, some long gone. And each leaf ahead is a potential, a hope, a vague dream, an anxious worry, a dread. Hours upon hours – leaves upon leaves – of relationship, interaction, places, longings . . .

Walking through the falling leaves in the woods of my world I am wrapped up in untouchable moments – invented pasts, fanciful futures. They sweep me along as I step in and out of myself – a body in becoming, always narrating to myself from the past as I'm brought into being by the next moment and the next – leaf upon leaf, hour upon hour. The leaves pile up through my life and gather around me as a comforting refrain, warming up my world, as if a summer season carried in on the wings of a fruit bat as it flies toward the promise of berries.

The four seasonal beats of Armidale's urban centre are predictable *only* if we ignore the tempo and cadence of their entire milieu, including the surrounding environment, historical agencies and many complex collaborations between beings of the present and the past. The transformation of Armidale's iridescent trees is a process of continual metamorphosis and becoming. The un-manicured generations of trees forming their own communities in surrounding bushland is just one example of an agency beyond human control – a creativity working to a temporal beat that is not easily measured in weekdays and calendar months.

Despite being envisioned in human abstract thought, Armidale's deciduous trees actively maintain their own lives and reproduce, extending lines of kin through space and time. They are helped in this by mutualistic relationships with other beings, such as birds who spread seeds, humans who plant them in their own private gardens, and a tourist industry that continues to promote autumnal aesthetics. An underground world of rhizomatic roots and soil organisms invisible to the human eye stretches each tree's life deep into the subterranean earth. Autumn colours are a celebration of this intimately entwined multi-species dance which paints the world red, gold and orange in patterns of transformation.

Light – elliptical, ungraspable, yet intensely material – is the source of all colour. Each of us are creatures of photosynthesis, converting sunlight into nourishment, into ideas, information and thoughts. The gene that opens our eyes for the first time, that signals the development of the visual organ in the human fetus, is the same gene found in fruit flies. James Hatley observes that 'our kinship with all other living entities runs deep, no matter how distantly related they may seem'.[79] Eyes open to an entangled world, where colour is made in intimate coevolutionary ecologies as flowers proposition bees, and birds choreograph exquisite dances in ultraviolet rays that humans cannot see.

Each of us evolve and learn to see in living webs of time. Alfred North Whitehead wrote that 'There is time because there are happenings, and apart from happenings there is nothing'. Time is deeply chronotopic and earthly, and trying to find time outside nature's becoming is like trying to 'find substance in a shadow'.[80] Attuning ourselves to the multispecies becomings of Armidale's autumn is a way to resist colonial temporality because time that is embedded in the earth, built on creaturely intra-action in dynamic affective ecologies, cannot be metronomic.

Deleuze and Guattari state that 'one of the most important characteristics of a rhizome is that it always has multiple entryways'.[81] Learning to be affected[82] by difference (the difference that makes a difference, that is, information)[83] is a process of following passageways into this dynamic and relational space of exchange and connection, a space where it is possible to become aesthetically sensitised to the pattern that connects. The pattern is made by an intra-active coevolutionary universe in becoming, the patterning of life that we witness in the dynamic multispecies event of a season.

At the beginning of this chapter I pondered what kind of an animal time might be. Michelle Bastian has playfully proposed that a turtle might be an appropriate way of measuring time in a world where clocks fail to alert us to the shifting patterns of a precariously balanced planet. She writes:

> Rather than coordinating our lives with and through a stable and predictable atom, augmented by the movements of a planet around a star, what if we tried coordinating our lives with something less predictable, but maybe more accurate for the times we live in? An animal perhaps, rather than a planet and an atom? A turtle?

Figure 13 A blue wren at my parents' property, Armidale, 2008 (Vic Wright)

Following the critters with which we share our world is a way of tapping into alternative rhythms hidden in the shadows. We are all wrapped up in this thing we call time. It binds us to the earth and is the meter of our lives. Perhaps it is hubristic to think we could measure it, except as it flows through the interaction between earthly bodies, where a season is not made of colour alone, but is a living poem, composed by movement and sound and light and life.

'Draw a picture of time,' Ben said.

Ben, I can draw you a picture of a tree, but I can't tell you who is in it. That is a surprise.

Notes

1 G. Bateson, *Mind and Nature*, 7.
2 Xanthophylls are yellow pigments that form one of two major divisions of the carotenoid group – organic pigments found in plants and some types of algae.
3 Beta-Carotene is a strongly-coloured red-orange pigment found in plants and fruits
4 Anthocyanins are water-soluble pigments that may appear red, purple or blue.
5 M. Bakhtin, *Dialogic Imagination*, 84.
6 Ibid., 84.
7 Ibid., 113.
8 Ibid., 115.
9 E. Casey, *Remembering*, 182.
10 M. Bakhtin, *Dialogic Imagination*, 208.

11   Ibid., 208.
12   H. Thoreau, *Autumnal Tints* (Massachusetts: Applewood Books, 1862), 272.
13   J. Arthur, *Default Country*.
14   M. Bastian, '"Fatally Confused": Telling the Time in the Midst of Ecological Crises,' in 'Temporal Environments: Rethinking Time and Ecology,' eds. J. Metcalf and T. van Doorn. Special issue, *Environmental Philosophy* 9, no. 1 (2012): 28.
15   E. Durkheim, *The Elementary Forms of Religious Life*, trans. J. W. Swain (New York: The Free Press, 1965), 23.
16   H. Thoreau, *Autumnal Tints*, 12.
17   Ibid., 35.
18   Ibid., 33.
19   Thom Van Dooren defines species as intergenerational achievements in *Flight Ways*.
20   A. Neimanis & S. Walker, 'Weathering', 571.
21   H. Thoreau, *Autumnal Tints*, 8.
22   Ibid., 39.
23   G. Bateson, *Mind and Nature*, 10 & 12.
24   H. Thoreau, *Autumnal Tints*, 47–48.
25   G. Deleuze and F. Guattari, *A Thousand Plateaus: Capitalism and Schizophrenia* (Minneapolis: University of Minnesota Press, 1987).
26   For more discussion on these ideas see T. Mastnak, J. Elyachar and T. Boellstorff, 'Botanical Decolonization'.
27   J. Metcalf and T. van Dooren, 'Editorial Preface', in 'Temporal Environments: Rethinking Time and Ecology,' eds. J. Metcalf and T. van Dooren. Special issue, *Environmental Philosophy* 9, no. 1 (2012): 1–22.
28   S. Muecke, *No Road*, 192.
29   S. Ryan, *The Cartographic Eye*, 101.
30   H. Thoreau, *Autumnal Tints*, 44.
31   Ibid., 62.
32   G. Bateson, *Ecology of Mind*, 459.
33   G. Bateson, *Mind and Nature*.
34   A. Tsing, 'Arts of Inclusion, Or, How to Love a Mushroom,' in 'Unloved Others: Death of the Disregarded in the Time of Extinctions,' eds. D. Rose and T. van Dooren, special issue, *Australian Humanities Review* 50 (May 2011), 19.
35   A. Jones, 'Fifty Years of Beautification and Tree Planting in Armidale,' *Armidale and District Historical Society: Journal and Proceedings* 37 (1994), 129.
36   Ibid., 129.
37   Ibid., 129.
38   Ibid., 134.
39   Ibid., 129.
40   Bastian, 'Fatally Confused', 31.
41   Environmental humanities theorist Rob Nixon developed the idea of 'slow violence' to explain incremental environmental devastation that does not receive attention in neoliberal, industrial societies in *Slow Violence*.
42   J. Benson, 'The Effect of 200 Years of European Settlement on the Vegetation and Flora of New South Wales,' *Cunninghamia* 2, no. 3 (1991): 350.
43   J. Wright, *Half a Lifetime* (Melbourne: Penguin, 1999), 296.
44   J. M. B. Smith, S. Borgis and V. Seifert, 'Studies in Urban Ecology: The First Wave of Biological Invasion by *Pistacia Chinensis* in Armidale, New South Wales, Australia', *Australian Geographical Studies* 38, no. 3 (2000): 272.
45   Ibid., 263.
46   Smith, Borgis & Seifert, 'Studies in Urban Ecology', 273.
47   Paul Robbins, 'Comparing Invasive Networks: Cultural and Political Biographies of Invasive Species', *Geographical Review* 94, no. 2 (2004): 139–156.

48 D. Rose, 'Val Plumwood's Philosophical Animism: Attentive Interactions in the Sentient World', *Environmental Humanities* 3 (2013), 104.
49 D. Rose, 'Rhythms, Patterns, Connectivities: Indigenous Concepts of Seasons and Change, Victoria River District, NT', in *A Change in the Weather: Climate and Culture in Australia*, eds. T. Sherratt, T. Griffiths & L. Robin (National Museum of Australia: Canberra, 2005), 39.
50 Bureau of Meteorology, 'Indigenous Weather Knowledge' (Commonwealth of Australiawww.bom.gov.au/iwk/climate_culture/Clim_Cult.shtml.
51 D. Kingsley, 'The Lost Seasons', *ABC Online* (14 August 2003), www.abc.net.au/science/features/indigenous/.
52 P. Clarke, 'Australian Aboriginal Ethnometeorology and Seasonal Calendars', *History and Anthropology* 20, no. 2 (2009): 87.
53 D. Rose, 'Rhythms, Patterns, Connectivities', 40.
54 Ibid., 40.
55 A. Lingis, *Dangerous Emotions* (Berkeley and Los Angeles & London: University of California Press, 2000), 29.
56 M. Lucashenko, 'All My Relations', 64.
57 Ibid.
58 D. Rose, 'On History, Trees, and Ethical Proximity', *Postcolonial Studies* 11, no. 2 (2008): 163.
59 G. Bateson, *Mind and Nature*.
60 N. Bateson, 'Practicality in Complexity', https://norabateson.wordpress.com/2016/01/02/practicality-in-complexity/.
61 E. Kohn, *How Forests Think*, 9.
62 Ibid., 5.
63 G. Bateson, *Ecology of Mind*, 459.
64 D. Rose, 'Rhythms, Patterns and Connectivities', 40.
65 Ibid.
66 C. Hustak and N. Myers, 'Involutionary Momentum: Affective Ecologies and the Sciences of Plant/Insect Encounters', *Differences: A Journal of Feminist Cultural Studies*, 23, no. 3 (2012): 105.
67 Ibid., 105.
68 Ibid., 104.
69 E. Kohn, *How Forests Think*, 81.
70 Ibid., 83.
71 A. Murphie, 'Deleuze, Guattari and Neuroscience', in *Deleuze, Science and the Force of the Virtual*, ed. P. Gaffney (Minneapolis: University of Minnesota Press, 2010), 20.
72 T. Cashman, 'What Connects the Map to the Territory', in *A Legacy for Living Systems: Gregory Bateson as Precursor to Biosemiotics*, ed. J. Hoffmeyer (Dordrecht: Springer, 2009), 51.
73 Bateson, *Ecology of Mind*, p. 316.
74 Latour builds on Stengers to argue that the world is full of 'propositions' waiting to be registered by interested bodies in 'How to Talk about the Body?', 205–229.
75 See G. Bateson, *Mind and Nature*.
76 H. Thoreau, 'Autumnal Tints', 57.
77 Ibid., 57.
78 D. Rose, 'When the Rainbow Walks,' in *Windows on Meteorology: Australian Perspective*, ed. E. K. Webb (Melbourne: CSIRO Publishing, 1997), 5.
79 J. Hatley, 'Temporal Discernment'.
80 A. Whitehead, *The Concept of Nature: The Tarner Lectures Delivered in Trinity College November 1919*. 1919. Reprinted as an eBook through Project Gutenberg (16 July 2006): www.gutenberg.org/files/18835/18835-h/18835-h.htm., 66.
81 G. Deleuze & F. Guattari, *A Thousand Plateaus*.
82 B. Latour, 'How to Talk about the Body?', 205.
83 G. Bateson, *Ecology of Mind*, 459.

Part III
Animals

Figure 14 Me and Lucy, 1996 (Vic Wright)

One of my favourite stories is Antoine de Saint-Exupéry's *The Little Prince*. This beautiful fable about friendship pays no heed to species barriers. Written with a child's imagination, the novel is about the way we make friends with the many earth others who share our world.

When the little prince, a lost boy from another planet, encounters a fox, he wants to play with him. The fox refuses to play until the prince tames him. To tame, says the fox, is to create ties to another, a bonding of co-presence built on responsibility.

> To me you are only a small boy, just like a hundred thousand other small boys. And I have no need of you. And you in turn have no need of me. To you I am just a fox like a hundred thousand other foxes. But if you tame me, then we shall need each other. To me, you shall be unique in the world. To you, I shall be unique in the world.[1]

At the age of ten I received the most wonderful gift – an 8-week-old Golden Labrador to tame and care for, called Lucy. This chapter is written in honour of the dog who became my dear friend. I hope that it carries with it a taste of the shared joy Lucy brought to my life, and translates some of the lessons she taught me. At a time of cascading extinctions, understanding how to develop strong ties with the earth and all of its inhabitants is vital. This part is written with the goal of fostering relationships of care, responsibility and love for the many nonhuman lives which are inextricably tied to our own.

Note

1   A. de Saint-Exupéry, *The Little Prince*, trans. T. V. F. Cuffe (London: Penguin, 1943/2000), 67.

5　Lucy

Lucy was born in Kentucky, New South Wales, on Boxing Day, 1995. She was the last in a litter of five Golden Labradors. A little too short to be a show dog, she was a hyperactive, golden ball of exuberance, and very, very naughty. Her first introduction to our nuclear New England family was a bowl of Weet-Bix mixed with cuddles and pats, as a television chattered monotonously in the background. Lucy was adopted into a human world of packaged cereals and electric lights.

Some of my earliest memories of Lucy are of quite tragic failings in inter-species communication and understanding. As she pined for her mother those first few weeks, crying like an abandoned child in the middle of the night, I felt criminal, and were it not for my parents and my anticipation of their anger and disappointment, I would have returned her to her family.

My father had a strict rule of no dogs in the house – 'my house will not be a kennel' – so she was kept far away at night, in the middle of the bush on a leash. I felt at the time that this was torturous for her, but I had neither the words nor the power to change the situation. Lucy was tied up most of the day on a 'run' – a piece of wire strung between two trees so that should could run up and down on her leash, although often the leash became stuck in a kink and she had to wait until we returned home to be able to move. This was quite normal in the area, and probably the best option, because many dogs did run away and my family were out of the house all day. There were times I seriously questioned, and still do, whether getting a Labrador was an incredibly cruel and selfish act.

But then there were all the things we got right and the tremendous joys I shared with my new friend. I used to set my alarm for 5:30 am so I could walk Lucy before getting ready for school. We ran along the wide dirt roads and through the bush, stumbling and twirling and panting. I'd never experienced the land like that before, and felt newly alive running recklessly with my best friend alongside me.

When I came home from school, we walked through the scrub looking for things to explore or chase and Lucy swam in the dams. Even now when I go swimming I sometimes imagine what it feels like to swim with a coat of fur and webbed dog feet.

I'd throw branches for her to collect and she'd pretend she was bringing them back, but then bow at me, cheekily, and run away, her whole body tilting to one side with a metre-long branch hanging out of her jaw. I'd chase her, but never catch up. When I laid on the grass in resignation or exhaustion she'd come and lie on me while she chewed the branch to splinters. She never gave it back to me!

At night while my parents watched television I'd mount a torch in her kennel and read a book by dim orange light while she fell asleep on my legs. I did this even when it was freezing cold. I think I did it because I felt needed, and, of course, because I loved her.

Lucy was an important part of my life, even when we weren't together. At primary school I wrote poems about her. For a school project I made a documentary film which starred Lucy as the ambassador for Labrador Retrievers.

As Lucy got older my family's treatment of her improved. There was little fear she would run away once grown, so she wasn't tied up during the day. She ate our chook when it escaped its pen, so received the deserted pen as a new sleeping place (some sort of justice?). This hay-filled old tree-house was warm and snug and for a birthday present one year I asked for insulation for Lucy's hut, and got it!

Dad softened with his years, and was worn down by Mum and me persistently flouting his rules. Lucy was always allowed inside by Mum until Dad got home from work, when she was rushed out. It wasn't long before Dad fell victim to her longing brown eyes and she was allowed inside until dinnertime, then she was inside until bed-time. Eventually she was sleeping on my bed, hogging the mattress so I slept contorted into all kinds of unnatural shapes and suffered from serious back pain in my final years of high school.

When I left home at 18 to go to university in Sydney I felt incredible guilt at leaving Lucy behind. I cried into my sheets at night with homesickness and my images of home were always of Lucy. She had come to embody my childhood, and my relationship with the New England block of land where I had grown up. She represented everything that I had loved about being young in the bush. I was devastated.

Four years later I got a phone call from my Dad when I was on the train home after working a shift as a veterinary nurse one evening. He sounded strange, sort of formal, and I knew something terrible had happened. He asked me to call him when I got home. I rang as soon as I got in the door.

Dad burst into tears at the end of the line and told me that Lucy was dead. She was only 11, and she was healthy. She had been kicked by a kangaroo that she was chasing. She had died at the vet's. My parents weren't there. I wasn't there. She had died alone.

I can't remember exactly how I felt, I just remember desperately wanting to go somewhere, and walking the streets of Newtown, a suburb in Sydney, well into the night. Dad told me later that he had never been so affected by a death before. Mum went into an obsessive state where she tried to rid the house of Lucy's hair. She vacuumed and washed for weeks. These were responses to the trauma of the unexpected death of a family member.

One could contend that the notion of a dog as a family member is an anthropomorphic delusion. Considering the imbalanced relationship between human and pet, the fundamental species difference, and the inability to consistently communicate and understand one another, such a notion can be viewed as sentimental and dangerously inappropriate.[1]

Following Kennan Ferguson I believe it is important to recognise that love between beings exists even within relationships where there are severe imbalances of power. 'That such a conception of love is politically troublesome does not mean that it has no legitimacy in human lives (it clearly does).'[2] It also seems clear to me that these relationships of love are mutualistic – that dogs are active players in these messy, intimate tunes of co-presence.

In her extended meditations on human and canine encounters, *The Companion Species Manifesto* and *When Species Meet*, Donna Haraway interrogates the ways human and nonhuman animals are relationally co-constituted. While Haraway believes that the human-pet relationship is 'inherently problematic' and 'puts dogs at risk' because they are vulnerable to the whims of human affection,[3] she also notes that criticisms of animal domestication forget that animals are engaged participants in the process. Instead of domestication being 'a kind of original sin separating human beings from nature,' domestication is built on mutuality and reciprocity.[4] Dominique Lestel refers to the important concept of 'mutual domestication' where 'the animal as well as the human are modified'.[5] Understood in this way, to speak of a pet, or using the term Haraway prefers, a companion species, is not to speak of a categorical form of life but an ongoing 'becoming with'.[6]

Becoming-dog

When Lucy entered my life she brought me a new understanding of corporeal existence. We spoke in the language of 'embodied communication' which Haraway tells us is 'more like a dance than a word'.[7] All these years later the feel of this dance, its rhythm, still lingers within my body, like the memory of riding a bike.

Vinciane Despret offers the term 'anthropo-zoo-genetic practice' to capture the way bodies can synchronise to create a cross-species conversation. New identities proliferate, on both sides, as human and nonhuman learn to articulate themselves in hybrid dialogues. Despret describes the way a human can engage in a 'becoming with a horse', by performing a body that 'a horse can read, acquiring a horse sensitivity'.[8] Examining the communications between skilled horse riders and horses, Despret notes that riders produce unintentional movements that are the same as the horse's body:

> The human's right hand imitates (and anticipates) what the horse's right front leg will do, the bottom of the back of the rider makes a jerk which is exactly the movement the horse will do to begin to canter, and so on...talented riders behave and move like horses. They have learned to act in a horse-like fashion...Human bodies have been transformed by and into a horse's body.[9]

Memories of my own body, once part-canine, flood back. I don't miss only Lucy, but also an embodied relation that was lost when dogs vanished from my life. Photographs cannot bring this back. The memory of movement is not only, or even primarily, visual – sounds and texture bring it closer. The muscular curve of a thigh flung across my shin, a furry, panting nuzzle loud into my neck and hair – this embodied communication was a far cry from the human contact I was used to, and I revelled in it.

Freya Mathews has suggested that the loss of animals from everyday human life is an estrangement from a mixed community of humans and animals which we have shared for thousands of years. She suggests that this may be causing deep feelings of loneliness and alienation in the post-industrial world. It is now well known that contact with animals can improve human health, and it has been estimated that pet ownership saves the Australian health care system one-and-a-half billion dollars per year.[10] Mathews infers that this may be, in part, the outcome of a long co-evolutionary history.[11] Perhaps we do not become-dog in embodied communications, but are born with the potential of being-dog within us.

Umwelt and the dog within

Nineteenth-century biologist Jakob von Uexküll outlined what Brett Buchanan has called an 'intersubjective theory of nature'.[12] Von Uexküll used the term *Umwelt* to describe the way organism and environment form a whole system. Each organism has its own *Umwelt* which is its meaningful environment. Each *Umwelt* is determined by the perceptions of the animal and '[e]very object becomes something completely different on entering a different Umwelt'.[13] Von Uexküll offers the example of a flower stem which in a human *Umwelt* is support for the flower, for the spittle bug is a pipe full of liquid, for the ant is an upward path connecting nest and hunting ground, and for the cow is food.[14]

Buchanan explains that the concept of the *Umwelt* implies that an organism is never 'just one':

> Instead, each organism has a context, an *Umwelt* in which it lives, and, in being so, the organism is always already more than itself...To know the organism requires knowing its other(s). But to what degree is the other, as other, a part of the subject?[15]

By way of an explanation, Buchanan offers these lines from a poem by Goethe:

> If the flower were not bee-like
> And the bee were not flower-like
> The unison could never be successful.

What von Uexküll is indicating is that the symbiosis between bee and flower is based on their becoming-other together, but that this becoming-other is already within them. Like Mathews' co-evolutionary argument for our closeness with companion animals, von Uexküll finds the basis of likeness within each organism, which could not fulfil its being without the other.

Buchanan explains:

> The bee in a sense *becomes* flower-like and the flower *becomes* bee-like through the relation that they create together, but they can only become the other insofar as they already have an affinity for the other. They thus become a new ontological unit together, a meaningful system greater than their 'individual' parts. At bottom, an organism *is* what it is capable of becoming, insofar as it already is the other that it becomes in the harmonious relation.[16]

The idea of a dog-ness within us that reaches its full expression in human-dog relationships, and a human-ness within dogs that does the same, raises a significant challenge to notions of discrete and separate species. As Anna Tsing eloquently writes, 'human nature is an inter-species relationship'.[17] This also mounts a formidable challenge against critiques of anthropomorphism as the basis for companionship between people and dogs – the 'dogs as fake children' argument. Instead of projecting human characteristics on to dogs in order to forge similar, but somehow deficient, intimacies with canines, humans are instead revelling in the opportunity to express their own inner dog through inter-species friendship.

Anthropomorphism as a kind of empathy

Many scholars have argued that charges of anthropomorphism affirm human superiority over animals, applying a Cartesian logic of the animal machine and denying humans the ability to share feelings with animals.[18] This form of human exceptionalism is a form of what Frans de Waal terms 'anthropodenial'[19] that severs empathic and ethical connections to nonhuman lives. Haraway argues that these claims that we cannot know a nonhuman Other 'is a denial of mortal engagements...for which we are responsible and to which we respond'.[20]

Ethologist Marc Bekoff promotes 'critical anthropomorphism' as a solution to problematic human projections, and attempts to be biocentrically anthropomorphic.[21] For example, he becomes a 'dogocentrist' when he is studying the behaviour of dogs to avoid losing the dog's point of view.[22] Finding the dog within himself, as the horse rider finds a horse body within her own, Bekoff is able to adopt a canine-centric perspective. But he does argue that without some kind of anthropomorphism, empathic engagements with animals are impossible.

Gregory Bateson observed that empathy is grounded in a metaphor of the self.[23] When we try to understand another's feelings, thoughts or way of being in the world, we necessarily refer to our own experience, imaginatively projecting ourselves into the body and life-world of the Other. Some of the worst examples of violence in human history have stemmed from a lack of empathy, and often from the culturally enforced rejection or obstruction of empathic connection to others. Anthropodenial is one means of severing empathy by denying similarity and forcing a rupture between nonhuman and human animals.

Instead of anthropodenial, which fixates on species and the separate-ness of the human, the embodied language of dog-human communication is based on becoming-other, on learning how to speak in a hybrid language. This is akin to the biological communication which Bateson argues illuminates 'the pattern that connects'[24] all earth life to each other. This multispecies language is not dependent on nouns, which refer to things, but instead concerns patterns and relationships.[25] All biological communication is, according to Bateson, focused on homology – how 'a hand resembles a foot or a paw or a flipper'.[26]

When I played the stick game with Lucy (which can't be called fetch because Lucy didn't play fair on that one), I was forced, by the nature of the play, to become dog-like. I chased her, then froze, stopped still. She bowed down and shook her bum and I crouched, and then lunged toward her. We mimicked each other, she becoming a little bit human, and I becoming a little bit dog, each of us becoming predator and then prey, until neither of us had any idea what we were! Immersed in the chase – the adrenalin of almost catching up, the silly and careless humour of falling, the frantic running through long grass – we were communicating by being alike. We were becoming more-than-human and more-than-dog by sharing joy.

Haraway observes that the joy of play 'breaks rules to make something else happen'.[27] In the 'joint dance of being' that is an inter-species game, human and nonhuman are 'bounded in significant otherness'[28] creating new forms of communication by becoming-other. Haraway describes significant otherness as the relational constitution of identity where beings 'are neither whole nor parts'[29] but rather are *made* in the fleshly space of encounter. This means that 'becoming is always becoming-with'.[30] Haraway argues that becoming-with is also a process of becoming worldly.

Glen Mazis describes how the relational qualities of play include the world, arguing that play is not only a socially binding activity, but also an activity that binds organisms to their environment because 'the natural world is a playmate'.[31] Bateson gives an evocative example of the way the environment is bound to relationships between beings. He describes a wolf demonstrating dominance over another by forcing the other to mimic puppy behaviour:

> the leader pressed the head of the junior male down to the ground in the same way, once, twice, four times, and then walked off. The communication that occurred was metaphoric: 'You puppy, you!' The communication to the junior wolf of how to behave is based on a syllogism in the grass.[32]

Here the wolf is engaging with the environment in which it is enmeshed to communicate about social roles by invoking the presence of an imaginary puppy via the grass. The wolf is not communicating about the grass, but about the relationship between himself and the puppy *through* the grass. The grass is part of the language, requiring 'fleshly acts of interpretation'[33] – part of the world of meaning, the *Umwelt*.

Von Uexküll's concept of *Umwelten* is deeply relational. It asserts that the essence of things is impossible to grasp beyond what they mean to particular individuals. A flower cannot be food for an ant as much as it cannot be a path for a cow. It makes sense, then, that communication should concern our relationships with the world, rather than a distant 'objective' reality. Not nouns, but patterns and connections.

Bateson writes:

> If we want to be able to talk about the living world (and ourselves), we need to master the disciplines of description and reference in this curious language that has no things in it but only differences and relationships. Only if we do so will we be able to think sensibly about the matrix in which we live, and only then will we recognise our affinity with the rest of that world and deal with it ethically and responsibly.[34]

Perhaps one of the best ways of learning this language is to begin to speak to the nonhumans we are closest to in a more-than-human tongue. Freya Mathews makes a persuasive argument for the indispensable value of intimate human–nonhuman relationships. She argues that animals can awaken us to 'new levels of awareness and responsibility'[35] for the natural world by acting as 'a principal bridge to communication with the unknowable subjectivity of the wider world'.[36] Having spent her youth surrounded by nonhuman animals, Mathews believes that this immersion in a world of more-than-human concern enlivened her sense of the world as responsive and alive. She writes, 'the ample opportunities for close communion with animals that were available to me throughout my childhood had opened me to a larger world, a world astir with presence or presences that vastly exceeded the human'.[37]

Looking at the photograph of Lucy and me (Figure 15), taken a few days after she had arrived, I am struck by the expression on both our faces. I am holding her

Figure 15 Me and Lucy no. 2, 1996 (Vic Wright)

as I would have been used to holding teddy bears. I wonder if she was uncomfortable or confused by it. She is looking down toward the ground. And I am looking to her, to see what she is seeing. I am wondering – what is she thinking?

This picture was taken at the beginning of a long journey. Over the next ten years we would become the best of friends. We would share morning and evening walks, we would swim in the dam together, we would give each other gifts and be upset when they weren't wanted, we would watch each other get sick and get better, we would have fights and stop playing, we would accidentally hurt each other, we would deliberately hurt each other, we would sleep curled together in beds, couches, tents and kennels, we would miss each other, we would play with, care for and love each other, and eventually, we would lose each other.

Sometimes I am angry at myself for getting so close to a friend I always knew I had to leave behind. It was irrational and unfair on both of us. But then I think of all the things Lucy has taught me, how my life has been shaped by my relationship with her and how she helped me to love the place where I grew up in a more intense, more-than-human way.

When Lucy died I lost a dear friend, and going home to my parents' house has never been the same. But Lucy has not stopped teaching me things, even in death. Remembering Lucy helps me to remember that we do not live in a world of mute creatures or aliens that speak only to each other. We live in knots of motion,[38] immersed in each other's stories and worlds. If, as James Hatley suggests, death is a gift to those left behind, part of Lucy's gift is a deeper love of my home-place, a home which she has now become a part of, buried in the soil, but always, in my mind, running beside me through the grass.[39]

After the little prince had tamed the fox, the time for him to leave was fast approaching.

> 'Oh!' said the fox. 'I am going to cry.'
> 'It's your own fault,' said the little prince. 'I never wished you any harm; but you wanted me to tame you...'
> 'I know,' said the fox.
> 'So you have gained nothing from it at all!'
> 'Yes, I have gained something,' said the fox, 'because of the colour of the corn'.[40]

For the fox, fields of corn which once seemed bland and meaningless will now always make him think of the prince's golden hair, and he will always love the sound of wind blowing through leaves of corn.

Notes

1   Paul Shepard, for example, criticises the human-pet relationship as a 'conquering of nature that turns animals into slaves (*The Others: How Animals Made Us Human* (Washington, DC: Island Press/Shearwater Books, 1996)).
2   K. Ferguson, 'I Love My Dog,' *Political Theory* 32, no. 3 (2004): 387.

3   D. Haraway, *The Companion Species Manifesto: Dogs, People, and Significant Otherness* (Chicago: Prickly Paradigm Press, 2003) 38.

4   D. Haraway, *When Species Meet*, 206.

5   D. Lestel, 'How Chimpanzees Have Domesticated Humans: Towards an Anthropology of Human-Animal Communication,' *Anthropology Today* 14, no. 3 (June 1998), 13.

6   D. Haraway, *When Species Meet*, 16.

7   Ibid., 26. Haraway writes: 'An embodied communication is more like a dance than a word. The flow of entangled meaningful bodies in time – whether jerky and nervous or flaming and flowing, whether both partners move in harmony or painfully out of synch or something else altogether…'

8   V. Despret, 'The Body We Care for', 122.

9   Ibid., 115.

10 F. Mathews, 'Without Animals Life Is Not Worth Living', *Between the Species* VII (August 2007), http://digitalcommons.calpoly.edu/cgi/viewcontent.cgi?article=1023 &context=bts, 16. I am unsure of the impact of pet ownership on pets themselves. It may be that the health benefits for humans come at a large cost for the animals, particularly those unwanted and mistreated pets who are victims of the pet industry. I am not suggesting that this abuse is just, but merely that the health benefits of pet ownership clearly indicate a human need for contact with nonhuman animals.

11 F. Mathews, 'Without Animals', 16. Haraway also believes that co-evolution is important in understanding human-canine relations, writing that '[c]o-evolution has to be defined more broadly than biologists habitually do…it is a mistake to see the alteration of dogs' bodies and minds as biological and the changes in human bodies and lives, for example in the emergence of herding or agricultural societies, as cultural' (*When Species Meet*, 31).

12 B. Buchanan, *Onto-Ethologies: The Animal Environments of Uexküll, Heidegger, Merleau-Ponty, and Deleuze* (New York: State University of New York Press, 2008), 28.

13 Ibid., 108.

14 Ibid., 108.

15 Ibid., 29.

16 Ibid., 34.

17 A. Tsing, 'Unruly Edges: Mushro0ms as Companion Species', *Environmental Humanities* 1 (2012): 144.

18 For more on this see M. Bekoff, *The Emotional Lives of Animals: A Leading Scientist Explores Animal Joy, Sorrow and Empathy – And Why They Matter* (California: New World Library, 2007); J. Fisher, 'The Myth of Anthropomorphism' in *Readings in Animal Cognition*, eds. M. Bekoff & D. Jamieson (Boston: MIT Press, 1999); M. Midgley, *Animals and Why They Matter* (Georgia: University of Georgia Press, 1998).

19 F. de Waal, 'Are We in Anthropodenial?' *Discover* 18, no. 7 (1997).

20 D. Haraway, *When Species Meet*, 226.

21 M. Bekoff, 'Animal Emotions: Exploring Passionate Natures', *BioScience* 50 (2000): 861–870.

22 M. Bekoff, 'The Public Lives of Animals,' *Journal of Consciousness Studies* 13, no. 5 (2006): 125.

23 G. Bateson and M. Bateson, *Angels Fear: Towards an Epistemology of the Sacred* (New Jersey: Hampton Press, 2005/1987), 198.

24 Ibid., 8.

25 Ibid., 188.

26 Ibid., 190.

27 D. Haraway, *When Species Meet*, 238.

28 D. Haraway, *Companion Species Manifesto*, 16.

29 Ibid., 8.

30 D. Haraway, *When Species Meet*, 244.

31   G. Mazis, 'The World of Wolves: Lessons about the Sacredness of the Surround, Belonging, the Silent Dialogue of Interdependence and Death, and Speciocide', *Environmental Philosophy* 5, no.2 (2008): 19.

32   G. Bateson & M. Bateson, *Angels Fear*, 28.

33   D. Haraway, *When Species Meet*, 250.

34   G. Bateson & M. Bateson, *Angels Fear*, 191.

35   F. Mathews, 'Without Animals', 19.

36   Ibid., 25.

37   Ibid., 25.

38   D. Haraway, *Companion Species Manifesto*, 6.

39   James Hatley uses the term 'death narrative' to describe the way the transmission of wisdom, memory and traditions is like a gift, on death, from generation to generation (Suffering Witness: The Quandary of Responsibility after the Irreparable, Albany: State University of New York Press, 2000). Val Plumwood also positions death as a gift: 'death is a gift of life to and from ecological others, a circle of reciprocity in which all take their turn' ('Cemetery Wars', 67). These ideas are discussed in detail in Chapter 7.

40   A. de Saint-Exupéry, *The Little Prince*, 71.

6   Down the rabbit burrow

The rabbit-hole went straight on like a tunnel for some way, and dipped suddenly down, so suddenly that Alice had not a moment to think about stopping herself before she found herself falling down what seemed to be a deep well.
—Lewis Carroll, Alice's Adventures in Wonderland

When Lewis Carroll's Alice follows a white rabbit into its burrow, she falls deeply into another world. Alice falls *down, down, down*, into the unknowable depths of a subterranean wonderland, filled with strange creatures, twisted physical laws and new ways of being in the world. Is it possible to take a similar journey in a non-fictional world? Can we enter the lives of others by following the paths they leave on the surface of our shared environments?

The block of land where I grew up was covered with rabbit burrows. I knew the shape of the burrows better than I knew the shape of rabbit bodies. Rabbits are flits of grey, always in motion, always beginning to disappear. But their burrows remain on the land's surface as enticing traces of rabbit life.

As a kid, these burrows provoked my sustained curiosity. I would peer into them, and as I walked over them I was intensely aware of a rich subterranean world buzzing beneath my feet. I imagined rabbits conversing in long twisting underground corridors, looking up when they heard the echo of my gumboots on their roofs. Lucy was often with me, straining her neck deep into the shadowy holes, scratching frantically at their sides to try to reach some delicious rabbity smell. But this underground world was inaccessible, deeply terrestrial, and I was always hoping that the rabbits would stay safe in their dark, unknowable tunnels.

In this chapter I position the rabbit burrow as an invitation into another world, and argue that these enticing underground tunnels are corridors into empathy – rhizomatic entryways to the pattern that connects.[1] While rabbit burrows can provoke empathic encounters that encourage wonder at the more-than-human world, sharing land with nonhuman life can also lead to intolerant violence. I believe that this violence does not stem from close physical proximity, but instead from conceptual distance, and the denial that nonhuman worlds and lives are in synchrony with the human. The unreachable shadowy twists and turns of the rabbit burrow reflect the ongoing decolonising project of witnessing the nonhuman worlds at the periphery of our own.

The burrow and violent inter-species conflict

While rabbit burrows can be an invitation into rabbit lives and worlds, they can also be an indication of the presence of 'vermin'. The presence of burrows on the surface of shared land does not always prompt pluralistic and inclusive ethics, and rabbit burrows are often sites of human violence against rabbits. Rabbits were introduced to Australia in the late 1800s. Adrian Franklin observes that the rabbit 'was held in great affection by the British, who liked the decorative way it completed woodland edge and hedgerow scenes'.[2] Over the past century, rabbits have caused economic and environmental damage across the continent, and so have been subject to violent control measures aimed at species eradication including shooting, the destruction of burrows, poisoning, ferreting, trapping and the well-known rabbit-proof fence in Western Australia. Particularly noteworthy in this slaughter has been the introduction of biological control measures with the release of the savage and painful disease, myxomatosis, in late December 1950, followed by the accidental release of the calicivirus (rabbit *hemorrhagic* disease, or RHD) in 1995, and its official release in 1996,[3] and the Australian Federal government has now approved the release of RHDV-K5, a Korean strain of the calicivirus, for 2017.[4]

Brian Coman observes that the spread of myxomatosis was rapid and effective. The rabbit population dropped from 600 million to 100 million. Coman writes that in some parts of Australia rabbits 'died in the millions and the stench…was unbearable'.[5] In these death spaces, the tortured bodies of infected rabbits lined the paddocks.

Myxomatosis causes painful tumours, acute conjunctivitis, blindness, pneumonia, inflammation of the lungs, loss of appetite and fever. Coman writes: 'A rabbit dying of myxomatosis is not a pretty sight. The eyes become swollen and purulent, blinding the animal in most cases. Some animals may linger on for many days, becoming emaciated.'[6] Myxomatosis continues to infect rabbits in Australia, despite genetic resistance in rabbits and alterations in the virulence of the virus.[7]

Like myxomatosis, calicivirus is highly infectious, spreads rapidly and kills rabbits en masse. Following the accidental release of calicivirus in 1995, 10 million rabbits were killed in eight weeks. While calicivirus appears to be more humane than myxomatosis, with little outward sign of suffering, there are indications that it causes rabbits pain and stress. Victims are described as becoming very quiet, refusing to eat, straining for breath, losing coordination, becoming feverish and excreting bloody nasal discharge.[8] Post-mortem dissection generally reveals a 'pale and mottled liver, many small streaks or blotches on the lungs and an enlarged spleen…small thrombi or blood clots'.[9] The new strain of the virus causes 'internal bleeding, rapid multiple organ failure and death within 6–12 hours of infection'.[10]

Public criticism of the cruel methods involved in killing rabbits is often assuaged with appeals to the greater good of the ecosystem. Rabbit-Free Australia Inc. states that:

though killing rabbits may sound inhumane, wild rabbits are affecting the survival of native Australian plants and animals. It is our responsibility to control them. We brought the European rabbit here in the first place – they are an invasive pest.[11]

The implication of this quote is that the suffering does not matter because rabbits are members of an introduced species. They are not regarded as individual animals with all the capacity of living creatures for joy and suffering, but rather as an environmental disaster.

Like the conifer, the rabbit has been implicated in the colonisation of Indigenous Australia, a vital part of the more-than-human imperialism that characterised the invasion of the continent.[12] Jay Arthur's analysis of the language used when describing the rabbit demonstrates the way rabbits have been positioned as though they were intentional colonial invaders into Indigenous land:

> The progress of the rabbit is described with the vocabulary of an army employing a scorched-earth policy. The rabbit extends its 'dominion', 'dispossesses' the indigenous bilby, causes sheep runs to be 'abandoned' and country 'forfeited', leaving the land in 'ecological tatters'. Conversation concerning the rabbit is dense with occurrences of terms of violence and struggle as the settlers dealt with the effects of the occupation of their fellow European which, like them, found Australia to its liking.[13]

Rabbit-Free Australia's answer to their self-posed question 'Why are rabbits a problem?' is simple: 'Rabbits do not belong in Australia.'[14] The rationale behind this statement involves the rabbit's exotic origin, the history of human interference in their relocation, their environmentally destructive impact and their economic cost. By these standards, settler Australians of non-Aboriginal origin also do not belong.

Colonial dualism

The more-than-human colonisation of Australia was not only physical, but ideological, as introduced life was privileged over the native. Val Plumwood explains that the colonial dynamic

> involved not only the devaluation of native plants, ecosystems and animals (the 'bright songless birds'), but the deliberate introduction of ferals by 'acclimatisation societies', and the privileging of traditional carnivorous pets such as cats and dogs over native animals, the latter treated as 'pests'.[15]

Eric Rolls explains how the rabbit transformed rapidly from a venerated animal into a pest:

Sometime in the 1850s a man was charged at the Colac (Victoria) Police Court with having shot a rabbit, the property of John Robertson of Glen Alvie. He was fined £10. A few years later, Robertson's son spent £5000 a year in an attempt to control rabbits.[16]

In the current narrative of the rabbit as an invasive pest, the cultural and economic benefits of the species are denied. There is little discussion of the rabbit's role in providing vital nourishment during the Great Depression, for instance, when a lot of hungry farmers lived on 'underground mutton'.[17] The rabbit is not celebrated for providing jobs in harsh economic times, when an entire industry developed around rabbiting employing generations of rural Australians. Conceptualised as a cultural outlier that has invaded the continent like an army, it is not often remarked that rabbits have also assisted Australia in military combat. During the First World War rabbit-canning factories were set up to send tinned rabbit to the troops fighting overseas. The parts of the rabbit species that align with a culturally supported ethos of Australian values are hidden because the introduced rabbit has come to be seen purely in opposition to native animals.

By assuming responsibility for fixing the rabbit situation – 'we brought the rabbits here in the first place, they are an invasive pest' – the settler-descended human assumes an almost Indigenous status as they defend the country against the exotic invader.[18] The apprehension of moral responsibility can, in this sense, be understood, in part, as the acquisition of settler indigeneity, as described in Chapter 1.

This does not negate the fact that assuming human responsibility for the native environment can be an act of genuine care. In a country scarred by a history of ecocide, many environmentally conscious Australians are seeking to rectify the negligent mistakes of the past. The problem is not the attempts to heal devastated environments, but the reactive devaluation of non-native life. This is unproductive because it preserves the basic structure of the native/invasive dichotomy by simplistically reversing its values, and fails to respond to more complex ecological contexts and requirements. This is also socially problematic because the native/invasive divide of nonhuman life overlays more complex human politics of colonisation in Australia, and devalues introduced life to the point of moral inconsiderability.

The devaluation of the rabbit in Australia is exemplified in the campaign to replace the imaginary Easter Bunny with the eco-politically correct Easter Bilby.[19] Catharina Landström observes that the Easter Bilby campaign performs 'cultural work' to assist in 'making the technoscience of rabbit control a success'.[20] Ali Garnett and Kaye Kessing's children's story *Easter Bilby*, co-published by the Anti-Rabbit Research Foundation, supports this mediated campaign to devalue the rabbit culturally. In the story, the illustrated rabbit offers to make itself disappear from the 'Easter job':

Easter Bunny says, 'Bilby, I want you to have my job.
You know about sharing and taking care. I think Australia should have an Easter Bilby.

We rabbits have become too greedy and careless.
Rabbits must learn from bilbies and other bush creatures.[21]

The reason for the rabbit's self-demotion is a despairing recognition of its 'greedy and careless' nature, and at the same time, its selfless offer to be replaced by the ecologically conscious Bilby. In this sacrificial gesture is the implicit offering of all rabbit life for the salvation of native ecosystems and animal life. In this tale the disappearance of the rabbit has insidious ramifications as an illustrated rabbit offers the flesh of real living animals, similar to the way cartoon chickens, depicted as alive and happy, are employed on chicken shop billboards to advertise the severed legs and wings of real birds which have been slaughtered.

On the website of the Anti-Rabbit Research Foundation, *Rabbit-Free Australia*, a rationale for the campaign to replace the Easter Bunny with the Easter Bilby claims that:

> Very young children are indoctrinated with the concept that bunnies are nice soft fluffy creatures whereas in reality they are Australia's greatest environmental feral pest and cause enormous damage to the arid zone.[22]

In this statement the lived corporeal presence of individual rabbits is denied as the 'soft, fluffy' body disappears behind the environmentally problematic species behaviour. The assertion that children are 'indoctrinated' to find rabbits loveable, and that this conflicts with the 'reality' of the rabbit as environmentally destructive, denies the complexity of the living animal and the multiple possible responses to it. That children find rabbits 'fluffy' is not the result of pro-rabbit propaganda, but because rabbits *are* fluffy! That Rabbit-Free Australia could construe this to be some kind of elaborate falsehood demonstrates the disappearance of the individual rabbit in the colonial allegory of invasive pest.

On Good Friday 2012, news organisation *Reuters Australia* quoted Mike Drinkwater of Wild Life Sydney Zoo on the zoo's support of the Easter Bilby campaign:

> Look, the reason that we want to highlight the bilby as an iconic Easter animal is, number one, rabbits are a pest in Australia. Secondly, the bilby has these lovely endearing rabbit-like qualities. And thirdly, the bilby is a beautiful, iconic, native animal that is struggling. It is endangered so it's important that we do all we can to support that.[23]

Drinkwater's appeal to the bilby's 'endearing rabbit-like qualities' reveals that an individual rabbit's embodiment sits in direct contrast to its problematic species behaviour. Rabbit-Free Australia therefore needs to conceptually remove the rabbits' fluff in order to teach children not to love rabbits, and to be grateful for the rabbit's disappearance from a pest-blighted country regardless of the suffering involved. There is no acceptance here of the rabbit as a complex animal that evokes ambivalent responses, being both worthy of moral consideration, care and love, and also environmentally destructive. Instead the rabbit is reduced to a fluff-less environmental disaster.

These media campaigns influence the way people treat and respond to living rabbits in the landscape. When I was growing up, rabbit life was entirely de-valued, and I was often told that rabbits were an ecological disaster. Despite the fact that my family did not live on a farm, the plight of rabbit-ridden farms was close by, and the rabbit hatred overflowed from the paddocks on to our tree-change block.

I have a visceral childhood memory of holding a dying baby rabbit that my dog, Lucy, had been 'playing with'. I must have been about twelve, and this memory slots into a context of both Lucy and our pet cat, Barney, being congratulated for killing 'another of the buggers' whenever a dead, usually mutilated, rabbit turned up at the family home. I remember pulling Lucy's excited body away when I realised she was throwing a baby rabbit up and down in the air. I picked the terrified creature up. I could feel by the way its body flopped and lolled that its bones were all broken inside. Its eyes were open, its fur soggy with dog saliva. The small grey chest heaved up and down desperate for breath. It looked at me with dilated pupils. I didn't want it to be frightened by me but I could see that it was, or maybe it was afraid of dying. I held the small body for some time, waiting for it to die. When it finally stopped breathing I was in tears, and threw the dead body in anger back to Lucy.

Deborah Bird Rose has written that '[d]eath makes claims upon all of us'.[24] These are claims of ethics and compassion, a claim that 'we look into the eyes of the dying and not flinch, that we reach out to hold and to help'.[25] When we watch the light of life in an animal's eyes flicker and go out we are left with this claim which is also a duty of remembrance, a duty to 'bear witness' to life and death.[26]

As organisations like the Anti-Rabbit Research Foundation seek to imagine and create Australia's rabbit-less futures they are also eradicating rabbits from Australia's past. At the heart of this supposedly Utopian vision of a rabbit-free nation is void and amnesia – a continent of dead rabbits that produces a 'deathful emptiness' in the landscape.[27]

These rabbits are discontinued in more ways than one. Their lives end and so do their deaths, as the dynamic synergies between life and death are severed.[28] Culled rabbits lie rotting en masse in fields, food for no one, and even their cultural impact in human society is sought to be annihilated and replaced with more appropriate native creatures. The rabbits' deaths do not turn back to life in transformative and regenerative processes that are ecological and cultural, but rather that death becomes 'an event with no future'.[29] This is true oblivion, as the rabbit is entirely removed from the world.

The ongoing, always failing, drama of annihilation that attempts to purge the country of rabbits in the vision of a Utopian rabbit-free future in Australia is a form of redemptive violence that seeks transformation through destruction, a cruelty that pursues the annihilation of others.[30] The rationalisation of rabbit slaughter as necessary, and the lesson taught to children that rabbit love is inappropriate because it conflicts with ecological politics, is an active process of denying what we experience and know but are forced to forget – that rabbits are living, affective earth others who share the world and are implicated in our lives. This is a process of 'anthropodenial'[31] which severs the 'interspecies ties that reverberate with us'.[32]

To dis-embed the rabbit from its phenomenological world, and to deny people emotional links with it, ensures that violent dramas of annihilation can be played out in rural Australia without too much controversy. The eco-nationalist politics of redemptive violence prevent emotional proximity to the rabbit which would promote ethical responses. One may stand close to a rabbit dying of myxomatosis and be able to look past the fluffy body, to mute the sound of pained whimpering and to place the rabbit's suffering as far away as possible. This is done for the greater good of the country.

Bare life and mere death

Mass slaughter with the goal of fostering life enacts a disturbing twist where death comes to signal life. This means, perversely, that a rabbit's dead body becomes a valuable sign of environmental health. Conservation researchers David M. Forsyth and Ben Reddiex observe that this leads to a situation where environmental managers are 'more interested in estimating how many pests they killed rather than the status of biodiversity they claimed to be able to protect'.[33] The idea of a live rabbit branded as vermin – the walking dead – makes me feel deeply uneasy. I think it has this effect because facile death signals a fundamental loss of meaning. The life that does not matter when it is born makes the tale of life itself emptier.

On the Rabbit-Free Australia website the section on biological controls states that 'the point is not how many rabbits are killed, but how many are left behind'.[34] This disturbing statement reveals that rabbits have been reduced to 'bare life' that cannot be murdered or sacrificed, but is instead 'the actualisation of a mere "capacity to be killed"'.[35] The life that can be extinguished without consideration is the bare life of the animal who does not exist, but merely lives; who cannot die, but can only perish.[36] The implication is that the millions upon millions of extinguished rabbit lives have vanished from the earth, and need not be remembered or considered. I am in agreement with Deborah Bird Rose, however, that 'all deaths matter'[37] and that 'no death is a mere death'.[38]

Every single rabbit is an individual being with its own unique life. Eduardo Kohn observes that humans tend to think that the only thing they have in common with nonhuman animals is a corporeal body, but reminds us that '[l]ives are more than bodies'.[39] A rabbit's selfhood derives not just from its embodied form, its genetic make-up or DNA code, but also from its unique experience of the world through its connection to other beings.

By considering the individual to be little more than a member of a devalued taxonomy, the individual rabbit, with all its capabilities for suffering and joy, is effaced. The singular rabbit becomes nothing more than a statistic in the war against the species.

Rabbits in a new ecology

To combat the violence of 'killing for conservation', ethologist Marc Bekoff proposes an ethic of 'compassionate conservation'. He opposes the 'numbers game' of taxonomic thinking where certain species are valued above others, and instead argues that ethically grounded conservation must 'respect all life; treat individuals with respect and dignity; and tread lightly when stepping into the lives of animals'.[40] This respect and compassion-based discourse is supported by research into wildlife conservation and the culling of introduced species which indicates that there is very little evidence to demonstrate the effectiveness of pest control on preserving native diversity.[41] The problematic justification of 'killing for conservation' becomes untenable when conservation outcomes are fundamentally uncertain.

The goal to entirely annihilate the rabbit from the ecosystem is predicated on the problematic native/invasive divide that informs much of Australia's conservation discourse. The demonstrated futility of attempting to eradicate the rabbit from Australia has not halted violent attempts at creating a rabbit-less future, as the name 'Foundation for Rabbit-Free Australia' indicates. Mark Davis et al. explain that the practical value of the native/invasive dichotomy in conservation programs is seriously diminished and in some cases is becoming counterproductive.[42] They note that 'classifying biota according to their adherence to cultural standards of belonging, citizenship, fair play and morality does not advance our understanding of ecology'.[43] Instead, they promote a more inclusive approach to conservation which accepts non-native species as part of Australia's 'new nature'.[44]

The native/invasive divide is an outcome of the 'chronological fracture' described in Chapters 1 and 2. Arthur explains that a plant or animal is called a 'native' when it 'belongs to a place understood by the colonist as being from . . . a complete biota, which existed before the arrival of the colonists'.[45] This is a 'temporal fracture' which places the 'introduced' to a 'time and place *after* the event' of colonisation.[46] But this is not necessarily the way Aboriginal Australian people approach introduced species. Arthur notes that Aboriginal Australians in Central Australia do not distinguish between 'native' and 'exotic' in the same way non-Aboriginal people do, and do not see cattle and rabbits of the region as a 'contaminant' to be eradicated. Instead they see exotic animals as having 'come out' of the place in the same way as native animals.[47]

The idea of nativism being measured by lifetimes rather than genetic inheritance aligns with a relational approach to decolonisation where emplaced interactions are more important than species designation. The combination of lived experiences of intimacy with both native and introduced Australian animals, and the knowledge and cultural memory of a history of violent and destructive colonisation, produced an interesting tension in my discussions with New England Elders. The Elders' personal experiences of animal life were not vastly different from my own, in the sense that they involved introduced as well as native animals. When we began discussing the native/introduced divide, Pat

Cohen declared 'Well, I like all animals', and Margaret Walford added, 'I like all animals too because I was brought up with all the animals. Dad had horses, and he had cows, and he had dogs. The only thing we didn't have was a cat,'

Pat Cohen explained to me that the European rabbit quickly became part of the Australian landscape and the food chain, stating 'Rabbits were all I was brought up on…through the Depression, back in the 30s and 40s'. Margaret Walford shared intimate memories of her childhood spent learning how to survive on the land from her father, where rabbits, just like kangaroos, were an essential part of living in a multi-species community and drawing nourishment from the land and its creatures. She did not seem to draw any distinction between the native and the introduced:

MARGARET WALFORD: Uncle George, he'd go out and kill a kangaroo, and they'd bring it back, and they taught me how to skin it…and in Dad and Mum's family I was the eldest so Dad taught me all those kind of things…We went trapping, and he taught me how to trap the rabbits, come home and skin them. So I did all that. And when he brought a porcupine home he taught me how to skin that as well, pluck it, all that. I really enjoyed all those kind of things. And he also taught me, when one of the cows was having a calf, he said: 'Now sometimes the calves get stuck, the mother can't deliver them properly.' So he taught me how to put my hand in, and help deliver that calf…I treasure all those wonderful things that he taught me.

At the same time the knowledge of colonisation problematises this personal experience of kinship with animals and emotional ties with a beloved father. Lorna Hague explained that rabbits, and other domestic animals such as cattle, became food out of necessity, when colonisers violently appropriated Aboriginal land, disrupting the native food sources:

LORNA HAGUE: In colonisation, the English came in, took over, pushed people off their land…and that's when the animals that they introduced became food for the people – when they couldn't go hunting and gathering like they were supposed to.

Steve Widders shared this view:

STEVE WIDDERS: Getting away from the animals, that was part of government policy too. They said if we remove the Aboriginal people from their traditional hunting ground, they won't be able to eat their proper foods, we'll just destroy their culture, take them away from the food chain, and we'll give them rations. We'll give them a little bit of flour, a little bit of sugar…
LORNA HAGUE: But they didn't think you would survive on that…
STEVE WIDDERS: Well, a lot of people didn't survive.
LORNA HAGUE: They didn't, but by gee there's still a lot of people around today.
STEVE WIDDERS: But look at all the illnesses people got from it.

PAT COHEN: Still today people get sick from that.

STEVE WIDDERS: That's where a lot of diets changed and that's where we got things like diabetes and poor nutrition, because Aboriginal people were used to having the traditional food all the time. People were going out and eating sheep and cows and rabbits instead of the traditional food. Over generations I think that's changed a lot of the diet and nutrition and health.

It was not only the impact on Aboriginal societies, health and culture that distressed the Elders, but also the impact on the land and the nonhuman animals themselves. Steve lamented:

> When settlement and colonisation happened a lot of the animals lost their habitat because [the colonisers] knocked down forests, ripped up the rivers, raped the land. Poor little animals had nowhere to live…Colonisation upset not only the Aboriginal people, but all the animals and everything. In the rivers it upset a lot of the fish when they introduced things like carp.

Despite this recognition of ecological damage and distress, the Elders' life-world, much like my own, was dominated by a mix of native and introduced animals, and the domestic home was particularly favourable to the introduced. After a lengthy discussion on the impact of settlement on Aboriginal relationships with animal life, and the effect of exotic introduced foods on health, Lorna playfully asked Steve, 'So did you have pets when you were young? What were your favourite pets?' Steve answered, with a grin, 'We only had dogs and cats'.

The obvious tension between the life-world of an individual growing up in post-settlement Australia and the native/invasive divide which hangs over from Australia's violent history suggest that the native/invasive dualism, while relevant, is not necessarily helpful. People live their lives immersed in a hybrid world, cohabiting with cats and dogs, while buying kangaroo at the supermarket, and remembering a childhood spent skinning rabbits and porcupines with a father. In this world a rigid native/invasive dichotomy seems to foster damage and death more than it does love and life.

It may well be that European rabbits in Australia need to be culled as a form of 'resilience facilitation' to recuperate devastated ecosystems.[48] Rabbits may need to be removed from certain environments to retain biodiversity and begin a process of 'environmental healing'.[49] But making these decisions outside the native/introduced dualism means that they would be place-specific, and based on evidence rather than ideology.

A dynamic understanding of ecology, as described in Chapter 3, dissipates the notion of an authentic, static 'nature'. This means that there can be no simple or comprehensive directives for how humans should interact with their environments. One of the most insidious aspects of the native/invasive divide is the way it makes violent death appear inevitable, as though rabbits *must* be culled. This obscures the many complex and contingent choices which determine the fate of nonhuman life.

Understanding the dynamism of ecology requires an acceptance that nature does not provide simple prescriptive responses to problems, and instead 'people are forced to choose the kind of environment they want' and then take actions to engender it.[50] Our entanglement with our earth others demands that we reject simplistic dualisms which offer illusory absolution from the consequences of the difficult choices humans make about life, ecologies and how to manage them. Living within a world of 'discordant harmonies', as Daniel Botkin evocatively describes it, environmental decisions are necessarily complex.[51]

By classifying certain lives as 'inappropriate', and therefore expendable, the process of rabbit slaughter becomes too easy. The idea that the rabbit should *disappear* is disturbing in its abstract approach to these living, sentient creatures who share with us place and time, and who burrow their way into our world.

An invitation into a world

Rabbit burrows are not just a sign of rabbit bodies, but also an essential part of a rabbit's life-world, folding rabbit lives into land. Rabbit burrows offer an alternative understanding of rabbit life beyond colonial projection and the native/invasive divide. Instead of species thinking which positions organisms according to DNA and genetics, focus on the burrow links the rabbit body to multi-species shared environments.

This organism-plus-environment understanding of species emphasises that each individual represents a unique way of being in the world. Biodiversity in an organism-plus-environment mode must take into account not only the diversity of bodies, but diverse interactions with place. As Freya Mathews observes, a species should be valued 'for the unique contribution it makes to the beauty or variety of the world'.[52] In the current mass extinction event, it is not the absence of bodies that will shroud the earth in a dark loneliness, but the absence of ways of seeing, a blindness born of lost perceptions and the destruction of *Umwelten* on a mass scale.

In her essay 'Arts of Inclusion, or, How to Love a Mushroom', Anna Tsing calls up a subterranean world of fungi to promote an immersive connection to the lives of nonhuman Others. Evoking the sensuous affectivity of a mushroom's world, Tsing awakens human experience to an unfamiliar earthly terrain. 'Reach down and smell a clot of forest earth', Tsing instructs readers: 'it smells like the underground city of fungi.'[53] To experience 'the way of the mushroom' is to be attuned to another world. The layering of human and rabbit *Umwelten* that I experienced as a child enabled me to sense the affective experience of the rabbit in an anthropocentric world. Rabbit burrows intensify the inter-corporeal connections between human and rabbit, decolonising humanised space.

The overlapping of my world and the rabbit world through holes in the Earth reveals the connected and enmeshed embodiment that human and nonhuman share. Glen Mazis defines embodiment as being 'interwoven with a surround', and, following Merleau-Ponty, the body, both human and animal, as a way into the world.[54] Watching Lucy the Labrador dig desperately at the rabbit's earthly home, following the digging of a rabbit that has burrowed into the country to make shelter, I witnessed a poetic interspecies dance. In this folding of earth and time, the inter-corporeality of human and nonhuman bodies is expressed through place and unique uses of the world. The 'lived world' of the rabbit is enfolded with my lived world and that of my pet dog, and this overlapping draws us all together.

The rabbit resonates through the burrow into a human world; its own experience of the burrow is an echo or reverberation in our own perception.[55] Glen Mazis observes that the body that is open to the world is also open to the affective life-world of the other, that 'within our own embodiment is a sense of others' bonds with the world, both human and animal'.[56]

Maurice Merleau-Ponty built on von Uexküll's work to describe the way organisms are interlaced with their surrounds. He used the term 'flesh' to describe the open and permeable embodiment that allows us to make contact with others and with the world. For Merleau-Ponty, the boundaries of the living body are like membranes that open possibilities for metamorphosis and exchange.[57] The body in this sense is an 'open circuit', that is in constant contact with others and with the earth, 'with the world, with things, with animals, with other bodies'.[58]

By 'flesh', Merleau-Ponty is referring to both the flesh of the body and the flesh of the world. He writes: 'my body is made of the same flesh as the world... and moreover that this flesh of my body is shared by the world, the world reflects it, encroaches upon it and it encroaches upon the world.'[59]

Flesh is not skin, but an extra dimension to the elements of life on earth. Flesh 'is the element that makes being possible'.[60] Glen Mazis applies Merleau-Ponty's ontology of flesh to help understand the cause of speciocide. He argues that processes of anthropodenial, like the denial of the lived experience of rabbits in favour of colonial allegory, detach human beings from the flesh of the world. Mazis writes, 'If we are part of the flesh of the world, then our interconnection with other species is part of the depth of our perception, and anthropodenial is the detaching from part of our own perceptual emplacement in the world'.[61]

Perception, according to Merleau-Ponty, is a process of recognising patterns between self and other through embodied connections and relationships.[62] He argued that human and nonhuman animals are in a lateral rather than a hierarchical relationship. He used the term inter-animality to refer to this continued kinship between human and nonhuman. For Merleau-Ponty inter-corporeality is not just a reality of life on Earth, but it also creates a longing in humans to be among other creatures of the world.

A rabbit-burrowing

Merleau-Ponty 'conceives of the body not as a thing, substance, or essence, but as an unfolding relation to an *Umwelt* through the phenomenon of behaviour'.[63] Behaviour is important in Merleau-Ponty's thought because he believes that it reveals the key to an animal's manner of being; for this reason he focuses on process and action – on the act of burrowing, rather than the rabbit body, for example. Burrowing is a kind of activity that 'acts as a cohesive bond between the organism and its *Umwelt*'.[64] A rabbit burrow is made by the rabbit, but then determines the rabbit's movements. '*The Umwelt* is the world implied by the movement of the animal, and that regulates the animal's movements by its own structure.'[65] Along with shaping the behaviour of the rabbit, the burrow, it must be remembered, is composed of living soil which is home to an underground community of microorganisms which nourish the soil and transform it into nourishment for others.

The rabbit, the burrow and the multi-species soil community all combine, and rabbit-burrowing connects animal flesh to earth flesh through movement and action. For Merleau-Ponty, movement is the principle means for 'how we understand the animal and the world as a cohesive structure'.[66] He writes,

> If we want to take the phenomenon of movement seriously, we shall need to conceive a world which is not made up only of things, but which has in it also pure transitions...For example, the bird which flies across my garden is, during the time that it is moving, merely a grayish power of flight and, generally speaking, we shall see that things are defined primarily in terms of their 'behaviour' and not in terms of their static 'properties'.[67]

What Merleau-Ponty describes here is the importance of recognising ways of being in the world, over the properties of any particular body, or organism. This is a relational focus on genre, rather than gene, where an organism's interaction with its environment defines it. Brett Buchanan explains: 'The bird-in-flight encounters scurrying-brown-mouse. The oily-otter-swimming emerges from the water to become slow-basking-otter. In each case, the animal-environment is transformed and takes on new meaning'.[68]

The grey-rabbit-burrowing becomes the tired-rabbit-resting, but the burrow remains, its opening bearing witness to another *Umwelt* in this shared world. This is more than a site of conflict or a structure that gives away the rabbit's location. This is an invitation into another way of being, another world – an entrance into the pattern that connects.[69] Unlike Alice I could not journey into those New England burrows which fascinated me. I could only imagine what a rabbit world might look like. But rabbits are not so restricted, and sometimes they enter human worlds with curious eyes.

Bunny

After Lucy died, a lone rabbit began to approach the house because there was no longer the threat of being eaten. Christened by my parents 'Bunny', this hungry little critter devoured my mother's strawberries from the garden. Bunny had transmigrated across the seemingly insurmountable divide between the wild and the domestic world.

While Bunny was chastised for his wayward nibbling of the strawberry bush, he was also watched with great intrigue as he calmly shuffled along the front porch.

Figure 16 'Bunny' eating my Mum's plants at my parents' house, Armidale, 2009

Bunny's imminent presence brought a rabbit phenomenology into a human view. As he nibbled away on Mum's carefully cultivated garden, 'two *Umwelten*, two rings of finality...[crossed] each other'.[70]

Von Uexküll used the image of a soap bubble or a circle to describe the *Umwelt* – a 'concentric circle lived naively [which] overlaps with the rings of other living beings, all together intersecting and crossing with each other, each a chiasm with the other'.[71] When a grey rabbit entered a human world, in an inversion of the logic of Alice's Wonderland, distinct *Umwelten* began to merge. Just as I peered into rabbit burrows as a child, Bunny peered through household windows, and was watched with equal intrigue from inside by a human family.

When Bunny appeared on the lawn, my parents, and I, too, when I was home for holidays, easily recognised him. This was not because of any bodily feature, a distinct colouring or a unique shape for instance, but because of *where he was*, his emplacement – how he had positioned himself in our world. Bunny was identifiable because of his location, suggesting that where we position ourselves in a field of relationships might be fundamental to how we identify one another. Bunny was recognised as an organism-in-environment. What this suggests is that our identities are relationally determined – not merely influenced, but defined – by where we are in the world.

Tim Ingold has proposed a relational model for understanding difference and similarity which conceives of the environment as a field of relationships. He argues that what makes people alike is not a genealogical proximity, like family or species history, but 'the extent to which their own life-histories are intertwined through the shared experience of inhabiting particular paths in an environment'.[72] Like the process of 'becoming-dog', sharing worlds is a way of becoming attuned to another life, of becoming similar and recognising 'the pattern that connects'.[73] Ingold believes that within this relational model, one's position in an environment is fundamental to their identity. He writes:

> There is no room [in relational thinking] for the kind of classificatory project that groups individuals on the basis of whatever intrinsic characteristics they might happen to possess, by virtue of their biogenetic inheritance or cultural heritage, irrespective of their life in the world. Thus ethnic and racial classifications are as foreign to relational thinking as are the genealogically conceived taxonomies devised by biologists for the classification of living things. It is not by their inner attributes that persons or organisms are identified, but by their positions *vis-à-vis* one another in the relational field…The relational model, in short, *renders difference not as diversity but as positionality.*[74]

When Bunny positioned himself within the human domestic circle he disrupted the moralised hierarchy of animal life that rendered his life valueless. In such close proximity the rabbit was a stranger, but not the tokenistic representative of a familiar taxonomic type. Bunny was considered a neighbour, rather than a 'nature' – an unfamiliar and exciting guest who was greeted with surprise and warmth. By being close, by eating Mum's strawberries, Bunny becomes a 'companion' in the sense evoked by Donna Haraway – another messmate at the table.[75] In this act of 'breaking bread' with humans, Bunny demands a regard which would not usually be afforded to an introduced 'pest'.

Bunny was not an allegory of human colonisation, but rather a very real and fleshly presence. As he watched me wander around the yard, I felt the warmth which comes from being observed by another, the loneliness of human isolation dissipating. The longing to be watched by an animal is what Paul Shepard has termed 'a widespread yearning for a sign from the Others'.[76] In this age of loneliness,[77] where animals have largely disappeared from our daily life, Shepard notes that humans 'seem frantic to contact some intelligence more assured than ourselves, to be blessed in their witness of our mutual presence, to be given the surety that life is real and purposeful, even if the purposes lie beyond our grasp'.[78]

To be watched curiously by a rabbit as he munches on strawberries in the garden is to be known by the world. The whole world warms up in the moment of more-than-human encounter which reminds us that life is made of inter-species connections and relationships.

Ethics of entanglement

In the midst of Earth's sixth mass-extinction event a more ethical approach to nonhuman life is clearly necessary. In my encounter with Bunny I recognised the potential for Bunny to exceed his species designation by his proximity and positionality – by where he placed himself in a human world and how he was encountered. This ethics of encounter follows phenomenological modes of ethical response, such as the face-to-face encounter promoted by Emmanuel Levinas. For Levinas, the appearance of the face of the Other is 'a fundamental event',[79] an epiphany[80] that calls one into ethical response. When considering ethics in relation to nonhuman lives and worlds, the immediate phenomenological encounter can fall short, however.

Leaving aside the arguments around the potential for including nonhumans in Levinas's ethical mode,[81] there are other significant problems with encounter and ethics more generally when applied to nonhuman life. Mick Smith has observed that phenomenologically grounded ethics rely on the *appearance* of the Other. Smith asks, within such ethical schema, 'what can we say about those beings that pass us by unnoticed…that are invisible to the naked eye, or even those whose existence…we are not even aware of?'[82]

That Bunny could be noticed at all was dependent on a number of very specific conditions. He needed to approach humans, he needed to have a body large enough to be seen, he needed to be a benign presence. If only a select few life forms are able to connect to human lives, how do we develop an ethical relationship, not built on abstract ethical maxims, but borne along lines of love and connectivity? For Smith the answer lies in the ability to extend the ethical concern that is prompted by immediate encounter beyond the mere face of the Other that is seen. Because we live in a richly vascularised world, intimately connected to many others we will never meet, it is possible to use understandings of this connection to fuel an engaged ethical response that is neither abstract nor reliant on visibility. Smith seeks a 'depth' in the immediate encounter that connects the face, or appearance, of the Other to a wider ecological community. Smith argues that ethical concern can be extended through an ecologically informed encounter with the Other, where moral concern overflows from ethical inclusion of an individual into a network of connections and relations.[83]

I am persuaded by this ethics of entanglement, because it recognises the intimate connections of lives and bodies to worlds promoted by Merleau-Ponty, von Uexküll and Bateson. Essential to an ethics of entanglement is a multi-species understanding of place that recognises that the individual is constituted, nourished and sustained by a community of earth others. The encounter is not with the body, although the body has integrity, but with the life process as it is materialised in the body.

When we consider ethics in the context of the appearance of Bunny, for example, not only are we aware of the individual rabbit, we are awakened to the living environment that Bunny is immersed in and which he requires to survive. His thin body reminds us of drought and soil degradation, his burrows draw us into a subterranean world of worms and soil and invisible micro-organisms. Through Bunny we become phenomenologically connected to worlds that may not be sensorially apparent to us at all. 'What appears to us is not all that appears',[84] as we engage in dialogical communion with Bunny and an entire ecologically connected system within which he is enmeshed. The burrows that invite us into a rabbit world also invite us to imagine rabbit faces that hide in the shadows. Both the burrow and the rabbit body become sites of ethical encounter that draws us into contact with the pattern that connects.[85]

The encounter with the life of the rabbit does not stop when Bunny hops off the porch and disappears into New England bush. Ethics of entanglement must exceed the individual body. If lives are more than bodies, ethical inclusion needs to be directed beyond the individual organism and into the many phenomenological worlds (*Umwelten*) that exist at the periphery of our own. Concern for Bunny does not stop at the tip of his fur but continues into the rabbit burrows. Just as buried companion animals charge the soil with memory, rabbit burrows bring nonhuman animal lives into view, ensuring that immersive connection to the other overflows from the body to constitute the flesh of the world.

Animals as ecology

Aboriginal understandings of Country, and of multi-species kinship, support an ethics of entanglement. Steve Widders expressed to me a strong adherence to the idea that the organism-plus-environment is inseparable, and mutualistic.

> I think it's very important to realise that animals are very much a part of the ecology, and that's why [Aboriginal people] had totems – to make sure that they lasted, and they were protected, they didn't die out. So certain people were only allowed to eat certain ones, so they would survive. But I think the relationship with the land has got a lot to do with the relationship with animals too. Because animals made the land really, they were very much a part of the ecology. And we're talking about water animals too. They made the rivers and...kept the life going, you know, the rivers and the land.

Here Steve speaks of connectivity in a way that embraces the extended environmental ethics that includes both rabbit and burrow. If fish are understood to make the rivers, they need to be protected for the rivers' sake – this ethics of interconnection does not approach faces as isolated, but as entangled participants in ecological communities. These communities also include the spirit world, and links between present and past.

Elder Pat Cohen explained, with a cheeky giggle, that she had, in the past, eaten her totem – the porcupine. She said it tasted wonderful – like fish. Then she told a story which illustrated the spiritual significance of the totem and its relationship to an ecological community that includes humans.

> [A porcupine] came right past the door one day, and all of us kids were jumping up and down singing out to Pop, who was my Grandfather who was initiated: 'Pop! Pop! Come and get this porcupine. Come and kill it for us.' He allowed us to eat porcupine, but not that one, because it was going past the door. We asked him, 'Why? Why won't you kill it?' He said, 'Because

he's…an old man passing through. And what better to turn himself into than the totem? Let him go, let him go on his way.' And he shooed him off.

On death, a man had transformed into an animal, crossing over from one kingdom of life to another. As I listened to this story I thought about the way death reveals its own kinds of truths: truths that are unclear, complex, at times mysterious. When I go to Lucy's grave I think about the way she too transformed into something else when she died. She has crossed over, and become part of the earth, nourishing a multi-species community.

My New England childhood spent in a mixed community has awoken me to other ways of being and seeing the world. Growing up surrounded by nonhuman life, in relationships which are messy, unfair, joyous, tragic and cruel, I have been shaped by signs from the Others. These relationships still live within me, as memory collects lost time together, in the chronotope of a childhood home.

Conclusion

This chapter began with the goal of exploring how intimate and responsible relationships between humans and nonhumans can be fostered, and made to flourish in an era of extinction. I have drawn on childhood experiences with animals to reveal the many ways that nonhuman animals enhance our relationship with place and self, making us more-than-human.

I am certain that the world is richer when we allow ourselves to wonder at the nonhuman lives we encounter, to become, like Alice in Wonderland, *curiouser and curiouser* as we enter into a dialogue with a rabbit, or learn how to play multi-species games with a dog. Donna Haraway regards 'provocation to curiosity' as 'one of the first obligations and deepest pleasures of worldly companion species'.[86] Growing up with Lucy I learned an 'art of curiosity' – the ability to allow an Other to exceed their species designation, to surprise, challenge and teach.

Paul Shepard has observed our deep interdependence with nonhuman animals from an evolutionary perspective. He writes:

> Our species…emerged in watching the Others, participating in their world by eating and being eaten by them, suffering them as parasites, wearing their feathers and skins, making tools of their bones and antlers, and communicating their significance by dancing, sculpting, performing, imaging, narrating, and thinking them.[87]

This suggests that the loss of species in this time of extinction, and the severing of human-animal relationships by processes of distance and denial, may be forcing a process of de-evolution.[88] As a community of dead rabbits disappears behind colonial allegory, each life and death forgotten, we enter more deeply into an 'age of loneliness'[89] – a 'darkened world' where everywhere humans encounter only projections of themselves.[90]

Deborah Bird Rose observes that this age of mass extinction is impoverishing life on Earth as the 'emptier Earth becomes, the emptier are those who remain alive'.[91] Emptiness is like a shadow within the self, heavy with the weight of space. This hollow feeling comes from the severing of inter-species ties: the dog within us which will never be expressed or fulfilled; the pleading eyes of a baby rabbit forgotten as a child swallows tears; the burrows that lead into other worlds, collapsed by shovels and dynamite.

The end of life is death. And yet, in remembering dead dogs and dead rabbits, death is not separated from life, but rather becomes part of it – a teacher for the living. Elie Wiesel has argued that memory is a reconciliatory force that creates bonds as mass annihilation seeks to destroy them. Memory ensures that no life becomes truly lifeless as it wrests the victims of mass slaughter from 'oblivion' and allows the dead to 'vanquish death'.[92] In a continent inhabited by dead rabbits – a community of the dead – remembering these lost individuals and their lost lives is an important task for making sure that no death is a mere death. While rabbits may be a target of speciocide, they will always exceed this designation, as their lives stretch out beyond their bodies, down into deep underground tunnels, then up, to emerge somewhere, in a sunny garden, munching on bright red, juicy, strawberries.

Notes

1   G. Bateson, *Mind and Nature*.
2   A. Franklin, *Animal Nation: The True Story of Animals and Australia* (Sydney: University of New South Wales Press, 2006), 97.
3   Calicivirus trials began on Wardang Island, off the coast of South Australia, in March 1995. The virus escaped and infected rabbits on the rest of the island in October 1995. The disease then spread to the mainland, and in September 1996 rabbit calicivirus was officially declared a legal biological control agent (C. Landström, 'Justifiable Bunnycide: Narrating the Recent Success of Australian Biological Control of Rabbits', *Science as Culture* 10, no. 2 (2001): 144–145).
4   P. Adams, 'RHDV-K5: New Strain of Pest Rabbit-killing Calicivirus Disease Given Green Light for 2017 Release', *ABC News*, www.abc.net.au/news/2016-04-29/new-strain-of-rabbit-killing-calicivirus-disease-approved/7367142.
5   B. Coman, *Tooth and Nail: The Story of the Rabbit in Australia* (Melbourne: The Text Publishing Company, 1999), 133.
6   Ibid., 132.
7   Ibid., 134.
8   D. Heishman, 'VHD Factsheet', *House Rabbit Network*, www.rabbitnetwork.org/articles/vhd.shtml.
9   B. Coman, *Tooth and Nail*, 173.
10 P. Adams, 'RHDV-K5'.
11 Foundation for Rabbit-Free Australia Inc., *Rabbit-Free Australia*, www.rabbitfreeaustralia.org.au/.
12 A. Crosby, *Ecological Imperialism*.
13 J. Arthur, *Default Country*, 130.
14 Foundation for Rabbit-Free Australia, *Rabbit-Free Australia*.
15 V. Plumwood, 'Decolonising Australian Gardens: Gardening and the Ethics of Place', *Australian Humanities Review* 36 (2005), www.australianhumanitiesreview.org/archive/Issue-July-2005/09Plumwood.html.

16   E. Rolls, *They All Ran Wild* (Sydney: Angus and Robertson, 1969), 21.
17   N. Smith, 'Thank Your Mother for the Rabbits: Bilbies, Bunnies and Redemptive Ecology.' *Australian Zoologist* 33, no. 3 (2000): 373.
18   Ibid., 134.
19   The first chocolate bilbies were made in 1982, but the concept really took off when major chocolate retailer Darrell Lea became involved in 2002. Since this time Haigh's chocolate, Cadbury and Pink Lady have also released chocolate bilbies as alternative Easter treats, and both Darrell Lea and Haigh's use their profits to support bilby assistance programs.
20   C. Landström, 'Bunnycide', 141.
21   A. Garnett & K. Kessing, *Easter Bilby* (Department of Environment and Heritage: Kaye Kessing Productions, 2006).
22   Foundation for Rabbit-Free Australia Inc., *Rabbit Free Australia*.
23   Cited by Reuters, ' "Easter Bilby" May Replace Easter Bunny in Australia to Stave Off Extinction', *Huffington Post* (April 2012), www.huffingtonpost.com/2012/04/05/easter-bilby-may-replace-easter-bunny_n_1407489.html.
24   D. Rose, *Wild Dog Dreaming*, 19.
25   Ibid., 20.
26   E. Wiesel, *From the Kingdom of Memory*, 160.
27   D. Rose, *Wild Dog Dreaming*, 25.
28   D. Rose, 'Judas Work: Four Modes of Sorrow', *Environmental Philosophy* 5, no. 2 (2008): 63.
29   D. Rose, *Wild Dog Dreaming*, 25.
30   Ibid., 57.
31   F. de Waal, 'Are We in Anthropodenial?'
32   G. Mazis, 'The World of Wolves', 77.
33   B. Reddiex and D. Forsyth, 'Control of Pest Mammals for Biodiversity Protection in Australia', *Wildlife Research* 33 (2006): 715.
34   Foundation for Rabbit-Free Australia Inc., *Rabbit-Free Australia*.
35   G. Agamben, *Homo Sacer: Sovereign Power and Bare Life*, trans. Daniel Heller-Roazen (Stanford: Stanford University Press, 1995), 114.
36   In *Being and Time* (Oxford: Blackwell, 1962), Martin Heidegger argues that animals do not die, but merely perish, because their lives simply come to an end, while the human's death is marked as significant and their deceased body continues to be meaningful after death.
37   D. Rose, *Wild Dog Dreaming*, 21.
38   Ibid., 22.
39   E. Kohn, 'How Dogs Dream: Amazonian Natures and the Politics of Transspecies Engagement', *American Ethnologist* 34, no. 1 (2007): 16.
40   M. Bekoff, 'First Do No Harm', *New Scientist* (28 August 2010): 24.
41   For more on this see A. Wallach et al., 'Predator Control Promotes Invasive Dominated Ecological States', *Biological Conservation* 142 (2009): 43–52; D. Bergstrom et al., 'Indirect Effects of Invasive Species Removal Devastate World Heritage Island', *Journal of Applied Ecology* 46 (2009): 73–81; B. Warburton & B. Norton, 'Towards a Knowledge-Based Ethic for Lethal Control of Nuisance Wildlife', *The Journal of Wildlife Management* 73, no. 1 (2009): 158–164.
42   M. Davis et al., 'Don't Judge Species on their Origins', *Nature* 474 (2011): 153.
43   Ibid., 153.
44   T. Low, *The New Nature: Winners and Losers in Wild Australia* (Melbourne: Penguin, 2002).
45   J. Arthur, *Default Country*, 75.
46   Ibid., 75.
47   Ibid., 75. This is based on Bruce Rose's 1995 survey of attitudes to introduced animals among Aboriginal people living in Central Australia. One interviewee raised

the penetrating question 'If white fellas don't want these [introduced/feral] animals then why don't they *all* move out?' (*Land Management Issues: Attitudes and Perceptions Amongst Aboriginal Peoples of Central Australia*, Alice Springs: Central Land Council, 13).

48 This concept is described in greater detail in Chapter 3.

49 Freya Mathews uses the term 'healing' to describe a synergistic approach to ecological health that draws on the strengths of the ecology already in place. Environmental healing 'might consist in the replenishment of exhausted soils or the removal of exotic organisms to enable the ecosystemic impulse towards biodiversification to be maintained. The wholesale "restoration" of an original suite of species however would constitute interventionism rather than healing' ('Letting the World Do the Doing', Australian Humanities Review 33 (2004), www.australianhumanitiesreview. org/archive/Issue-August-2004/matthews.html).

50 D. Botkin, *Discordant Harmonies: A New Ecology for the Twenty-First Century* (New York & Oxford: Oxford University Press, 1990), 189.

51 Ibid.

52 F. Mathews, 'Planet Beehive', Australian Humanities Review 50 (2011), www. australianhumanitiesreview.org/archive/Issue-May-2011/mathews.html.

53 A. Tsing, 'Arts of Inclusion', 5.

54 G. Mazis, 'The World of Wolves', 70.

55 Ibid., 75.

56 Ibid., 77.

57 D. Abram, *The Spell of the Sensuous* (New York: Vintage Books, 1996), 46.

58 M. Merleau-Ponty cited in Mazis, 'The World of Wolves', 242.

59 M. Merleau-Ponty, *The Visible and the Invisible*, trans. Alphonso Lingis (Evanston: Northwestern University Press, 1968), 248.

60 B. Buchanan, *Onto-Ethologies*, 140.

61 G. Mazis, 'The World of Wolves', 76.

62 The concept of Flesh is central to Merleau-Ponty's understanding of perception which he defines as an ongoing interchange between the body and its surrounds. There is a reciprocity to the flesh because being able to perceive is necessarily being also able to be perceived; to be sentient is also to be sensible; 'the presence of the world is precisely the presence of its flesh to my flesh' (Merleau-Ponty, *The Visible and the Invisible*, 127).

63 B. Buchanan, *Onto-Ethologies*, 115.

64 Ibid., 134.

65 M. Merleau-Ponty cited in Buchanan, *Onto-Ethologies*, 134.

66 B. Buchanan, *Onto-Ethologies*, 134.

67 M. Merleau-Ponty, *Phenomenology of Perception* (London & New York: Routledge, 2002), 320.

68 B. Buchanan, *Onto-Ethologies*, 135.

69 G. Bateson, *Mind and Nature*.

70 M. Merleau-Ponty cited in B. Buchanan, *Onto-Ethologies*, 136.

71 B. Buchanan, *Onto-Ethologies*, 145.

72 T. Ingold, *The Perception of the Environment: Essays on Livelihood, Dwelling and Skill* (London and New York: Routledge, 2000), 148.

73 G. Bateson and M. Bateson, *Angels Fear*, 8.

74 T. Ingold, *Perception*, 149.

75 D. Haraway, *When Species Meet*, 4.

76 P. Shepard, *The Others*, 141.

77 E. O. Wilson, *The Creation: An Appeal to Save Life on Earth* (New York: W. W. Norton & Co., 2006), 61.

78 P. Shepard, *The Others*, 141.

79   T. Wright et al., 'The Paradox of Morality: An Interview with Emmanuel Levinas', trans. A. Benjamin and T. Wright, in *The Provocation of Levinas*, ed. R. Bernasconi and D. Wood (London and New York: Routledge, 1988), 168.

80   E. Levinas, *Totality and Infinity: An Essay on Exteriority* (Duquesne University Press: Pittsburgh, 1969), 194.

81   Levinasian ethics are distinctly anthropocentric. Levinas believed that while '[o]ne cannot entirely refuse the face of an animal' the human face has 'priority'. He wrote: 'The phenomenon of the face is not in its purest form in the dog' ('Paradox', 169). Debates about whether it is possible to include the nonhuman animal in Levinasian ethics are ongoing.

82   M. Smith, 'Dis(appearance): Earth, Ethics and Apparently (In)Significant Others', in 'Unloved Others: Death of the Disregarded in the Time of Extinctions', eds. D. Rose and T. van Dooren, special issue, *Australian Humanities Review* 50 (May 2011): 25.

83   Ibid., 41.

84   Ibid., 42.

85   G. Bateson, *Mind and Nature*.

86   D. Haraway, *When Species Meet*, 7.

87   P. Shepard, *The Others*, 11.

88   Val Plumwood also made this observation: 'I think that we are definitely diminished by a lack of contact with the more-than-human world, and we are diminished as thinkers as well as emotionally' ('Place, Politics, and Spirituality: An Interview', in *Pagan Visions for a Sustainable Future*, ed. de Angeles et al. (Woodbury, MN: Llewellyn Publications, 2005), 251.

89   E. O. Wilson, *The Creation*, 61.

90   M. Rowlands citing Heidegger in *Animals Like Us* (London: Verso, 2002), 196.

91   D. Rose, *Wild Dog Dreaming*, 146.

92   E. Wiesel, *From the Kingdom of Memory*, 21.

Part IV

Water

Figure 17 Dam on my parents' property after heavy rain, 2010 (Vic Wright)

Water is the blood of life, the blood of the land.

Uncle Steve Widders

Dam

The water was lukewarm for a centimetre on the surface, and like ice below. Mud was snuggling into the gaps between my toes. After paddling into deep water on his boogie board, my older brother turned back to yell: *Come on – sook!*

I pictured myself sinking into the mud like quicksand, swallowing the cold black water until I drowned.

I'm staying here.

He turned around and paddled toward me with a menacing grin and pulled me in. I fell forward into the dark ice water, and then ran back to the house screaming.

I could'a been drowned – he tried to kill me!

Dam, in drought

Lucy loves to swim but the dams have dried up. The whole block is brown and parched. When we walk together on the grass it splits and crunches like old brittle bones.

She used to run and dive into the dam. The brown water seemed electrified by her joy – whipping up white against her fur. Now she runs in but she can't make the dive. The water never covers her back. I want to fill it up for her, but I don't even know how to ask Dad for something like that.

Garden

I was back from uni for holidays one year and Mum said to me: 'I don't wanna fuckin' grow old here. Some old woman wandering around watering dying plants in the dry dirt. I can't bear the bloody thought of it.'

Farm

On the long dirt drive through my Grandfather's farm the car windows fill with the vision of starving sheep. Bones poke through freshly sheared wool pulled tight over their delicate suffering frames like nylon. They look so desperate and doomed. I don't say anything because I know I'm not meant to. I was taught very young that some deaths do not matter, that farm animals don't die, they merely perish. But those living perishing bodies of sheep stain my memory with a shadow, a shadow that sits in silence in the back of a white sedan as it rolls along a dirt drive and over a cattle grid up to the farmhouse.

Gully

Before we knew who we were we rode our bikes here. The world was younger then and I could say 'what say you gully?' without philosophy and without cynicism. And the gully would answer in tones of swishing water, glistening rock – in the disappearance of a lizard coloured like a stone. My brother said I was too young to play with, but we played together anyway, in tiny waterfalls.

Water is not youth but after all this heavy rain I am following my footsteps in the mud, plodding through hours of my life gloriously lived by these rushing gully waters 25 years ago, as if it were just yesterday.

In my New England, Australian home, water was not blue like the ocean, but brown like a muddy dog, and green like trees and grass. Water pumps through the veins of the places we love, and it cannot be removed or extracted without unmaking those places and bringing death. We are now living in the midst of a water crisis which may be 'the most pervasive, most severe, and most invisible dimension of the ecological devastation of the earth'.[1] As we are called to respond to yet another great unmaking of places and lives in the Anthropocene, I am persuaded by environmental philosopher Thom Van Dooren's observation that 'we are required to make a stand for some possible worlds and not others, we are required to take responsibility for the ways in which we help to tie and retie our knotted multispecies worlds'.[2]

In this time of 'dying water'[3] I am writing to call up water's livingness, and to celebrate it as a vital, connected and tangible part of all life on Earth. The situated waters I know best – the waters of my homeland – provide the focus for a collaborative storying where I attempt to write in dialogue with this language of life, to trace something of the cadence of water in my words and arguments. I feel it is important to acknowledge that the creeks and gullies and rains that I write of, and with, have an Indigenous history and Indigenous ethos – they are already 'rich with stories, ceremonies and life',[4] and I do not intend my stories to overwrite Aboriginal Australian water dreaming. On the contrary, I hope that my water stories help to sing up Indigenous Country, and that my writing can form part of a collaborative decolonising dialogue that affirms Aboriginal people's immanent sovereignty in place.

Notes

1 V. Shiva, *Water Wars: Privatization, Pollution, and Profit* (London: Pluto Press, 2000), 1.
2 T. Van Dooren. 'Vultures and their People in India: Equity and Entanglement in a Time of Extinctions' *Australian Humanities Review* 50 (2011), www.australian humanitiesreview.org/archive/Issue-May-2011/vandooren.html.
3 D. Rose, 'Justice and Longing', in *Fresh Water: New Perspectives on Water in Australia*, eds. E. Potter, A. Mackinnon, S. McKenzie and J. McKay (Carlton: Melbourne University Press, 2007), 12.
4 Ibid., 8.

7   Petrichor: lessons from a lost gully

Before rain falls, the earth releases a scent. The Australian Commonwealth Scientific and Industrial Research Organisation (CSIRO) termed it 'petrichor'.

> The smell itself comes about when increased humidity – a pre-cursor to rain – fills the pores of stones (rocks, soil, etc.) with tiny amounts of water. While it's only a miniscule amount, it is enough to flush the oil from the stone and release petrichor into the air. This is further accelerated when actual rain arrives and makes contact with the earth, spreading the scent into the wind.[1]

Petrichor is the longing of the soil. Petrichor describes an Earth remembering rain. Petrichor is memory, tinged with anticipation.[2] Petrichor is the past in the present that speaks of the yet-to-come. Petrichor is in my memory too; it is a memory of the living world shared across bodies and lives.

It smells like a childhood summer. It smells like the sound of rain hammering down on a tin roof.

The scent lingers in the air, an echo in my thoughts, awakening in me a desire to return to something untouchable, some prior self, an earlier feeling lost with age. Petrichor … it flows through the rivers of my mind.

Petrichor is the scent of an old record player and the scratchy warmth of familiar songs by fireside.
Petrichor is the scent of my father with a wheelbarrow full of wood escaping a stormy sky.
Petrichor is kangaroos at dusk.
Petrichor is gumboots and slushy undergrowth, an overflowing creek.
I follow the scent of rain on a Proustian journey through gulleys, down watercourses.
Petrichor, collecting kindling, my small body tilting with the weight of the wood.
Petrichor, ankle-deep in mud, fishing for trout.
Petrichor, the laundry bucket full of yabbies.
Petrichor, that cubby I built out of bark in the bush but could never find again.

Petrichor – it must be in my blood, running wild through this country like an unruly stream. And my blood is in these rains that wash through the gully, descending down all the years I spent here, rivers of time carrying me back to some ancient sea... back to a place I never return to, and yet never seem to truly leave. Back to my blood's country.

Petra, in ancient Greek, means stone. *Ichor* is blood – the blood of the gods: an ethereal fluid, a tenuous essence.

Uncle Steve Widders told me that *Water is the blood of life, the blood of the land.* Petrichor is the blood of stone, blood pumping through Country awoken by the promise of rain.

Our ancestors, they think, learned to love this smell. Petrichor said 'nourishment', said 'survival', said 'relief'. It is the aroma of life, a tenuous essence, an ethereal hope. It disappears, flitting in and out of perception, but repeats as a refrain carried by the waters of the world.

Petrichor is an address and a response. It is a meeting, a greeting, a chemical reaction, an intra-action, a proposition, a becoming-with. In an affective ecology of mind, petrichor is a living thought in the world.

The rains have been talking to the earth since it began. The gorge country of my childhood was carved by the flows and intensities of rushing waters. In this dialogue between stone country and sky country, petrichor is a memory as old as life itself.

In India, they call it *matti ka attar,* earth's perfume, as if dry lands sprayed it across their bodies to attract a suitor of rain. And like perfume it awakens the senses to a longed for future through a fragrance from the past. *I have smelt this before, I have known this before.* Bodies retrace exquisite memories that cannot be placed, and yet replace, take over place, are all that remain. Petrichor is a scent as ephemeral as attraction, as ancient as desire.

I know this language of the earth, we all do. It is part of our ecology of mind. It awakens in me a longing for rain, but not just that. It awakens longing itself, poising me on the tip of desire, wanting and waiting, leaning in to a moment with the next moment lightly touching... the future brought closer by mind and flesh coming to meet it, somewhere in the lingering air.

The eucalypt trees, do they smell it too? Their leaves outstretch, as if hands, ready to cup rain.

There is some evidence that drought-stricken cattle respond in a restless manner to this 'smell of rain'.[3] The starving sheep of my youth, the cracked soils of the dry dam, they must have remembered the scent. In a country as old as this, baked in heat and sun, petrichor says 'mercy'.

Immersed in a living ecology of mind, this effusion is a web of memories, and of hope. When I smell it, it beckons me toward arterial waters, the waters that run in my blood.

The country of memory is a country of rivers. Some wide and flowing, some dry and deserted. Some you can follow, but with some, the country is too harsh and too threatening. Some you can only just hear they're so far off, and some carry you away completely.

How distant I have become from this everywhen!⁴ What direction is the rain? Is it south of here? Rivers run to the sea but they split and diverge too. Follow them too long and you could find yourself in backcountry, trapped in a current of time, a thousand miles away from the effortless pleasures of home.

The lost gully

The ancient Greek philosopher, Hereclitus, said that no man could ever step twice into the same river. Conceptualising life as 'flow', 'as a river', Heraclitus introduced the concept of becoming into Western philosophy, an ontological understanding that the world is composed of states of change, that 'everything flows, nothing stands still'.

When I was a child our home had a flowing river. It was really a trickling gully, but in the vivid fancies of youth, it gushed like a waterfall. My earliest memories are of playing by the gully's side with my older brother – memories of gumboots, slushy muddy undergrowth and noisy brown running water.

I cannot step into this river again – not only because of the ongoing flow of becoming, because the river has changed and so have I, making a genuine return impossible – but because the river no longer flows. At the age of nine or ten, the river of my youth disappeared. Drought descended on the country, evaporating the waters that nourished the land, and taking with them the river's song of place.

In moments of nostalgia I sometimes find myself longing for this impossible river of childhood. And every time I pass the barren, dry earth gully where it used to flow, a remembered country slips from my thoughts into my footsteps, and I walk in the rhythm of the rushing waters, in the shadows of a past alive in a place it can never return to.

As synapses connect to flowing gulleys, and storm clouds gather in mnemonic atmospheres, my personal journey into remembered waters becomes a journey into connectivity, because the waters I remember have not actually left the earth. The flowing water from my Proustian journey along a childhood river, water that is 'real without being actual, ideal without being abstract',⁵ is still cycling through Earth's hydrological system as an immanent, material memory that carries both the past and the future.

Writing with the droughts and rains that are within me, with the waters that have enveloped my life, either by their presence or by their absence, I am working to situate my own water memories and encounters within the immanent material memories of a living world. Inspired by the effusion of petrichor – a scent that awakens memory and desire in multispecies ecologies – I am conceptualising memory as part of a broader ecology of mind that enables and nourishes co-evolutionary processes of life on earth. Memory, in this sense, is both a becoming, and a becoming-with.

Lynn Margulis and Dorion Sagan articulate the way life works productively with time, as life is always 'preserving the past, making a difference between past and present; life binds time, expanding complexity and creating new problems for itself'.[6] Memory and becoming are therefore at the heart of reproduction and evolution, maintained through iterative and generative re-articulations of the past.

Gregory Bateson understood evolution to be an all embracing learning process and a form of ongoing memory.[7] Situating epistemology within this evolutionary process, Bateson argued that the human mind is nested in larger thinking systems, and that our knowledge of the world depends on a 'wider knowing'[8] of Earth's systems. Inspired by the connections drawn by Bateson between an ecology of mind and the iterative processes of evolution, I am looking at water as a substance that reveals and enables the time-binding quality of matter to explore a more-than-human ecology of memory, becoming, communication and learning.

I develop this discussion in dialogue with Deborah Bird Rose's work on multispecies knots of ethical time. Rose applies James Hatley's research into aenocide – 'the mass murder of individuals that constitutes a sustained attack on the future of the group, and thus an attack on ethical time' – to a biosocial context, in order to understand the enormity of our current anthropogenic mass extinction event. She argues that ethical time is sustained through intersecting temporal patterns of sequence and synchrony that depend on more-than-human connectivity because life is a gift shared across species and generations.[9] Because water helps to create the 'great patterns of life, death, sustenance and renewal that intersect...to form flows of life-giving life',[10] anthropogenic alterations of waterways undermine many situated sets of relationships that maintain patterns of ethical time.

At the heart of this understanding of water in relation to memory, time, becoming, biodiversity, evolution and ethics is a politics of possibility, as water contains and can help to enact alternative futures. The past embodied in water, and in memory, does not recede into the distance toward a state of oblivion, but is enlivened as it is actualised in the present that opens up yearnings for the yet-to-come.

Memory is a country of hope and of connectivity. In its mysterious becomings we find an abundance of life-giving rivers, a flow of wild and unknown pasts and futures patterned through our shared world.

A creek-scar

> No rain yet, and the creek drying, and no rain coming;
> and I remember the old man, part of my childhood,
> who knew all about cattle and horses. In the big drought,
> he said, the mares knew when their milk gave out,
> and I've seen a mare over a dead foal
> with tears coming out of her eyes. She kept on standing;
> she wouldn't go near water or look for grass,
> and when the rain came she stayed where the foal died,
> though we dragged it away and burned it.
> —Judith Wright, Unknown Water[11]

Drought lingers in the memory like a scar. An evaporated creek can carry wounds that are decades old. When Judith Wright writes of witnessing a mare unable to save her starving foal in a drought, she writes of pain imprinted on her own memory, on the memory of the mare, and on the memory of the land. *When the rain came she stayed where the foal died, though we dragged it away and burned it.* In an eco-mental ecology of trauma, suffering is shared across human and nonhuman lives as water's absence carves grief into the places we love.

Droughts are a recurrent and frequent feature of Australia's climate. Wright's poem refers to the nation-wide droughts of the late 1930s and 1940s. Like Judith Wright, I grew up in a country of droughts. Immersed in webs of multispecies suffering, I witnessed the more-than-human world longing for waters that never came. Drought makes a lack of water exquisitely tangible. I remember seeing the shape of bones poking through wool on the bodies of starving sheep; the dried-up dams, the cracked soils, the grey-brown of parched grass and trees.

When I hear the word drought my mind returns to visceral, layered and emplaced bouts of trauma in my water-starved New England life world. Memories of water deprivation in the ecologies that surrounded me as a child are memories of moments where I witnessed connectivity between water and lives being broken. The feeling of helplessness that my dog couldn't swim in the dam anymore; noticing that my mother looked older and tired beyond her years while she told me of her distress at watching her garden die; staring out the car window at the starving bodies of sheep as we drove through my Grandfather's property; never really noticing the green being sucked out of the block until all that was left was an almost colourless grey. What these experiences indicate is that water is primarily experienced through encounter with a relational world – that is, as an emplaced and vital part of more-than-human life, memory, emotion and thought.

While water is globally distributed, evaporating from earth, where clouds transform gullies and dams into rains, this fluid transformative process does not negate the way water inheres in, and helps to make, place. Writing from an arid country that is dancing with El Niño – a country of extremely variable rainfall – my own bio-geographical and historio-cultural inheritance of water attunes me to its place-making quality, and to the dangers of treating water as an abstract and anonymous substance in a relational world where the specific conditions of a place matter vitally.

Much of the devastation wreaked by drought in Australia, including the emotional wrench of watching plants and animals suffer and die, is caused not by water scarcity in the sense of having an unusually low amount of water, but by an imbalanced, delusional relationship, where settlers have failed to respond to the environmental conditions of the continent. Jay Arthur writes that Australia is a country 'stained with the memory of water'[12] – a memory that has been carried over from the watery environments of a colonial homeland.

The United Nations Convention to Combat Desertification Working Group notes that '[w]hile agricultural and pastoral activity are critical components of our national economy, Australian landscapes are generally not well suited to many of the land use and management practices imported from other continents over the last 200 years'.[13] The 'double vision' of a well-watered Australia leads to land degradation which damages the hydrological cycle and dries out the continent. 'Drought becomes then a particularly colonial experience.'[14]

Waters of connectivity

Aboriginal Australian Elder and descendant of the Anaiwan people Steve Widders expresses the importance of water to Aboriginal people living on Country before colonisation. He says that 'Aboriginal people always lived near the water, because that was life, the blood of life, the blood of the land. You don't have that, you can't survive'. Understanding water as the blood of living places, that pumps through them and helps to sustain them, is a form of 'connectivity thinking'[15] that acknowledges and celebrates water's ability to create 'nourishing terrain' that both gives and receives life,[16] and resists water's conceptual and physical abstraction from place.

In a water-based ecology of life on Earth, the waters that flow in our own blood are part of the connected networks of life on Earth that bring us into being. If water is the blood of life, the trees that water grows are life's breath, the animals water sustains are life's children and our kin, and the stone and soil water enlivens are life's body and nourishment. This means that it is not the abstract formulation of H_2O that we require to survive. If the unit of survival is the organism-plus-environment, the drought-ridden farms, too, are within us, as are the suffering animals, and the dry and cracked soils of dying rivers.

Stephen Muecke argues that connectivity is a mode of reasoning that leads to commitment[17], and Deborah Bird Rose observes that 'entanglements give us grounds for action'.[18] From a connectivity perspective, water is the lifeblood of ethical time, as it helps to create nourishing interfaces that can birth new life and support biodiversity. This means that one way to respond to the global water crisis is through an 'ethics of particularity'[19] that cultivates response-ability to emplaced, situated waters that support multispecies ecologies. At the same time, the waters that run in our blood open us up to porous relation with many distant earth others, as water moves through the hydrological cycle, and flows into countless bodies and lives, making and unmaking places across the world. Within this radical entanglement is the potential to understand, through our shared, embodied porosity, the ways we are implicated in hydrological networks of social and environmental justice.

In keeping with this book's engagement with entangled ethics in the Anthropocene, I am bringing an understanding of emplaced waters into dialogue with water's radical distribution in order to make sense of how discrete places across the globe are made with and through each other. Understanding this inter-implication requires attentiveness to the way human memory is nested in the memories of the living world.

Water remembers

Contemplating the dry earth of my lost childhood gully, as rain begins to fall around me, I am reminded that water never truly disappears. It continuously transforms into the rivers and rains of the Earth, just as my own memories continue to flow through a living ecology of mind. Water has been cycling through Earth's hydrological system since the beginning of the planet – a perennial circulation of matter and information through the world. As a form of immanent material memory that is both retentive and communicative,[20] water holds chemical and molecular memory traces of what it has touched 'for our past follows us, it swells incessantly with the present that it picks up on its way'.[21] Janine Macleod writes of the way our porous ecological bodies[22] connect us to multiple species and multiple beings, as the hydrological cycle carries memories through time and place:

> The promiscuous waters that have bathed me and irrigated my cells have been everywhere, animating Amazonian centipedes, Antarctic jellyfish, depression-era schoolteachers, and Xia-dynasty farmers. They are the moisture we exhale with our breath, the blood, sweat, urine, and breast milk that flows or evaporates from openings in our bodies. At the same time, these waters have the capacity to make things new, to act as agents of birth, rebirth, purification, and germination. All matter is ultimately shared across generations. However, as the medium that carries away the dead and nurtures the unborn, water is uniquely capable of symbolising multi-generational time. In some sense, it actually *is* multi-generational time.[23]

Because water is the 'blood of life', the memories it carries are intimately linked to the futures it will create. Memory traces carried in water are part of a bio-semiotic communicative system, where the 'past no longer exists...but it insists, it consists, it *is*'.[24]

Thinking water as memory and becoming in multispecies ecologies prompts us to frame questions about responsibility, inheritance and ethics in ways that are attuned to the multi-temporal complexities of our geological moment. Where has the water you bathe in been? What lives has it touched over the vast stretches of time in which it has flowed through networks of life on Earth? Where are you positioned in this intimate pattern of hydrological connection? Are you upstream or downstream, or both at one and the same time? How does your use of this water now impact on what this water will become in the future? What memory traces do you leave behind in lakes, rivers and oceans? How are the memories carried in the molecular structure of the water you drink interacting with the memories of your own waterlogged body?

In the material-semiotic flows of life on Earth, our past is not an object of whimsical reflection, but a real fleshly becoming that will condition the present and the future, reminding us that time is not a passive milieu in which we are arbitrarily situated, but something we actively help to make with others.[25]

The lost river of my childhood offers lessons in how to live with loss and permanence, memory and becoming, in the Anthropocene. Knowing that we can never step twice into the same river is essential for understanding a world composed of states of change, especially as our species faces a period of unprecedented change. But knowing too that the waters of a river will never truly disappear is fundamental for understanding our responsibilities to the earth others that share our waterways. While one cannot step in the same river twice, we should step lightly into the waters of the world, aware that where and how we step has consequences for other places and beings that are made and unmade by water's flow. This dance of presence and absence forms the basis for an ethics of hydrological connection as water patterns itself across all earthly life and death.

Water and ethical time

When Uncle Steve Widders told me that he saw water as the blood of life, the blood of the land, he added that the land was his mother. 'That's the earth, the land, my mother – gives you everything. Just as your mother gives birth, the land gives life – to everything.' Water is the blood that keeps the land living, and water is what enables the maternity of the Earth to birth the new as it emerges from creative differentiations of the old – the proffering of time as a gift from one body to another.

Deborah Bird Rose develops a concept of multispecies knots of ethical time that is intimately entwined with webs of connectivity, sustained by water. Rose writes that ethical time depends on synchronous multispecies encounters 'where each interface is a site of flow, a place of mutuality and gift'.[26] Water helps to nurture multispecies interfaces where life experiments with new forms of becoming, generating new forms of being in the world. Margulis and Sagan explain:

> Life is the representation, the 'presencing' of past chemistries, a past environment of the early Earth that, because of life, remains on the modern Earth. It is the watery, membrane-bounded encapsulation of space-time. Death is part of life because even dying matter, once it reproduces, rescues complex chemical systems and budding dissipative structures from thermodynamic equilibrium.[27]

As life works to transform death into new forms of life in processes of negentropy, it sustains memory in the bodies of living beings. Through memory and becoming, 'death is given a future'.[28]

Rose observes that because life is a gift, the result of 'an on-going series of ethical relationships',[29] all living beings are 'entangled with and responsible to and for others – both nourishing and being nourished'.[30] Responsibility and multispecies ethics is the basis of relational evolutionary processes that enable life. 'Time', writes James Hatley, 'is articulated as a differentiation across which and by means of which responsibilities are born'. This means that relationships of responsibility to others in a time-binding world are 'the very articulation of the "real."'[31] Hatley explains: 'Time, as it is given to humans to live is not only determined but also creative, not only necessity but also gift, particularly as its significance is articulated in our witnessing of time's wild and earthly fruits.'[32]

I turn now to two emplaced sites of multispecies nourishment from my childhood home where time is proffered as a gift to the wider earth community. At both of these places, water helps to weave the past into the present by helping to create nourishing interfaces where matter binds time in webs of ethical and ecological connectivity.

Mum's garden

My mother spends a lot of her time tending her garden. In a pair of shorts, flip-flops and a T-shirt, she carries around a green plastic watering jug, filled with recycled water from the washing machine, to water her plants. She will often talk to them, saying things like 'Would you like a drink? You look very thirsty'. As she wanders around the house she seems to have a sense of calm purpose. In her interactions with these beloved cultivated plants she expresses responsibility, compassion, curiosity and occasionally pain, when the plants get sick, are eaten by surrounding wildlife or die of unknown causes.

Watching my mother devote so much time to these nonhuman others, I see the garden as a site of love, connection and the cultivation not only of life but of relationships where water is a vital player in a life-sustaining pattern of multispecies ethical time. In this context water is not an abstract resource but a fundamental part of an emotional and embodied backyard ecology. Mum's care to use recycled water reflects her understanding of water's life-creating and life-affirming character. Research indicates that gardens often inspire extensive conservation efforts to preserve both plants and water.[33] My Mum's own use of 'grey' water from the washing machine is not a necessary response to water scarcity, as she continues to do this even when water levels on the property are high (water tanks overflowing). Instead it is an emotional response to the value of water as a life-sustaining presence.

In the garden my Mum, and many others who tend to their own gardens, enter what Jessica Weir has described as 'an expanded connectivity'[34] where humans situate themselves within a 'web of life sustaining relationships'.[35] This intimate space of encounter with the more-than-human world fosters response-ability where humans become responsive to 'the role of water as one element within a complete "lifeworld" of both living and non-living things'.[36]

Watching Mum speak gently to her cultivated botanies I am aware that she is deeply attuned to their growth – to the way their plant bodies reflect thirst or fullness. She is aware of the affective conditions of their lives – of whether it's been a hot day or a cold one, of how the wind is whipping against their skin like it is her own. The water is taken up by their bodies and expressed in healthy greens and reds, full shapes, outstretched leaves towards sun.

Michael Marder observes that plants are always open to the other, that 'their unique ensouled existence enjoins plants to be the passages, the outlets, or the media for the other'.[37] Plants embody radical hospitality, and in water we witness a self-effacing ethics of becoming-other to the point of disappearance. Mielle Chandler and Astrida Neimanis write that water:

> subsists as and for the other, which it also is, and which it also nourishes. As sea grass water is 'invisible.' When we look at sea grass, we see the manifestation we call sea grass; we do not see the water. The water is hidden, covered over, forgotten, in the shape and manifestation of the other.[38]

Water is a pet dog's joy, a growing plant, a row of clean clothes flapping in the wind. In this radical becoming-with, water embodies gestational ethics,[39] where its very being is constituted in the nourishment of others, in the birthing of new forms of life.

I am filled with love for my mother when I see her tending a patch of strawberries. As she stands over the bright red berries with her watering can, I see her body in a 'posture of openness' to the earth, and to the earth others that share it with us.[40] The water flows from her hands to the dirt and becomes enlivened, nourishing soils and moving into bodies and lives, so that we can witness it as the source of life, endlessly giving. She expresses her gratitude for this life with her careful conservation of the water that she carries from a household ecology of pipes and pumps to a garden ecology of 'wild and earthly fruits'.[41] The mother – the earth – the water that brings it all into being – are glued together in my mind by a memory of Mum in a sunny garden with her green watering can.

Lucy's grass

When Lucy died, my parents buried her in the backyard. They placed some rocks from the property around her grave, and Mum planted some plants nearby to form a kind of memorial grove. Last time I went home grass was growing between the rocks, with a single stem of brown wheatgrass reaching up into the air. It was the same colour as Lucy's fur, and its tip almost the same texture. Her blood and bones and organs now nourish and feed new forms of life. Lucy's grass teaches me that water is vital not only for life, but for death conceived as a part of an immanent life process sustained by patterns of differentiation and creative becoming. Water allows inter-species transformations to take place, ensuring that death is creative and productive.

Another way to put this would be to say that water ensures life, irrespective of individual bodies or organisms. Water ensures the continuation of life as a process, not a property one possesses. As anthropologist and philosopher Tim Ingold puts it, 'Co-presence may be temporally bounded, but existence is not…Death punctuates, but does not terminate, life'.[42] Val Plumwood has referred to this ecological continuity as a form of 'materialist spirituality' where 'on death we become a part of the earth, we nurture other species in a process of mutual life giving'.[43] Individual deaths are gifts to an ecological community that is nourished in processes of birth, life, death, decay and multispecies rebirth. The patch of dirt where my beloved dog Lucy is buried is something I cherish, not because it preserves her soul, or body, but because it is the place where she transformed into 'nourishing terrain',[44] and grew into other lives.

Plumwood's 'materialist spirituality' challenges where we traditionally locate self and identity. The idea that we are of the earth transforms the perception of death as the end of the line. Plumwood observes that this perception of finality 'comes from having a sense of identity that is very cut off from other beings, so your story cannot continue in another form'.[45] Unlike Christian Heavenism[46] which focuses on a transcendent afterlife, Plumwood develops an 'ecological concept of the sacred' that invests matter with life – locating continuity of self within the earth.[47]

Water is an essential part of nourishing matter and, within this ecological discourse, is intrinsically emplaced. Water grows plants in a particular garden and turns a single cherished grave into a site of renewed life. Lucy's grass is the product of bodies and water combining in a specific site in the world. In that strand of new grass I find both the consolation and the continuity which Plumwood finds in materialist spirituality. My beloved friend is nurturing a place we have both loved. She has become 'a material part of the land, blending stories'.[48]

Water as the blood of the land takes on new resonances when I think of Lucy's dead body birthing new lives in an ecological circle of reciprocity. Water runs in our blood until we become part of the earth, and our blood becomes the blood of the land.

The Anthropocene as a threat to ethical time

In a conference paper delivered in 2009, subaltern historian Dipesh Chakrabarty[49] spoke powerfully on the relationship between emplaced water and the transformative agency of death and memory in a world of Hereclitan flux. Standing knee-deep in the river Ganges in India, as it flows past the city of Calcutta, Chakrabarty was honouring his father through funerary rites when he noticed that alongside him hundreds of men were practising the same rites. As he watched family upon family release the personal effects of their loved ones into the river, Chakrabarty began to situate human flows of memories, pasts and futures within the continuity and permanence of the flowing water.

> The river felt eternal; the rituals felt eternal; Hinduism felt eternal. I knew that one day I would die, and my son would perhaps do the same thing at the same point in the river. I know that once in the past my father had done similar things for his parents. Suddenly, I realised that most people in that river doing the same rituals as I was engaged in probably felt the same way: that our tradition, like the river, was there forever.[50]

Indian environmental activist Vandana Shiva explains that the Ganges River is sacred in Hindu mythology, where 'the very possibility of life on earth is associated with the release of heavenly waters by Indra, the god of rain'.[51] Because the Ganges is understood to have descended from the heavens, 'she is a sacred bridge to the divine'[52]. Shiva notes that the spiritual significance of water is seen in many cultures across the world, and that 'the sacredness of water has been inspired both by the power of rivers and by water as a life force'.[53] The eternal flow of the river provides material grounding for a cosmology where human life is positioned in a 'world of ecological death, gifts and flows'.[54]

When Chakrabarty recounts his experience of releasing his father's possessions to the flow of the river, he positions himself within an ongoing intergenerational process of life and death. 'I knew that one day I would die, and my son would perhaps do the same thing at the same point in the river. I know that once in the past my father had done similar things for his parents'.[55] This is a form of what James Hatley terms a 'death narrative'. A death narrative situates the dead within a historic community, so that any given group or population

> can be seen as a wave of memory, insight, and expectation coursing through time, a wave that lifts up and sustains the individuals of each succeeding generation, even as those individuals make their own particular contributions to or modifications of that wave.[56]

Through the flow of the Ganges river, Chakrabarty experiences the eternal flow of death and life as immanent processes of intergenerational nourishment, where 'one experiences one's time as a gift, the proffering of one's own existence from out of the bodies and lives of the beings who preceded one. One in turn offers this gift to those who come after one'.[57] For this reason, learning that anthropogenic activity might destroy the river had a strong impact on Chakrabarty:

> It was quite a shock...to be told by climate scientists that the river may not be there forever, that the Himalayan glaciers are melting, that there might be flash floods or drought, that changes in the weather could become extreme. But, the harder shock to absorb...was the news that human beings have become a geological agent on this planet. In other words, that fact that the climate of the planet is changing has something to do with what we are doing as a species, as a collectivity.[58]

In this observation Chakrabarty notes something quite profound about the uneasy temporal horizons of the Anthropocene. Humans, by inserting themselves into the deep time of the planet as a geological agent, are in the process of destroying patterns of ethical time sustained by the immanent, living, material memories of that planet that nourish life processes of ongoing renewal. These memories live in rhizomatic networks – they are the memories of cultures and traditions, memories of multiple species and the memories of the river itself.

As the river undergoes radical upheaval, the underlying flow of the river ruptures, and this ruptures 'flows of being, energy and information'[59] that allow the proffering of life as an intergenerational and multispecies gift.

Dipesh Chakrabarty's lament at the loss of this river of time resonated with me, because I too have lost a river that held my past, and unknowable futures. To mourn the loss of a waterway that is as small as a local gully might seem sentimental, but in the context of radical anthropogenic alteration of the environment, distress at the destruction of beloved homeplaces is becoming increasingly common.[60] I believe that personal psychological distress can be seen as an ethical call to respond to the distress of the larger living world, and to recognise that we, and many other critters, are at stake in this distress which signals the breakdown of an ecology of mind that nurtures the future and the past.

Disremembering water

In the era of the Anthropocene water is undergoing a process of 'disremembering', where the ability of life to transform the past in order to nourish the future is being attacked. I use the term 'disremembering' here in a similar mode to the discussion of anthropogenic assaults on environmentally embodied memories in Chapter 3, in connection with deforestation and the harvesting of plantation timber. Anthropogenic alteration of waterways can violate human memories that are nurtured in their dynamic flow.

Disremembering also refers to the way conceptual and physical processes of abstraction reduce the complex living process of water to a commodity, so that water comes to be understood as a measured, displaced, substitutable and homogeneous 'resource' that can be bought and sold in the market.[61] Through infrastructures of convenience, such as tap water, bottled water and the invisibility of sewerage and 'discarded water',[62] a commodity regime is manipulating the way humans perceive water, erasing bio-cultural memories and evaporating ethical patterns of hydrological connection. This can lead to water abuse and misuse, as people fail to connect their own watery interactions with hydrological patterns through time and place that nourish multispecies communities across the world.

Val Plumwood observes that the capitalist-based form of trade that dominates today's market eliminates 'place patterns'. She claims that 'the commodity form is part of the fracturing of place' because it fails to develop responsibility for the places that support our lives and instead presents the world as a collection of anonymous resources.[63] Commodification of water fractures not only place patterns, but temporal patterns, as it reduces the human capacity to perceive water in its living multitemporal complexity.

The past carried by water does not disappear in this conceptual and physical displacement, but is 'dismembered, cut up and off, and not-remembered'. This past can resurface in devastating bouts of recursive damage – for example as toxic waste and pollution carried in water; or floods, tsunamis, droughts caused by atmospheric changes. Disremembering thereby undermines the ability of water to create nourishing interfaces where the past is transformed, through patterns of ethical time, into a future of convivial, multispecies flourishing.

All over the globe humans have transformed waterways into what Martin Heidegger termed 'standing reserve', where the more-than-human world comes to be seen purely as a collection of resources available for human consumption, subject to regulation, measurement and control.[64] This is nowhere more clearly symbolised than in the figure of an anthropogenic dam, where an assemblage of infrastructure creates 'new natures and new landscapes: giant reservoirs and catchment areas, mountains pierced with pipelines and aqueducts'[65] in order to divert water away from the multispecies commons. Waters flow through spatio-temporal patterns of hydrological connection, its nourishment of innumerable species on Earth over vast expanses of co-evolutionary history, has been banked by a commodity logic where 'water that replenishes ecosystems is considered water wasted'.[66] With its relational living complexity denied, water becomes a motionless and timeless product, waiting to be propelled by human infrastructure into an assemblage where human consumption and exchange dominate all other ethical patterns of time, and all other modes of water being.

With water perceived as a measurable commodity, as standing-reserve, humans have not simply ignored its non-anthropocentric, non-utilitarian values, but have damaged water's capacity to fulfil them. Through centuries of human exploitation of environments, water's hydrological cycle – the ecological process through which water is received by the ecosystem – has been corroded. In the hydrological cycle, falling moisture in the form of rain and snow recharges streams, aquifers and groundwater sources, but modern humans have destroyed some of the Earth's capacity to receive, absorb and store water. Vandana Shiva writes:

> Deforestation and mining have destroyed the ability of water catchments to retain water. Monoculture agriculture and forestry have sucked ecosystems dry. The growing use of fossil fuels has led to atmospheric pollution and climate change, responsible for recurrent floods, cyclones and droughts.[67]

This disremembering is an attack on the nourishing interfaces and situated sets of multispecies relation that sustain patterns of ethical time. Water helps to create the possibility for life and matter to bind the past to the present and so is a gestational milieu of co-evolution, a womb for the birthing of multispecies futures. If the 'whole ongoing process of evolution is a "knowing" that includes and enables our own knowing'[68] then relationships and connections with our co-evolutionary kin are fundamental to our ability to understand and respond to the complex living systems in which we are immersed; they are the 'species of possibilities' that define our 'sense of the world'.[69] This means that creating nourishing interfaces that nurture the diversity of life on Earth is vital for protecting an ecology of mind necessary for our survival.

Fostering waters of lively abundance means protecting immanent processes of death and life shared with our multispecies kin, as an act of modest biocultural hope.[70] Our responsibility to recuperate and preserve waters of diversity across the world is a responsibility to sustain an interspecies ecology of mind – the web of life and meaning in which all our futures and pasts are nested.

Petrichor as a living thought in the world

Gregory Bateson used the notion of an ecology of mind to capture the way mental processes are active in the living world, and the human mind is nested within these larger systems, where thinking occurs 'in a great many other places besides what is in my head and yours'.[71] In Bateson's expansive understanding of mind, a mind can be understood as any 'aggregate of interacting parts and components' that is sufficiently complex, where interaction between parts of the mind is triggered by difference'.[72] In this mode, an effusion such as petrichor can be understood as a living thought in a co-evolutionary ecology of mind, sustained by situated multispecies intra-actions.

In keeping with the Environmental Humanities' emphasis on dismantling unhelpful mind/body dualisms, I am looking to petrichor to demonstrate that water's role in helping to create life-sustaining patterns of ethical time is entangled with the 'wider knowing' that Bateson understood to be at the heart of coevolution. Petrichor is a language of the earth that speaks in creaturely tongues, reminding us that biodiversity is an essential part of our epistemology. If becoming-with is becoming-worldly,[73] our attention to the diverse range of beings that surround us is fundamental to how we come to understand and respond to a dynamic living world.

Petrichor is the scent of coming rain that emerges from a conversation between sky country and stone country. Humidity carried in the atmosphere releases an oil that is held in particular stones embedded in particular places on the Earth. And as the clouds and water and sky and stone speak to one another, other species tune into the conversation. Cattle become restless. Humans become nostalgic. Currawongs are known to sing louder before rain, and ants appear indoors as they begin to gather food. In this immanent affective ecology, the living world is wrapped up in a moment of dynamic difference, and multispecies bodies help to bring 'news of difference'. Noel Charlton explains that in Bateson's understanding of mind:

> Information can be any sort of indication of change or '*difference*' that can inform the system that something has happened. It might be a chemical change in the environment of a cell, a nervous impulse within an organism, symptoms of illness or recovery in a human or other animal, the temperature changes and diminution of daylight that signal the onset of winter to a forest ecosystem, or news of an attack on a nation.[74]

The bodies that respond to the mood and atmosphere of petrichor are functional parts of this ecology of mind. The 'world communicates itself as it creates itself',[75] and bodies are living thoughts in the world, at the same time as agents in the world's dynamic, multispecies becoming. Following Karan Barad and Donna Haraway, I am referring here to the way agential more-than-human life is implicated in the 'ongoing reconfigurings of the world'.[76] Petrichor is a moment of collaborative worlding, and the bodies it wraps up in an affective ecology are both signals and agents because everything in the world 'is a kind of immanent process of mediation or communication'[77] and an active participant in the world's becoming.

Because petrichor is a refrain in a communicative world, its familiar scent awakens memories in others, who respond to the subtle atmospheric changes of an anticipating, hopeful Earth. This living thought is a product of memory and desire shared across multiple more-than-human bodies and lives. To perceive this 'news of difference', a change must be registered, and so the past must be remembered. And that living memory is not in any one isolated organism. It is a memory that circulates through all the interconnected beings that share place and time, awakening intimate and private desires and longings and fears, where the stakes for each entity are very different. What the smell of rain means to me (inconvenience, nostalgia, relief at not having to water the garden) is very different to what rain means to an ant. But this difference is productive, in fact it is vital, because the ant can teach me things I cannot possibly learn alone, or from a member of my own species.

Aunty Frances Bodkin, a D'harawal Elder from the Sydney region, and climatologist, explained to me that ants respond to weather conditions months in advance. 'Their nests go down to the groundwater', she said. 'And groundwater is connected to air pressure – it rises and falls as the air pressure changes.' The changing shape of an ant mound can tell us which direction the rain is coming from. These insect ambassadors connect us to unknowable rhizomatic underworlds, communicating environmental information that we ourselves cannot possibly perceive alone.

Paying attention to ants, like rabbits, could help us to trace scented paths into other worlds, to forage at the periphery of deeper narratives. Ants can teach us about the pattern that connects[78] because their behavior is regular enough to reliably communicate information about changing conditions. At the same time, individual ants are dynamic agents of virtual potential – there is no predicting what path they will take next. Deborah M Gordon explains:

> In its ordinary meaning, 'network' evokes a fairly regular array of connections, like chicken-wire or a honeycomb. But to speak of a network of interactions in an ant colony (or a brain or an immune system) is not to say that the interactions are patterned in any simple or regular way. It is colonies, not ants, that behave in a predictable way...The patterns or regularities in ant colony behaviour are produced by networks of interaction among ants. The networks of interactions are complicated, irregular, noisy, and dynamic. The network is not a hidden program or set of instructions. There is no program – that is what is mind-boggling, and perhaps why, at the beginning of the twenty-first century, there is so much we do not understand about

biology. It is very difficult to imagine how an orchestra could play a symphony without a score.[79]

Bateson tells us that 'the right way to begin to think about the pattern that connects is to think of it primarily as a dance of interacting parts and only secondarily pegged down by various sorts of physical limits and by those limits which organisms characteristically impose'. He likens this moving and dynamic pattern to patterns one might find in music – not fixed, but in motion.[80]

The Anthropocene is an era of shifting patterns, and critters have evolved to respond to changes in a world of Hereclitan flux and flow – a world of becoming. Attunement to our multispecies kin could be vital for allowing us to 'catch the rhythm'[81] of a radically changing planet.

As black ants swirl around my feet, each bite says 'rain, rain, rain'. A cacophonous conversation, this unpleasant assault scatters across my flesh as if to foreshadow falling raindrops. A past change in the atmosphere that speaks of the rains to come is communicated through birdsong. The appearance of ants, the smell of petrichor, the call of a currawong – it is a living poem, and I am dwelling in it. Each stanza is carried by the movements of the body of another being, another species that brings 'news of difference'. The deep sensorial pulse of lives being lived together, in particular places, at particular times, teaches against atomism, isolation and disremembering. In its rhythm and its cadence we can learn to live in a world made of states of change.

What a gully can teach you

As a child I was always learning from the more-than-human world. I have forgotten many of these lessons, but sometimes they are awoken by living memories that flow like rivers through an intimate ecology of mind.

The loss of my childhood gully led me to begin this journey into emplaced waters of connectivity, and when I walk beside the dry earth where life-affirming water once gushed, it feels like I am walking through a scar on the land, and a scar in my life. Yet through water, and through memory, the past is brought alive in its infinite materiality, its immanent vitality and its creaturely call to responsibility.

Slavoj Žižek observes, via Deleuze, that 'to perceive a past phenomenon in becoming...is to perceive the virtual potential in it, the spark of eternity, of virtual potentiality which is there forever'. In a world of Hereclitan flux, the possibilities for the future held in the time-binding matter of the earth are wild and unknown, carving out a space for hope, even in the darkest of times.

Memory is a becoming-with that is at the heart of entangled ethics in the Anthropocene. It is through memory that I come to understand my responsibility to innumerable others that have created the possibility of my life. The more-than-human womb from which I have been birthed and will continue to be nourished is itself a living memory – a co-evolutionary tangle of ideas in deep time – where life's creative and generative spark, its experimentation with material thought in the world, has produced the abundant array of diverse beings that surround me.

And it is through memory that I come to understand my radical entanglement with this exuberant array of kin, the same kin that communicate vital information about the system in which I am immersed – a system that will always remain mysterious, and outside my full comprehension. Through attention to memory and becoming I am able to recognise that as I move through time and place I create living memories in our shared material semiotic ecology. These memories can be carried into the bodies of many others who I may never meet, as I collaboratively participate in chemical and atmospheric becomings that circulate through vast patterns of connection, making and unmaking watery environments across the globe.

The lost gully of my youth is a scar on the land and a scar in my mind. Through this eco-mental scar I travel from the first rains to fall on our planet to our deep water past as an earlier incarnation of our species emerging from the sea. My indebtedness to my biogenic inheritance of all life processes in the vast expanse of ethical time is with me on my journey into childhood memory – the mysterious awakening of who I once was in relation to a long ago evaporated waterway. These memories of the memories of the world call me into ethical relation and command responsibility.

From the last drip in a drying gully to the tears in my eyes as I watched the suffering of starving sheep, water floods the most visceral archives of my body, and courses through the blood in my veins. So deep is its flow, so vital its presence, that it is an immutable ethical call – an arterial obligation to the co-evolutionary creature languages of the earth, and their abiding tales of memory, anticipation, desire and longing.

Following ants

Petrichor fills the air. Immersed in its effusive web, the child I once was is telling me a story about rain and gullies and lizards and stones. As she speaks, ants pattern themselves at my feet. I trace the lines of movement with a stick – the stopping and starting, the backtracking and twisting. I don't know the scent-ways, and this improvised primitive map tells me little of the territory.

Deleuze and Guattari wrote that they watched lines of flight migrate 'like columns of tiny ants'.[82] These ants aren't metaphors. They are embodied signals and agents in the worlds becoming. Each path taken is a proposition – 'I'll go this way.'

I'd love to keep following them but I'm too big – I can't get down into the nest. I get frustrated but the child reminds me that it's important not to go everywhere, not to know everything. I reluctantly agree. What's most important is to pay attention, we conclude, as the ants disappear into their hidden world.

The ants and the rain – to think them separately is pathological. Laying my waterlogged body down by this dry gully I wonder, where do the rains end and where do they begin?

Figure 18 Sunrise reflected in a dam on my parents' property, Armidale, 2011

Water is part-human, indeed part-everything, and it is part of us on death as well as in life. Water is the blood of the land in relationships. Water is Lucy swimming, then becoming grass. Water is my mother's joy at bringing new life into being. Water is the sound of a rushing creek and childhood memories in a country of rivers. Water can be found beneath the reflection of a eucalypt tree, deep in the echo of a currawong's song.

Watching tiny moving black dots pattern themselves across my feet, I hear hammering rain, while the snore of thunder on the horizon warms up the world.

Notes

1   H. Poynton, 'The smell of rain: how CSIRO invented a new word', *The Conversation* (31 March 2015), http://theconversation.com/the-smell-of-rain-how-csiro-invented-a-new-word-39231.
2   A. N. Whitehead, *The Concept of Nature*, 53.
3   H. Poynton, 'The smell of rain'.
4   Deborah Bird Rose uses the term 'everywhen' to describe the Aboriginal dreaming to capture its enduring temporality in *Nourishing Terrains*.
5   See G. Deleuze on the virtual, inspired by Marcel Proust's reflections on memory, in *Difference and Repetition* trans. P. Patton (London: The Athlone Press, 1994), 208.
6   L. Margulis and D. Sagan, *What is Life*, 86.
7   N. G. Charlton, *Understanding Gregory Bateson: Mind, Beauty and the Sacred Earth* (Albany: Suny Press, 2008), 65.
8   G. Bateson, *Mind and Nature*, 4–5.

 9 D. Rose, 'Multispecies Knots of Ethical Time'.
10 Ibid., 139.
11 Judith Wright, *Collected Poems 1942–1970* (Sydney: Angus & Robertson Publishers, 1971), 110.
12 J. Arthur, *Default Country*, 139.
13 *Commonwealth Intergovernmental Working Group for the UNCCD, Australian Actions to Combat Desertification and Land Degradation: National Report by Australia on Measures Taken to Support Implementation of the United Nations Convention to Combat Desertification (April 2002)*, www.environment.gov.au/land/publications/actions/summary.html.
14 J. Arthur, 'Default Country', 144.
15 J. Weir, 'Connectivity', *Australian Humanities Review* 45 (November 2008), 154. In her extended study of the ecological crisis in the Murray-Darling Basin and the importance of Australian Aboriginal ecological knowledge and philosophy, Weir advocates a kind of 'connectivity thinking' that focuses on relationships and connections over substance.
16 D. Rose, *Nourishing Terrains*.
17 S. Muecke, *No Road*, 184–185.
18 D. Rose, *Reports from a Wild Country*, 22.
19 J. Metcalf and T. Van Dooren, 'Editorial Preface', vii.
20 J. Macleod, 'Water and the Material Imagination: Reading the Sea of Memory against the Flows of Capital', *Thinking with Water* eds. C. Chen, J. Macleod and A. Neimanis (Montreal, London & Ithica: McGill-Queens University Press, 2003), 49
21 H. Bergson, *Introduction to Metaphysics*, trans. T. E. Hulme (Indianapolis: Hacket Publishing, 1999).
22 D. Rose, 'Dialogue with Place'.
23 J. Macleod, 'Water and the Material Imagination', 49.
24 G. Deleuze, *Difference and Repetition*, 82.
25 For more discussion of this see A. Neimanis and S. Walker, 'Weathering'.
26 D. Rose, 'Multispecies Knots', 137.
27 L. Margulis and D. Sagan, *What is Life*, 86.
28 J. Hatley. *Suffering Witness*, 62.
29 Ibid., 60.
30 D. Rose, 'Multispecies Knots', 137.
31 J. Hatley, *Suffering Witness*, 61.
32 J. Hatley, 'Temporal Discernment', 18.
33 F. Allon and Z. Sofoulis, 'Everyday Water: Cultures in Transition', *Australian Geographer* 37, no. 1 (2006): 45–55; L. Head and P. Muir, 'Changing Cultures of Water in Eastern Australian Backyard Gardens', *Social and Cultural Geography* 8, no. 6 (2007): 889–902.
34 J. Weir, 'Connectivity', 154. In her extended study of the ecological crisis in the Murray-Darling Basin and the importance of Australian Aboriginal ecological knowledge and philosophy, Weir advocates a kind of 'connectivity thinking' that focuses on relationships and connections over substance.
35 Ibid., 154.
36 F. Allon and Z. Sofoulis, 'Everyday Water', 52.
37 M. Marder, *Plant-Thinking*, 42.
38 M. Chandler and A. Neimanis, 'Water and Gestationality: What Flows beneath Ethics' in *Thinking with Water* eds. C. Chen, J. Macleod and A. Neimanis (Montreal, London & Ithica: McGill-Queens University Press, 2013), 61–83.
39 Ibid.
40 V. Plumwood, 'Nature in the Active Voice', *Australian Humanities Review* 46 (May 2009), www.australianhumanitiesreview.org/archive/Issue-May-2009/plumwood.html.
41 J. Hatley, 'Temporal Discernment', 18.
42 T. Ingold, *Perception*, 143.

43   V. Plumwood, 'Place, Politics and Spirituality', 245.

44   D. Rose, *Nourishing Terrains*.

45   V. Plumwood, 'Place, Politics and Spirituality', 246.

46   Val Plumwood critiques 'Heavenism' as a form of ecological denial and alienation. Heavenism is the notion that the self is split into 'an embodied and perishable part belonging to earth, and a thinking imperishable 'spirit' part belonging to heaven' (Plumwood, 'Cemetery Wars', 56).

47   V. Plumwood, 'The Cemetery Wars', 55.

48   Ibid., 58.

49   D. Chakrabarty, 'Breaking the Wall of Two Cultures: Science and Humanities After Climate Change', Falling Walls Conference, Berlin, 9 November 2009, http://falling-walls.com/lectures/dipesh-chakrabarty/.

50   Ibid.

51   V. Shiva, *Water Wars*.

52   Ibid.

53   Ibid.

54   D. Rose, 'Embodied Knots of Multispecies Time', 135.

55   D.Chakrabarty, 'Breaking the Wall of Two Cultures'.

56   J. Hatley, Genos, *Suffering Witness*, 61–62.

57   Ibid., 61.

58   D. Chakrabarty, 'Breaking the Wall of Two Cultures'.

59   D. Rose, 'Multispecies Knots of Ethical Time', 136.

60   See Glenn Albrecht 'Solastalgia: A New Concept in Health and Identity', *Philosophy, Activism, Nature* 3 (2005): 41–55.

61   M. Kaika, *City of Flows: Modernity, Nature, and the City* (London: Routledge, 2005), 143.

62   See Gay Hawkins and Kane Race, 'Bottled Water Practices: Reconfiguring Drinking in Bangkok Households', in Material Geographies of Household Sustainability, eds. R. Lane and A. Gorman-Murray. (Farnham & Burlington: Ashgate Publishing, 2011), 113–124.

63   V. Plumwood, 'Place, Politics and Spirituality', 229.

64   M. Heidegger, 'The Question Concerning Technology'.

65   F. Allon, 'Dams, Plants, Pipes and Flows: From Big Water to Everyday Water', *Reconstruction* 6, no. 3 (2007): http://reconstruction.eserver.org/063/allon.shtml.

66   V. Shiva, *Water Wars*.

67   Ibid., 2.

68   N. Charlton, *Understanding Bateson*, 67.

69   M. Smith, 'Ecological Community, the Sense of the World, and Senseless Extinction', Environmental Humanities 2 (2013): 21–41.

70   S. Eben Kirksey, Nicholas Shapiro and Maria Brodine, 'Hope in Blasted Landscapes'.

71   G. Bateson, *Mind and Nature*.

72   Ibid., 92.

73   D. Haraway, *When Species Meet*, 3.

74   N. Charlton, *Understanding Bateson*, 48.

75   A. Murpie, 'The World as Medium: Whitehead's Media Philosophy', in *Immediations*, eds. Erin Manning, Anne Munster and Bodil Marie Stavning Thomsen (Open Humanities Press, forthcoming).

76   K. Barad, *Meeting the Universe Halfway*, 141.

77   A. Murphie, 'The World as Medium', 13.

78   G. Bateson, *Mind and Nature*.

79   D. M. Gordon, *Ant Encounters: Interaction Networks and Colony Behaviour* (Princeton & Woodstock: Princeton University Press, 2010).

80   G. Bateson, *Mind and Nature*.

81   N. Bateson, 'Practicality in Complexity'.

82   G. Deleuze and F. Guattari, *A Thousand Plateaus*, 22.

Part V

Sky country

Figure 19 Lightning storm, Armidale, 2016 (Andrew Pearson)

One of my strongest memories from childhood is of being outside during a thunderstorm. I am standing at a barbed wire fence at the edge of our property with my older brother, Ben. It is dusk and big nebulous grey clouds are congregating on the horizon. When the lightning strikes the clouds they glow orange, red and purple. The thunder bellows out and shakes the ground beneath us. We are laughing at the bombastic light and noise. I am usually terrified by such close thunder, but the laughter seems to protect us. Each reverberation of thunder seems to call out and our laughter is a kind of response – one that acknowledges our vulnerability. Then the rain comes. We run through pelting wet and tripping dark scrub toward the house. The house is like a lamp shining down the black night. I am desperate to get inside it, to dry my body in its warm yellow glow.

In this book I have aspired to recuperate the magic of the home-place I experienced in my childhood. This magic was not the product of childhood fantasy, but the result of being immersed in a living and communicative world. The thunder was able to shake the ground beneath me that night because my stance was fertile, my posture open to the agency of a more-than-human world. Throughout my research I have argued that such enchanted horizons come from a celebration of connectivity – the bonds that tie us to 'the pattern that connects'.[1]

Donna Haraway observes that 'the world is a knot in motion'.[2] Over the past seven chapters I have journeyed back and forth in place and time tracing over rhizomatic patterns of connection between people, their earth others and the places they share.

I have decided to end this journey in sky country because each of the more-than-human encounters described in the previous chapters occurred beneath New England clouds and stars. My life, and all the lives I meet, are hyphenated between two encompassing bodies: the ground-the sky. I use sky here, particularly the immersive experience of storms, to describe a feeling of wonder at the more-than-human world which occurs when the bonds between earth and sky are cultivated and cared for. I understand this wonderment to produce a relational state of enchantment.

Jane Bennett describes the experience of enchantment as 'an energising feeling of fullness or plenitude – a momentary return to childhood joie de vivre'.[3] In this book I have returned to the place of my childhood and attempted to immerse myself in landscapes alive with memory. Trawling the past for encounters, situating myself in places which seemed to call out to me, sites where 'signs from the Others'[4] are strong, I hope I have been able to recapture something of the enchanted world I grew up in.

Freya Mathews describes an enchanted land as a place which has been 'called up'. Making reference to Aboriginal Australian ideas of 'singing up' the country, she writes: 'World is experienced as enchanted when it has been invoked, awoken, by self in this way; and self is in turn enchanted by its engagement with such an awakened world.'[5]

Being wakeful in a living world is part of an 'art of noticing' which calls up the world so that it becomes responsive to us and us to it. Enchantment is relational – a move toward intimacy and connectivity. Jane Bennett claims that enchantment is 'a state of openness to the disturbing-captivating elements in everyday experience'.[6]

Enchantment, like a thunderstorm, arrives unexpectedly to light up the world in incendiary patterns. It is possible to cultivate an open stance, to situate oneself on fertile ground which is receptive to the agency of the more-than-human world. But enchantment is more than openness. It emerges from a relationship as the world reaches out to captivate, to inspire wonder, to make the stable ground beneath us shudder.

Notes

1   G. Bateson and M. Bateson, *Angels Fear*, 8.
2   D. Haraway, *Companion Species Manifesto*, 6.
3   J. Bennett, *Enchantment*, 104.
4   P. Shepard, *The Others*, 141.
5   F. Mathews, *For Love of Matter*, 18.
6   J. Bennett, *Enchantment*, 131.

Conclusion
Thinking like a storm

The environmentalist author Aldo Leopold encouraged humans to think like a mountain in order to develop a relational understanding of life and connectivity. For Leopold thinking like a mountain would develop an ethics of interconnection viewed over time which could stop the cascades of human intervention that wash 'the future into the sea'.[1]

Australian environmental historian Libby Robin has adopted Leopold's phrase to describe the destructive practices of settler Australians and their alienation from the environment. Robin argues that settlers should begin 'thinking like a Banded Stilt' in order to adapt to their variable and unpredictable climate.[2]

The banded stilt is a nomadic wetland bird found primarily in southern and western parts of Australia. Just as the rabbit burrows into a life-world unlike anything we have experienced, banded stilts exist in an *Umwelt* where unpredictable seasonal cycles are the norm. They breed immediately after rain, instead of nesting annually or seasonally. Robin presents the banded stilt as a teacher of lessons in how to live with uncertainty:

> Thinking like a Banded Stilt forces us to reconsider how European Australians make assumptions about 'annual cropping and breeding' that are imported from lands of regular seasons and annual cycles. Australia's arid-zone biologists are increasingly infiltrating the idea of 'variability' into discussions, perhaps in an echo of uncertainty and chaos in the physics of the new millennium. Banded Stilts are a species that can teach Australians much about living with boom-and-bust ecologies: how to take opportunities as they arise, but never to expect regularity.[3]

Inspired by both Leopold's and Robin's more-than-human empathic exercises, I have been wondering what it would mean to think like a storm. In a climate changing world, extreme weather events are becoming more common, and humans are implicated in the precarious patterns of unstable skies. Storms are immersive and direct experiences of Earth's changing systems. Thinking like a storm could therefore be a valuable exercise for revealing how we might develop entangled ecological ethics in the era of the Anthropocene.

Thinking like a storm involves thinking collaboratively – in terms of assemblages. A storm is an amorphous conglomeration of water, wind, electricity. Thinking solely from the perspective of rain, for example, would neglect the totality of the storm. Thinking like a storm pushes us away from atomism and into relationality, a shift which has formed the theoretical basis of this book.

Storms understand the importance of connections, because they themselves are born out of interaction. They emerge from the collision of two opposing forces – low-pressure cells and high-pressure cells. A storm combines rain and electricity, wind and hail. But a storm is not a *thing*, it is a process, a becoming-with. Storms do not descend from the sky as fully formed events, but emerge from situated dialogue with the earth. 'Typical mechanisms that initiate thunderstorms are fronts, troughs and regions of low pressure. Features of topography such as hills and mountains may also enhance storm development.'[4]

Storms are relational, situated and chthonic – creatures of the earth as much as creatures of the sky. While the storm has its own localised integrity, it is also the outcome of global atmospheric conditions. Thinking like a storm is therefore useful for understanding how discrete places are affected by, and affect, global environmental patterns – an understanding that is vital for living ethically in a rapidly changing world.

The interaction between the local and the global does not end at the edge of the atmosphere, either. The most localised and direct weather experiences are connected to the burning gas of the sun, and to the twinkling radiances of ancient stars which light up New England's crisp country nights.

Margulis and Sagan explain that '[l]ife, a local phenomenon of Earth's surface, can in fact be understood only in its cosmic milieu. It formed itself out of star stuff, shortly after Earth 4,600 million years ago congealed from a remnant of a supernova explosion.'[5] The global is embedded in the local at the most intimate level: the human body is made of stardust.

When I was young I thought the stars were holes in a black balloon sky. Now I see planets exploding in a past that is so far from me that it becomes my present. The stars of the New England sky are like dots in a dot painting. Stories tell you what the dots mean, and each dot you enter becomes a world. Each dot could, in fact, be a whole world, and a spark at the periphery of this world. When we look up at the stars we see other worlds at the same time as we see our own. We see the past at the same time as we see the present. This kind of stargazing illustrates what Doreen Massey describes as 'a global sense of the local, a global sense of place'.[6] Thinking like a storm means thinking in terms of these rhizomatic patterns and relationships that stretch across the universe.

Deborah Bird Rose reminds us that while all life connects to something, not everything is connected to everything:[7] the connections are messy, tangled-up spider webs of life and death that criss-cross over the land like lightning strikes. From space this enchanted world must look like a knot of light in motion.[8]

An enchanting conversation

I love watching storms roll in across New England skies. Sketchy electrical scribbles flash against the crow-black night as the world is enlivened by a moment of dynamic difference. Sometimes the shock of the loud thunder causes me to laugh with exultant abandon, as the mood of the storm becomes my own mood, my body enlivened by the 'charged yearnings'[9] of an enchanted world.

A storm sings up place, creating a lively conversation. Like petrichor, this emergent and anticipating dialogue between sky country and stone country entangles earthly critters in webs of desire. Karan Barad writes: 'Lightning is an energising play of a desiring field...Not a trail from the heavens to the ground but an electrifying yearning for connection that precedes this and that, here and there, now and then.'[10]

Just before a lightning storm, air is ionised – it 'breaks down,' as electrons are stripped from positive ions, creating a more conducive flow for electricity.[11] Air that is ionised is the space of the virtual, an air thick with propositions.[12] Vicky Kirby observes the way lightning forms as a kind of 'stuttering chatter between ground and sky'[13] because a lightning strike does not come down from the clouds in a continuous motion, but is formed in communication with the earth. Barad writes, '[i]t is as though objects on the ground are being hailed by the cloud's interpellative address',[14] where an upward response meets a downward proposition, and the electrical circuit closes to form a lightning strike. This becoming-with aligns with Barad's agential realist ontology, where the world is not composed of discrete 'things,' but 'phemomena-in-their-becoming' – 'a radical open relatingness of the world worlding itself'.[15]

The desiring of a lightning storm draws other critters into an affective ecology of shocks and discharges. Ionised air electrifies bodies, including the human body. Immersed in the enchanting dialogue of a lightning storm, my own flesh is electrified, to the point where, if I were to touch my finger to another, I could cause an electric shock through the same intra-active mechanism that forms a lightning strike. I am, through my porosity to a world of charged desire, becoming-lightning.

An electric ecology of mind

When I was a kid I knew when a thunderstorm was coming because ants would appear on the kitchen bench, and Lucy would become storm-like, running madly up and down our dirt driveway, her own body electrified by the ionised shift in the atmosphere. Alphonso Lingis writes:

> emotions get their force from the outside, from the swirling winds over the rotating planet, the troubled ocean currents...the continental plates shifting and creaking...the nonsensical compostions of mockingbirds, the whimsical fluttering of butterflies...Their free mobility and energies surge through us; their disquietudes, torments, and outbursts...[16]

Our affective response to storms speaks to a vital component of our ecology of mind – an attention to the 'difference that makes a difference'[17] through embodied responsiveness to a living world.

Throughout this book I have charted the ways humans learn about the world not through abstract, disconnected knowledge – as if it were possibly to survey it from an outside position, but from intimate more-than-human encounters in shared and entangled relation. Our flesh is inscribed with the patterns of deep co-evolutionary becoming-with. We are, what Deborah Bird Rose calls, 'embodied knots of multispecies time'.[18] It makes sense, then, that the pattern that connects[19] might be best articulated through the poetry of interspecies relations, reverberating through affective responses to environmental change.

From this multispecies perspective, encounters with the more-than-human world form an essential part of our epistemology. This undermines solipsistic thinking because we learn about our position in a complex system not through abstract knowledge, but through the affective capacities of our own bodies and the bodies of the more-than-human world. This is an understanding that is prominent in Aboriginal Australian philosophy. Yolngu Elder Laklak Burrarwanga explains:

> This lightning and thunder is sending out messages to other countries and other homelands telling everyone – Yolngu, animals, plants, everyone – that barra'mirri mayaltha [a particular season] is coming. Are you listening? Are you looking, smelling, feeling, tasting it? Quick baru [crocodile], there's a message here for you, don't miss it. It's very hot and humid during the day now and we're starting to sweat during the night. The night sweating is a message telling us fruit like larrani, apple, is getting ripe.[20]

In the West, a fixation on human subjectivity and Cartesian rationality, which supposedly separates anthropos from the rest of the living world, blinds us to the intricate patterns of connection in which we are entangled and prevents us from registering vital information about our world. The rational mind is made irrational when it fails to recognise its limitations in a complex system – a system that, in the words of Frank Egler, may not just be more complex than we think, but more complex than we *can* think.

This book has been a journey into a beloved homeplace that advocates the importance of situated knowledges at a time when global distress indicates the pathology of abstract and displaced systems of knowledge. I have charted numerous cases where disconnection from the more-than-human world, and processes of distance and concealment, facilitate violence and environmental destruction. Alienation from the deep temporal forces of the land, distance from deforestation and the denial of botanical agency, abstract distortions of local weather conditions and knowledges, the devaluation of nonhuman animal life, and damage to the hydrological cycle through processes of disremembering, have each been interrogated to demonstrate how failure to protect patterns of ecological connection is often the result of hyper-separation and delusional detachment.

The Anthropocene is an epoch characterised by a systemic pathology – it is the geological manifestation of the madness of a species disconnected from the conditions of their world. Gregory Bateson argued that the unit of survival is the organism plus environment and that human neglect, damage and devastation of environmental systems, our failure to respond to feedback loops in the larger living ecological system of thought in which our own thoughts are nested, is suicidal and insane.

Stephen Muecke has argued that it is anthropocentric hubris to believe that humans are the only creatures who can present arguments,[21] and it seems to me that responding to the arguments of the more-than-human world is vital for our survival on an entangled planet. Elder Steve Widders told me about a New England storm which had presented a powerful argument:

> A friend of mine did some work with National Parks years ago, and they were preserving, noting, documenting Aboriginal sites – where they were, and how you get there – to be put into an Aboriginal culture and heritage document.[22] He was telling me that in New England National Park, one of the Elders went through there and led these people to an area in the middle of the scrub on a really clear sunny day. And they came across an open area and it was completely in contrast to the surrounding area. It was smooth and it was circular – no growth on it, no roots of the trees, nothing like that on there. And when they walked out onto it a big thunderstorm came over. The sky turned grey and black and there was lightning and rain just over the top of them. And when they walked away from that area, the sun was shining. Now that tells me that there's some connection there. And they were scared because none of them knew what was happening… They all knew it was sacred ground, but couldn't understand what it meant – why it was sacred. But they had obviously gone somewhere where they shouldn't have gone.

Steve then explained to me what he thought the storm was saying that day, what lessons it was offering.

> Keep in your own place. It also tells you about spirituality. It tells of a spiritual connection with the land that people had, and if you're out of place, you're going to be told, and that's the land reacting there. The land's got its own way. The land is part of nature, as the weather is. I think the weather, the climate, reacts to human intervention, just the same as the land did that day when people were there and out of place. The land and the temperature change, so there's some connection there.

Here the weather is an expression of connectivity, where human beings are made accountable to the environment by their connection with it. The storm presented an argument for relational ethics; it proffered a direction to be humble because we are immersed in mysterious and highly complex systems. We should tread lightly and take care because we are small and vulnerable in the face of this larger whole, but also because we are interconnected and caught up in an entangled dance of co-presence with our many earth others.

The Anthropocene through the eye of a storm

Donna Haraway has implored humans living in the Anthropocene to 'think the world we are actually living' and to respond to the worldings we are engaged in.[23] Thinking like a storm is not only a celebration of the vibrancy of more-than-human agency in a living, connected world, but an acknowledgement of humans' role in producing a dark and unpredictable ecological moment that threatens the future of our own, and many other, species. Thinking like a storm is thinking against fragmentation, isolation and hyper-separation. This is vital because it is no longer possible for Western thought to evade the fact that humanity is ethically implicated within all that transpires on Earth.

Throughout this book I have traced patterns of connection that criss-cross over place and through time like spider webs. Life on Earth is sustained by webs of connectivity, but in the era of the Anthropocene many of these multispecies webs are unravelling. Our inattention to the connectivities we emerge from, and are sustained by, has caused such environmental devastation that we are now the agents of Earth's sixth mass extinction event. In this darkening world, I have advocated arts of noticing that call up the pattern that connects.[24] I believe it is only through radical exposure to this pattern – woven in a coevolutionary experimental nest of togetherness – that we might be able to 'catch the rhythm' of our changing world.

Dancing with a storm

Kate Rigby suggests that 'dancing with disaster' could be a useful metaphor for articulating and enacting the kind of rationality that can respond to an unpredictable and changing climate. She explains:

> The kind of 'dance' that I have in mind here is not a formal dance, whether ballroom or barnyard, where everybody knows the steps in advance. It's more improvisational than that. But nor is it the quasi-solo style of improvisation that I learnt to engage in, alluringly, or so I thought, in my teens. It's more like the practice of 'contact improvisation'...In this kind of dance, you cannot enjoy the comfort of distance, but are obliged to endure the risk of constant touch. To do it well – and nobody can do it perfectly – you need to be responsive, but not passive; ready to take the initiative, but able to go with the flow; strong, but flexible; and, above all, you need to know how to fall in a way that causes minimum harm both to yourself and your partner.[25]

In a world of 'discordant harmonies', where no rhythm is absolutely knowable, improvisation is a mode of being that responds to unpredictability.[26] Being caught in a storm requires this kind of contact improvisation, as the storm wraps the body and the world up into an unfamiliar, often chaotic, rhythm.

We live in a precariously balanced world with melting ice sheets, species extinction and extreme weather events now daily occurrences on the planet. This is a time of exceptional climate – a time where uncertainty is the only rational response to rapidly changing environmental conditions.

Despite the fundamental uncertainty of climate and weather, there is still a fervent desire to map the future of our skies using the detached methods of meteorological science. It seems to me that if we remain bound to the predictable beat of this anthropocentric metronome, our dance steps will continue to be out of step with the world, a denial of the reality of our lives.

Jody Berland argues that abstract observational technology has produced a 'phenomenological split'[27] between weather as it is lived – 'the most tangible of experiences' and the way we think about weather as the 'most abstract of concepts'.[28] We no longer trust our life-world, our everyday sensorial experience of immersion in a multispecies communicative ecology:

> [U]naided human perception and memory – and therefore, local tradition, the wisdom of elders, and the everyday deduction of aural and visual signs, including the bodies of humans or animals – are no longer used to interpret or forecast the weather. The human eye cannot detect complex systems, we learn. Rather, these require the instruments and experimental resources of science…[29]

A lack of confidence in the multispecies ecology of mind that communicates the weather speaks to the heart of the disenchantment of contemporary life. Jane Bennett explains that '[d]isenchantment does not mean that we live in a world that has become completely counted up and figured out but rather that the world has become calculable in principle'.[30] If enchantment requires openness to the world, deafness to the arguments and voices of nonhuman agents that inhabit our shared world deals a fatal blow to a posture of openness.[31]

Berland observes that the weather maps produced by meteorological technologies are often 'stunningly beautiful' coloured and patterned photographs of the earth from satellites.[32] But, she notes, they are 'completely silent' and lack the vibrant sound of insects' wings, bird calls and rustling leaves that once alerted us to weather changes.[33] We are unable to hear these auditory patterns of transformation – the storm has lost its song. Freya Mathews explains that a state of enchantment

> means to have been wrapped in chant or song or incantation. A land or place is enchanted if it has been called up, its subjectivity rendered responsive to self by self's invocation of it. Similar expressions exist in indigenous parlance: in Aboriginal English, for instance, one speaks of 'singing up' country, awakening it to the presence of its people.[34]

The song of a storm is not confined to percussive rain and bass thunder. It is an entire orchestra of birds, winds, insects – everything that signals an interconnected and communicative multispecies world. In the midst of Earth's sixth mass-extinction event, it is clear that we are in danger of irreparably destroying this song. In Chapter 2, Steve Widders lamented that each time an older Aboriginal person dies, a part of the culture dies. When a species dies we lose not only a song, but an entire instrument. The age of loneliness[35] is also an age of silence. I imagine this dystopian emptiness as a flat plateau where monotonous human voices beat like arrhythmic drums against an empty, birdless sky.

How to remember the song of a storm

Freya Mathews despairingly asks, 'How can we sing back to life a world which has been so brutally silenced?'[36] In this book I have used memory in an attempt to 'sing up' the forgotten songs of my homeland so that they are not lost forever. Memory is a powerful force for restoring the world's songs because silence and forgetting go hand in hand. In a country plagued by colonial disremembering, memory is imperative for decolonisation and the recuperation of culture.

In addition to the recuperative and resistant goal of fighting amnesiac colonial processes, this book has also promoted memory as a means of restoring counter-colonial approaches to the world. I have fought against the tide of finitude which would leave dead dogs (and rabbits) lie, and have returned to a childhood home to remember what it was like to embody a posture of openness to a living world.

Throughout this book I have written of remembered moments of connectivity, points at which the world became alive to me, called out to me. These memories are not like photographs. They are sensorial recollections, a far cry from veridicality, and yet they mean more than any photograph could because they register a relationship – the way the self is shaped by the world at that moment.

Situating my own autobiographical memories in a broader ecology of mind, I have looked to organic modes of remembrance beyond the human to demonstrate that remembering is not an isolated and internalised process, but a multispecies becoming-with. The country I have written from is, for me, a country of memory. Its skies and waters, its stones and animals and plants, carry some of the most intimate moments of my life, weaving my past into the present, and my body and mind into the pattern that connects.[37] In my journey into beloved blood's country I have attempted to bring my home-place, and the many creatures which inhabit it, alive on the page, just as they continue to live within me.

In an era of more-than-human distress, I have attempted to write place through more-than-human encounters, with the deep 'ecological imagination' evoked by Mark Tredinnick in his *Blue Plateau*. This involves sensorial engagement with even the most hidden of rhythms – a writing which traces the patterns between 'atoms, geological movements, winds, seasons, sap, salt, microbes, thoughts of animals, rotation of leaves'.[38] I have written with the aim of decolonising inter-lapping ecological and social realms. In a mode of experiential and dialogical

30 J. Bennett, *Enchantment*, 59. Bruno Latour and Stephen Muecke reject the notion that modernity is disenchanted, both arguing that it is based on the disjunctive illusion that modernity has broken away from the ancient world. I argue that disenchantment is not a necessary outcome of modernity, but the result of rapid change which destroys connectivities or, at least, the perception of connections.

31 V. Plumwood, 'Nature in the Active Voice'.

32 J. Berland, 'On Reading', 107.

33 Ibid., 107.

34 F. Mathews, *For Love of Matter*, 18.

35 E. O. Wilson, *The Creation*, 61.

36 F. Mathews, *For Love of Matter*, 8.

37 G. Bateson, *Mind and Nature*.

38 M. Tredinnick, *The Blue Plateau*, 16.

Works cited

Abram, David. *The Spell of the Sensuous: Perception and Language in a More-Than-Human World*. New York: Vintage Books, 1996.

Adams, Prue. 'RHDV-K5: New Strain of Pest Rabbit-killing Calicivirus Disease Given Green Light for 2017 Release', *ABC News*, www.abc.net.au/news/2016-04-29/new-strain-of-rabbit-killing-calicivirus-disease-approved/7367142.

Agamben, Giorgio. *Homo Sacer: Sovereign Power and Bare Life*. Trans. Daniel Heller-Roazen. Stanford: Stanford University Press, 1995.

Albrecht, Glen. 'Solastalgia: A New Concept in Health and Identity', *Philosophy, Activism, Nature* 3 (2005): 41–55.

——. 'The Age of Solastalgia', *The Conversation* (7 August 2012), https://theconversation.com/the-age-of-solastalgia-8337.

Allon, Fiona. 'Dams, Plants, Pipes and Flows: From Big Water to Everyday Water', *Reconstruction* 6, no. 3 (2007), http://reconstruction.eserver.org/063/allon.shtml.

Allon, Fiona and Zoë Sofoulis. 'Everyday Water: Cultures in Transition', *Australian Geographer* 37, no. 1 (2006): 45–55.

Anderson, Benedict. *Imagined Communities*. London & New York: Verso, 1991.

Armidale Dumaresq Council. 'Pine Forest Stakeholder Analysis, 2009', www.armidale.nsw.gov.au/files/134201/File/F.pdf.

——. 'Supplementary Management Plan: Armidale State Forest, 2009'.

Arthur, Jay. *The Default Country: A Lexical Cartography of Twentieth Century Australia*. Sydney: UNSW Press, 2003.

Atkinson, Michael. *Ghosts in the Machine: The Dark Heart of Pop Cinema*. New York: Proscenium Publishers, 1999.

Bachelard, Gaston. *The Poetics of Space*. 1958. Reprint. Trans. Maria Jolas. Beacon Press: Boston, 1969.

Bakhtin, Mikhail. *The Dialogic Imagination*. Austin: University of Texas Press, 1981.

Barad, Karen. *Meeting the Universe Halfway: Quantum Physics and the Entanglement of Matter and Meaning*. Durham and London: Duke University Press, 2007.

——. 'Nature's Queer Performativity', *Women, Gender, and Research* 1–2 (2012): 35.

——. 'Transmaterialities: Trans/Matter/Realities and Queer Political Imaginings', *GLQ A Journal of Lesbian and Gay Studies* 21, no. 2 (2015): 387–422.

Bastian, Michelle. 'Fatally Confused: Telling the Time in the Midst of Ecological Crises', in 'Temporal Environments: Rethinking Time and Ecology', eds. Jacob Metcalf and Thom van Doorn. Special issue, *Environmental Philosophy* 9, no. 1 (2012): 23–48.

Bateson, Gregory. *Mind and Nature: A Necessary Unity*. New York: E.P Dutton, 1979.

——. *Steps to an Ecology of Mind*. San Francisco: Chandler Publishing, 1972.

Bateson, Gregory and Mary Catherine Bateson. *Angels Fear: Towards an Epistemology of the Sacred*. 1987. Reprint. New Jersey: Hampton Press, 2005.

Bateson, Nora 'Practicality in Complexity', https://norabateson.wordpress.com/2016/01/02/practicality-in-complexity/.

Baudrillard, Jean. *America*. London and New York: Verso, 2010.

Bayet-Charlton, Fabienne. 'Overturning the Doctrine: Indigenous People and Wilderness – Being Aboriginal in the Environmental Movement', in *Blacklines: Contemporary Critical Writing by Indigenous Australians*, ed. M. Grossman. Carlton: Melbourne University Press, 2003, pp. 171–180.

Bekoff, Marc. 'Animal Emotions: Exploring Passionate Natures', *BioScience* 50 (2000): 861–870.

——. 'First Do No Harm', *New Scientist*, 28 August 2010, 24–25, www.projectcoyote.org/bekoffnoharm.pdf.

——. *The Emotional Lives of Animals: A Leading Scientist Explores Animal Joy, Sorrow and Empathy – And Why They Matter*. California: New World Library, 2007.

——. 'The Public Lives of Animals', *Journal of Consciousness Studies* 13, no. 5 (2006): 115–131.

Bengton, David and Michael J. Dockry. 'Forest Futures in the Anthropocene: Can Trees and Humans Survive Together', *The Futurist* 48, no. 4 (2014): 34–39.

Bennett, Jane. *The Enchantment of Modern Life: Attachments, Crossings and Ethics*. Princeton, NJ: Princeton University Press, 2001.

Benson, J. 'The Effect of 200 Years of European Settlement on the Vegetation and Flora of New South Wales', *Cunninghamia* 2, no. 3 (1991): 343–370.

Benterrak, Krim, Stephen Muecke and Paddy Roe; with Ray Keogh and Butcher Joe. *Reading the Country: Introduction to Nomadology*. Fremantle: Fremantle Arts Centre Press, 1984.

Bergson, Henri. *Creative Evolution*. Trans. Arthur Mitchell. New York: Henry Holt and Company, 1911.

——. *Introduction to Metaphysics*. Trans. T. E. Hulme. Indianopolis: Hacket Publishing, 1999.

Bergstrom, Dana M., Arko Lucier, Kate Kiefer, Jane Wasley, Lee Belbin, Tore K. Pederson and Steven L. Chown. 'Indirect Effects of Invasive Species Removal Devastate World Heritage Island', *Journal of Applied Ecology* 46 (2009): 73–81.

Berland, Jody. 'On Reading "The Weather"', *Cultural Studies* 8, no. 1 (1994): 99–114.

Biermann, Soenke. 'Knowledge, Power and Decolonisation: Implication for Non-Indigenous Scholars, Researchers and Educators', in *Indigenous Philosophies and Critical Education: A Reader*, ed. George J. Sefa Dei. New York: Peter Lang, 2011, pp. 386–398.

Blomfield, Geoffrey. *Baal Belbora – The End of Dancing: The Agony of the British Invasion of the Ancient People of Three Rivers, The Hastings, the Manning & the Macleay, in New South Wales*. Alternative Publishing Co-operative: Sydney, 1981.

Botkin, Daniel. *Discordant Harmonies: A New Ecology for the Twenty-First Century*. New York & Oxford: Oxford University Press, 1990.

Braudel, Fernand. *On History*. Trans. Sarah Mathews. Chicago: University of Chicago Press, 1980.

Buchanan, Brett. *Onto-Ethologies: The Animal Environments of Uexküll, Heidegger, Merleau-Ponty, and Deleuze*. New York: State University of New York Press, 2008.

Bureau of Meteorology. *Indigenous Weather Knowledge*. Commonwealth of Australia, 2010, www.bom.gov.au/iwk/index.shtml.

Burke, Edmund. *A Philosophical Enquiry into the Origin of Our Ideas of the Sublime and Beautiful*. 1757. Reprint. Oxford: Oxford University Press, 1999.

Byrne, Denis. 'Deep Nation: Australia's Acquisition of an Indigenous Past', *Aboriginal History* 20 (1996): 82–107.

Campbell, Sue. 'Our Faithfulness to the Past: Reconstructing Memory Value', *Philosophical Psychology* 19, no .3 (2006): 361–380.

——. 'The Second Voice', *Memory Studies* 1, no. 1 (January 2008): 41–48.

Carter, Paul. *The Lie of the Land*. London and Boston: Faber and Faber, 1996.

——. *The Road to Botany Bay: An Essay in Spatial History*. London: Faber and Faber, 1987.

Casey, Edward S. *Remembering: A Phenomenological Study*. Second Edition. Bloomington: Indiana University Press, 2000.

——. *The Fate of Place: A Philosophical History*. Berkeley: University of California Press, 1997.

Cashman, Tyrone. 'What Connects the Map to the Territory', in *A Legacy for Living Systems: Gregory Bateson as Precursor to Biosemiotics*, ed. Jesper Hoffmeyer. Dordrecht: Springer, 2009.

Chakrabarty, Dipesh. 'Breaking the Wall of "Two Cultures": Science and Humanities After Climate Change', paper presented at the Falling Walls International Conference on Future Breakthroughs in Science and Society, Berlin, 9 November, 2009, http://falling-walls.com/lectures/dipesh-chakrabarty/.

——. 'The Time of History and the Times of Gods', in *The Politics of Culture in the Shadow of Capital*, eds. Lisa Lowe and David Lloyd. Durham, NC: Duke University Press, 1997, pp. 35–60.

Chandler, Mielle and Astrida Neimanis. 'Water and Gestationality: What Flows beneath Ethics', in *Thinking with Water* eds. Cecilia Chen, Janine Macleod and Astrida Neimanis. Montreal, London & Ithica: McGill-Queens University Press, 2013, pp. 61–83.

Charlton,Noel G. *Understanding Gregory Bateson: Mind, Beauty and the Sacred Earth*. Albany: Suny Press, 2008.

Chew, Matthew K. and Andrew L. Hamilton. 'The Rise and Fall of Biotic Nativeness: A Historical Perspective', in *Fifty Years of Invasion Ecology: The Legacy of Charles Elton*, First Edition, ed. David M. Richardson. Oxford: Blackwell Publishing Ltd, 2011, pp. 35–47.

Clarke, Philip A. 'Australian Aboriginal Ethnometeorology and Seasonal Calendars', *History and Anthropology* 20, no. 2 (2009): 79–106.

Colebrook, Claire. 'Stratigraphic Time, Women's Time', *Australian Feminist Studies* 25 (59) (2009): 11–16

Collins, Julie. '"Caring for Country" in NSW: Connection, Identity, Belonging', PhD thesis, Southern Cross University, 2006.

Coman, Brian. *Tooth and Nail: The Story of the Rabbit in Australia*. Melbourne: The Text Publishing Company, 1999.

Commonwealth Intergovernmental Working Group for the UNCCD. *Australian Actions to Combat Desertification and Land Degradation: National Report by Australia on Measures Taken to Support Implementation of the United Nations Convention to Combat Desertification*, April 2002, www.environment.gov.au/land/publications/actions/summary.html.

Connell, Jeff and Barbara Rugendyke. 'Creating an Authentic Tourist Site? The Australian Standing Stones, Glen Innes', *Australian Geographer* 41, no. 1 (2010): 87–100.

Cooke, Stuart. '*Speaking the Earth's Languages: A Theory for Australian-Chilean Postcolonial Poetics*. Amsterdam & New York: Rodopi, 2003.

Crosby, Alfred W. *Ecological Imperialism: The Biological Expansion of Europe, 900–1900*. Second Edition. Cambridge: Cambridge University Press, 2004.

188   *Works cited*

Curthoys, Ann. 'An Uneasy Conversation: The Multicultural and the Indigenous', in *Race, Colour and Identity in Australia and New Zealand*, eds. John Docker and Gerhard Fischer. Sydney: UNSW Press, 2000, pp. 21–36.

David, Bruno, Marcia Langton and Ian McNiven. 'Re-Inventing the Wheel: Indigenous Peoples and the Master Race in Philip Ruddock's "Wheel" Comments', *Philosophy, Activism, Nature* 2 (2002): 31–45.

Davis, Mark, Matthew Chew, Richard Hobbs, Ariel Lugo, John Ewel, Geerat Vermeij, James Brown, Michael Rosenzweig, Mark Gardener, Scott Carroll, Ken Thompson, Steward Pickett, Juliet Stromberg, Peter Del Tredici, Katharine Suding, Joan Ehrenfield, J. Philip Grime, Joseph Mascaro and John Briggs. 'Don't Judge Species on their Origins', *Nature* 474 (2011): 152–154.

Deleuze, Gilles. *Difference and Repetition*. Trans. Paul Patton. London: The Athlone Press, 1994.

——. *Foucault*, trans. and ed. Seán Hand. New York & London: Continuum, 2006.

Deleuze, Gilles and Felix Guattari. *A Thousand Plateaus: Capitalism and Schizophrenia*. Minneapolis: University of Minnesota Press, 1987.

——. *What is Philosophy?* London & New York: Verso, 1994.

Despret, Vinciane. 'The Body We Care for: Figures of Anthropo-zoo-genesis', *Body and Society* 10, no. 2–3 (2004): 111–134.

de Waal, Frans. 'Are We in Anthropodenial?', *Discover* 18, no. 7 (1997): 50–53.

Durkheim, Émile. *The Elementary Forms of Religious Life*. 1912. Reprint. Trans. J. W. Swain. New York: The Free Press, 1965.

Fabian, Johannes. *Time and the Other: How Anthropology Makes Its Object*. New York & Sussex: Columbia University Press, 2002.

Ferguson, Kennan. 'I Love My Dog', *Political Theory* 32, no. 3 (2004): 373–395.

Ferrier, Elizabeth. 'Mapping the Space of the Other: Transformations of Space in Postcolonial Fiction and Postmodern Theory', PhD thesis, University of Queensland, 1990.

Fisher, John Andrew. 'The Myth of Anthropomorphism', in *Readings in Animal Cognition*, eds. Marc Bekoff and Dale Jamieson. Boston: MIT Press, 1999, pp. 3–16.

Foundation for Rabbit-Free Australia Inc. *Rabbit-Free Australia*. www.rabbitfreeaustralia.org.au/.

Fowler, H. W. and F. G. Fowler, eds. *The Concise Oxford Dictionary of Current English*. Fifth Edition. London: Oxford University Press, 1964.

Franklin, Adrian. *Animal Nation: The True Story of Animals and Australia*. Sydney: University of New South Wales Press, 2006.

Fuller, Robert. 'How Ancient Aboriginal Star Maps have Shaped Australia's Highway Network', *The Conversation* (2016), https://theconversation.com/how-ancient-aboriginal-star-maps-have-shaped-australias-highway-network-55952.

Gagliano, Monica. 'In a Green Frame of Mind: Perspectives on the Behavioural Ecology and Cognitive Nature of Plants', *AoB Plants* (2015), http://aobpla.oxfordjournals.org/content/7/plu075.

Gagliano, Monica, M. Renton, M. Depczynsky and S. Mancuso. 'Experience Teaches Plants to Learn Faster and Forget Slower in Environments where it Matters', *Oecologia* 175: 63–72.

Gaia, Vince. *Adventures in the Anthropocene: A Journey to the Heart of the Planet We Made*. Minneapolis: Milkweed Editions, 2014.

Gane, Nicholas. 'When We Have Never Been Human, What is to be Done?: Interview with Donna Haraway', *Theory Culture Society* 23 (2006): 135-158

Garbutt, Rob. 'Local Order', *M/C Journal of Media and Culture* 7, no. 6 (2005), http://journal.media-culture.org.au/0501/08-garbutt.php.

——. 'The Locals: A Critical Survey of the Idea in Recent Australian Scholarly Writing', *Australian Folklore* 21 (2006): 172–192.

——. 'Towards an Ethics of Location', in *Landscapes of Exile: Once Perilous, Now Safe*, eds. Anna Haebich and Baden Offord. Bern: Peter Lang, 2008, pp. 175–192.

——. 'White "Autochthony"', *ACRAWSA e-journal* 2, no. 1 (2006), www.acrawsa.org.au/files/ejournalfiles/88RobGarbutt.pdf.

Garbutt, Rob, Soenke Biermann and Baden Offord. 'Into the Borderlands: Unruly Pedagogy, Tactile Theory and the Decolonising Nation', *Critical Arts* 26, no. 1 (2012): 62–81.

Garnett, Ali and Kaye Kessing. *Easter Bilby*. Department of Environment and Heritage: Kaye Kessing Productions, 2006.

Gelder, K. and J. M. Jacobs. *Uncanny Australia: Sacredness and Identity in a Postcolonial Nation*. Carlton South: Melbourne University Press, 1998.

Gibson-Graham, J.K. 'A Feminist Project of Belonging for the Anthropocene', *Gender, Place, and Culture* 18, no. 1 (2011): 1–21.

Gibson, Ross. *Seven Versions of an Australian Badland*. St. Lucia: University of Queensland Press, 2002.

——. *South of the West: Postcolonialism and the Narrative Construction of Australia*. Bloomington and Indianapolis: Indiana University Press, 1992.

Glen Innes Tourism. 'Australian Standing Stones Brochure', Glen Innes and Severn Shire Tourist Association, www.gleninnestourism.com/pages/australian-standing-stones/.

Gordon, Deborah M. *Ant Encounters: Interaction Networks and Colony Behaviour*. Princeton and Woodstock: Princeton University Press, 2010.

Graham, Mary. 'Some Thoughts about the Philosophical Underpinnings of Aboriginal Worldviews', *Australian Humanities Review* 45 (2008): 181–194.

Griffiths, Tom. 'Deep Time and Australian History', *History Today* 51, no. 11 (2001): 20–25.

——. *Hunters and Collectors: The Antiquarian Imagination in Australia*. Melbourne: Cambridge University Press, 1996.

Hage, Ghassan. *Alter-Politics: Critical Anthropology and the Radical Imagination*. Melbourne: Melbourne University Press, 2015.

——. *White Nation: Fantasies of White Supremacy in a Multicultural Society*. Annandale: Pluto Press, 1998.

Hall, Matthew. 'Plant Autonomy and Human-Plant Ethics', *Environmental Ethics* 31, no. 2 (2009): 169–181.

Hamacher, D. W., R. S. Fuller and R. P. Norris. 'Orientations of Linear Stone Arrangements in New South Wales', *Australian Archaeology* 75 (2012): 46–54.

Haraway, Donna. 'Anthropocene, Capitalacone, Chthulucene: Staying with the Trouble', *Anthropocene: Arts of Living on a Damaged Planet* (2015), http://opentranscripts.org/transcript/anthropocene-capitalocene-chthulucene/.

——. 'Anthropocene, Capitalocene, Plantationocene, Chthulucene: Making Kin' *Environmental Humanities* 6 (2015): 159–165.

——. 'Staying with the Trouble: Sympoiesis, String Figures, Multispecies Muddle', lecture, University of Alberta, 25 March, 2014, accessed 5 June, 2014, www.new.livesteam.com/aict/DonnaHaraway.

——. *The Companion Species Manifesto: Dogs, People, and Significant Otherness*. Chicago: Prickly Paradigm Press, 2003.

——. *When Species Meet*. Minneapolis and London: University of Minnesota Press, 2008.

Harvey, David. *The Condition of Postmodernity: An Enquiry into the Origins of Cultural Change*. Oxford: Blackwell Publishers, 1990.

Hatley, James. 'Naming Coyote in Hebrew: A Memoir', *TEXT Special Issue 20: Writing Creates Ecology and Ecology Creates Writing*, eds. Martin Harrison, Deborah Bird Rose, Lorraine Shannon and Kim Satchell (2013): 1–11.

——. *Suffering Witness: The Quandary of Responsibility after the Irreparable*. Albany: State University of New York Press, 2000.

—— 'The Virtue of Temporal Discernment: Rethinking the Extent and Coherence of the Good in a Time of Mass Species Extinction', *Environmental Philosophy* 9, no. 1 (2012) 1–21.

Hawkins, Gay and Kane Race. 'Bottled Water Practices: Reconfiguring Drinking in Bangkok Households', in *Material Geographies of Household Sustainability*, eds. Ruth Lane and Andrew Gorman-Murray. Farnham & Burlington: Ashgate Publishing, 2011, pp. 113–124.

Haworth, Robert. 'The Rocks Beneath', in *High Lean Country: Land, People and Memory in New England*, eds. Alan Atkinson, J. S. Ryan, Iain Davidson and Andrew Piper. Crows Nest: Allen and Unwin, 2006, pp. 23–34.

Head, Lesley and Pat Muir. 'Changing Cultures of Water in Eastern Australian Backyard Gardens', *Social and Cultural Geography* 8, no. 6 (2007): 889–902.

Heidegger, Martin. *Being and Time*. Oxford: Blackwell, 1962.

——. 'The Question Concerning Technology', in *The Question Concerning Technology and Other Essays*, ed. Martin Heidegger. New York: Harper and Row, 1977, pp. 3–35.

Heishman, Darice. 'VHD Factsheet', *House Rabbit Network*, www.rabbitnetwork.org/articles/vhd.shtml.

Horne, Ross. 'The Philosophy and Practice of *P. Radiata* Plantation Silviculture in New South Wales', School of Forestry, Melbourne University (Beecroft: Forestry Commission of New South Wales, 1986), www.dpi.nsw.gov.au/__data/assets/pdf_file/0009/389925/The-Philosophy-and-Practice-of-P-Radiata-Plantation-Silviculture-in-NSW.pdf, accessed 30 December 2012.

Hustak, Carla and Natasha Myers. 'Involutionary Momentum: Affective Ecologies and the Sciences of Plant/Insect Encounters', *Differences: A Journal of Feminist Cultural Studies*, 23, no. 3 (2012) 74–117.

Ingold, Tim. *The Perception of the Environment: Essays on Livelihood, Dwelling and Skill*. London and New York: Routledge, 2000.

Instone, Lesley and Affrica Taylor. 'Thinking about Inheritance Through the Figure of the Anthropocene, from the Antipodes and In the Presence of Others', *Environmental Humanities* 7 (2015): 133–150.

Irigiray, Luce. 'Animal Compassion', in *Animal Philosophy: Essential Readings in Continental Thought*, eds. Mathew Calarco and Peter Atterton. London and New York: Continuum, 2004, pp. 195–202.

Jones, Alwyn. 'Fifty Years of Beautification and Tree Planting in Armidale', *Armidale and District Historical Society: Journal and Proceedings* 37 (1994): 129–134.

Kaika, Maria. *City of Flows: Modernity, Nature, and the City*. London: Routledge, 2005.

Keller, John. 'The Celticising of Glen Innes', *Australian Folklore* 16 (2001): 202–210.

Kelly, Lynne. *Knowledge and Power in Prehistoric Societies: Orality, Memory and the Transition of Culture*. New York: Cambridge University Press, 2015.

Kennedy, Brian. *Australian Place Names*. Sydney: ABC Books, 2006.

Keulartz, Josef. 'The Emergence of Enlightened Anthropocentrism in Ecological Restoration', *Nature and Culture*, 7, no. 1 (2012): 48–71.

Kingsley, Danny. 'The Lost Seasons', *ABC Online*, 14 August 2003, www.abc.net.au/science/features/indigenous/.

Kirby, Vicki. *Quantum Anthropologies: Life at Large*. Durham: Duke University Press, 2011.

Kirksey, S. Eben, Nicholas Shapiro and Maria Brodine. 'Hope in Blasted Landscapes', *Social Science Information* 52, no. 2 (2013): 228–256.

Kohn, Eduardo. 'How Dogs Dream: Amazonian Natures and the Politics of Transspecies Engagement', *American Ethnologist* 34, no. 1 (2007): 3–24.

——. *How Forests Think: Toward an Anthropology Beyond the Human*. Berkeley, Los Angeles, London: University of California Press, 2013.

Kolbert, Elizabeth. 'Enter the Anthropocene – Age of Man', *National Geographic* (2011), http://ngm.nationalgeographic.com/2011/03/age-of-man/kolbert-text/2.

Kristeva, Julia. *Powers of Horror: An Essay on Abjection*. Trans. Leon S. Roudiez. New York: Columbia University Press, 1982.

Landström, Catharina. 'Justifiable Bunnycide: Narrating the Recent Success of Australian Biological Control of Rabbits', *Science as Culture* 10, no. 2 (2001): 141–161.

Langton, Marcia. 'What Do We Mean by Wilderness? Wilderness and *Terra Nullius* in Australian Art', *The Sydney Papers* 8, no. 1 (1996): 11–31.

Latour, Bruno. 'How to Talk about the Body? The Normative Dimensions of Science Studies', *Body and Society* 10, no. 2 (2004): 205–229.

——. *Pandora's Hope: Essays on the Reality of Science Studies*. Cambridge & London: Harvard University Press, 1999.

——. *We Have Never Been Modern*. Cambridge & London: Harvard University Press, 2001.

Leopold, Aldo. 'Thinking Like a Mountain', in *A Sand County Almanac and Sketches Here and There*. New York: Oxford University Press, 1949, pp. 129–141.

Lestel, Dominique. 'How Chimpanzees Have Domesticated Humans: Towards an Anthropology of Human-Animal Communication', *Anthropology Today* 14, no. 3 (1998): 12–15.

Levinas, Emmanuel. *Totality and Infinity: An Essay on Exteriority*. Pittsburgh: Duquesne University Press, 1969.

Lindenmayer, David, Michael McCarthy, Kirsten Parris and Matthew Pope. 'Habitat Fragmentation, Landscape Context, and Mammalian Assemblages in Southeastern Australia', *Journal of Mammalogy* 81, no. 3 (2000): 787–797.

Lingis, Alphonso. *Dangerous Emotions*. Berkeley and Los Angeles & London: University of California Press, 2000.

Low, Tim. *The New Nature: Winners and Losers in Wild Australia*. Melbourne: Penguin, 2002.

Lucashenko, Melissa. 'All My Relations: Being and Belonging in Byron Shire', in *Landscapes of Exile: Once Perilous, Now Safe*, eds. Anna Haebich and Baden Offord. Bern: Peter Lang AG, International Academic Publishers, 2008, pp. 61–68.

MacGill, Bindi, Julie Mathews, Aunty Ellen Trevorrow, Aunty Alice Abdulla and Deb Rankine. 'Ecology, Ontology and Pedagogy at Camp Coorong', *M/C Journal of Media and Culture* 15, no. 3 (2012), http://journal.media-culture.org.au/index.php/mcjournal/article/viewArticle/499.

Macleod, Janine. 'Water and the Material Imagination: Reading the Sea of Memory against the Flows of Capital', in *Thinking with Water* eds. Cecilia Chen, Janine Macleod and Astrida Neimanis. Montreal, London & Ithica: McGill-Queens University Press, 2013, pp. 40–60.

Malm, Andreas and Alf Hornborg. 'The Geology of Mankind? A Critique of the Anthropocene Narrative', *The Anthropocene Review* (2014): 62–69.

Marder, Michael. *Plant-Thinking: A Philosophy of Vegetal Life*. New York: Columbia University Press, 2013.

Margulis, Lynn and Dorion Sagan. *What is Life?* Berkeley and Los Angeles: University of California Press, 2000.

Massey, Doreen. 'A Global Sense of Place', in *Space, Place and Gender*, ed. Doreen Massey. Minneapolis: University of Minnesota Press, 1994, www.unc.edu/courses/2006spring/geog/021/001/massey.pdf.

Mastnak, Tomaz, Julia Elyachar and Tom Boellstorff. 'Botanical Decolonization: Rethinking Native Plants', *Environment and Planning D: Society and Space* 32 (2014): 363–380.

Mathew D Ua, John H. *The History of the Australian Standing Stones*. Glen Innes: The Australian Standing Stones Management Board, 2012.

Mathews, Freya. *For Love of Matter: A Contemporary Panpsychism*. Albany: State University of New York Press, 2003.

——. 'Letting the World Do the Doing', *Australian Humanities Review* 33 (2004), www.australianhumanitiesreview.org/archive/Issue-August-2004/matthews.html.

——. 'Planet Beehive', *Australian Humanities Review* 50 (May 2011), www.australianhumanitiesreview.org/archive/Issue-May-2011/mathews.html.

——. 'Without Animals Life is Not Worth Living', *Between the Species* VII (August 2007): 1–28, http://digitalcommons.calpoly.edu/cgi/viewcontent.cgi?article=1023&context=bts.

Mazis, Glen. 'The World of Wolves: Lessons about the Sacredness of the Surround, Belonging, Silent Dialogue of Interdependence and Death, and Speciocide', *Environmental Philosophy* 5, no. 2 (2008): 69–91.

McBryde, Isabel. *Aboriginal Prehistory in New England: An Archaeological Survey of Northeastern New South Wales*. Sydney: Sydney University Press, 1974.

——. *Records of Times Past: Ethnohistorical Essays on the Culture and Ecology of the New England Tribes*. Canberra: Australian Institute of Aboriginal Studies, 1978.

Memmi, Albert. *The Colonizer and the Colonized*. New York: Orion Press, 1965.

Merleau-Ponty, Maurice. *Phenomenology of Perception*. London & New York: Routledge, 2002.

——. *The Visible and the Invisible*. Trans. Alphonso Lingis. Evanston: Northwestern University Press, 1968.

Metcalf, Jacob and Thom van Dooren. 'Editorial Preface', in 'Temporal Environments: Rethinking Time and Ecology', eds. Jacob Metcalf and Thom van Dooren. Special issue, *Environmental Philosophy* 9, no. 1 (2012): 1–22.

Midgley, Mary. *Animals and Why They Matter*. Georgia: University of Georgia Press, 1998.

Moore, Jason W. *Capitalism in the Web of Life: Ecology and the Accumulation of Capital*. London And New York: Verso Books, 2015.

Moreton-Robinson, Aileen. 'Introduction', in *Sovereign Subjects: Indigenous Sovereignty Matters*, ed. Aileen Moreton-Robinson. Crows Nest: Allen and Unwin, 2007, pp. 1–11.

——. 'I Still Call Australia Home: Indigenous Belonging and Place in a White Postcolonising Society', in *Uprootings/Regroundings: Questions of Home and Migration*, eds. Sara Ahmed, Claudia Castañeda, Anne-Marie Fortier and Mimi Sheller. Oxford: Berg, 2003, pp. 23–40.

Muecke, Stephen. *Ancient and Modern: Time, Culture and Indigenous Philosophy*. Sydney: University of New South Wales Press, 2004.

——. 'Can You Argue with the Honeysuckle?', in *Halfway House: The Poetics of Australian Spaces*, eds. Jennifer Rutherford and Barbara Holloway. Crawley: UWA Publishing, 2010, pp. 34–42.

——. *No Road (Bitumen All the Way)*. Fremantle: Fremantle Arts Centre Press, 1997.

——. 'What the Cassowary Does Not Need to Know', *Australian Humanities Review* 39–40 (2006), www.australianhumanitiesreview.org/archive/Issue-September-2006/muecke. html.

Murphie, Andrew. 'Deleuze, Guattari and Neuroscience', in *Deleuze, Science and the Force of the Virtual*, ed. Peter Gaffney. Minneapolis: University of Minnesota Press, 2010.

——. 'The World as Medium: Whitehead's Media Philosophy', in *Immediations*, eds. Erin Manning, Anne Munster and Bodil Marie Stavning Thomsen. Open Humanities Press, forthcoming.

Myers, Natasha. 'Photosynthesis', Theorizing the Contemporary, *Cultural Anthropology* website, 21 January 2016. https://culanth.org/fieldsights/790-photosynthesis.

Nagel, Thomas. 'What Is It Like to Be a Bat?' *The Philosophical Review* LXXXIII, no. 4 (October 1974): 435–50.

Neidjie, Bill. *Story about Feeling*. Broome: Magabala Books, 1989.

Neimanis, Astrida and Stephanie Walker. 'Weathering: Climate Change and the "Thick Time" of Transcorporeality', *Hypatia* 29, no. 3 (2013) 557–575.

New South Wales National Parks and Wildlife Service. *Heritage Walk: Mount Yarrowyck Nature Reserve Rock Art Site*. Information Pamphlet. NSW National Parks and Wildlife, no date.

Newton, Isaac. Scholium to the Definitions in *Philosophiae Naturalis Principia Mathematica*, Bk. 1. 1689. Trans. Andrew Motte (1729). Revised by Florian Cajori. Berkeley, CA: University of California Press, 1934, pp. 6–12, http://plato.stanford.edu/entries/newton-stm/scholium.html.

Nixon, Rob. *Slow Violence and Environmentalism of the Poor*. Cambridge: Harvard University Press, 2011.

Offord, Baden. 'Landscapes of Exile (and Narratives on the Trauma of Belonging)', in *Landscapes of Exile: Once Perilous, Now Safe*, eds. Anna Haebich and Baden Offord. Bern: Peter Lang, 2008, pp. 5–18.

O'Loughlin, Colin. 'Environmental Services Provided by Plantations', Guest Editorial. *New Zealand Journal of Forestry* 49, no. 4 (2005): 2.

Oxley, John. *Journals of Two Expeditions into the Interior of New South Wales, By Order of the British Government in the Years 1817–18*. 1820. Reprint. eBooks@Adelaide: updated 10 November 2012, http://ebooks.adelaide.edu.au/o/oxley/john/o95j/part2.html.

Parliament of New South Wales. 'Full Day Hansard Transcript', Legislative Assembly (8 June 2000), www.parliament.nsw.gov.au/prod/parlment/hanstrans.nsf/V3ByKey/LA 20000608?Open&refNavID=.

Pitcher, Wallace S. *The Nature and Origin of Granite*. London: Chapman and Hall, 1993.

Plumwood, Val. 'Decolonising Australian Gardens: Gardening and the Ethics of Place', *Australian Humanities Review* 36 (2005), www.australianhumanitiesreview.org/archive/Issue-July-2005/09Plumwood.html.

——. 'Decolonising Relationships with Nature', *Philosophy, Activism, Nature* 2 (2002): 7–30.

——. *Environmental Culture: The Ecological Crisis of Reason*. London: Routledge, 2002.

194 *Works cited*

——. 'Journey to the Heart of Stone', in *Culture, Creativity and Environment: New Environmentalist Criticism*, eds. Fiona Becket and Terry Gifford. Amsterdam & New York: Rodopi, 2005, pp. 17–36.

——. 'Nature in the Active Voice', *Australian Humanities Review* 46 (May 2009), www.australianhumanitiesreview.org/archive/Issue-May-2009/plumwood.html.

——. 'Place, Politics and Spirituality: An Interview', in *Pagan Visions for a Sustainable Future*, eds. Ly de Angeles, Emma Restall Orr and Thom van Dooren. Woodbury, MN: Llewellyn Publications, 2005, pp. 225–258.

——. 'Shadow Places and the Politics of Dwelling', *Australian Humanities Review* 44 (March 2008), www.australianhumanitiesreview.org/archive/Issue-March-2008/plumwood.html.

——. 'The Cemetery Wars: Cemeteries, Biodiversity and the Sacred', *Local-Global: Identity, Security, Community* 3 (2007): 54–71.

Poynton, Howard. 'The Smell of Rain: How CSIRO Invented a New Word', *The Conversation* (31 March 2015), http://theconversation.com/the-smell-of-rain-how-csiro-invented-a-new-word-39231.

Pugliese, Joseph. 'Forensic Ecologies of Occupied Zones and Geographies of Dispossession: Gaza and Occupied East Jerusalem', *Borderlands* 14, no. 1 (2015): 1–37.

Read, Peter. *Belonging: Australians, Place and Aboriginal Ownership*. Cambridge: Cambridge University Press, 2003.

——. *Haunted Earth*. Sydney: University of New South Wales Press, 2003.

——. *Returning to Nothing: The Meaning of Lost Places*. Cambridge, New York & Melbourne: Cambridge University Press, 1996.

Reddiex, Ben and David M. Forsyth. 'Control of Pest Mammals for Biodiversity Protection in Australia', *Wildlife Research* 33 (2006): 711–717.

Rigby, Kate. 'Dancing with Disaster', *Australian Humanities Review* 46 (May 2009), www.australianhumanitiesreview.org/archive/Issue-May-2009/rigby.html.

Robbins, Paul. 'Comparing Invasive Networks: Cultural and Political Biographies of Invasive Species', *Geographical Review* 94, no. 2 (2004): 139–156.

Robin, Libby. *How a Continent Created a Nation*. Sydney: UNSW Press, 2007.

Roediger, David. *Towards the Abolition of Whiteness: Essays on Race, Politics and Working Class History*. London & New York: Verso, 1994.

Rolls, Eric. *They All Ran Wild*. Sydney: Angus and Robertson, 1969.

Rose, Bruce. *Land Management Issues: Attitudes and Perceptions Amongst Aboriginal Peoples of Central Australia*. Alice Springs: Central Land Council, 1995.

Rose, Deborah Bird. 'Aboriginal Life and Death in Australian Settler Nationhood', *Aboriginal History* 25 (2001): 148–162.

——. 'Connecting Nature and Culture: The Role of the Humanities', presentation in the Fenner School of Environment and Society seminar series, Australian National University, Canberra, 31 May 2007.

——. 'Dialogue with Place: Toward an Ecological Body', *Journal of Narrative Theory* 32, no. 3 (2002): 311–325.

——. 'Judas Work: Four Modes of Sorrow', *Environmental Philosophy* 5, no. 2 (2008): 51–66.

——. 'Justice and Longing', in *Fresh Water: New Perspectives on Water in Australia*, eds. Emily Potter, Alison Mackinnon, Stephen McKenzie and Jennifer McKay. Carlton: Melbourne University Press, 2007, pp. 8–20.

——. 'Multispecies Knots of Ethical Time', *Environmental Philosophy* 9, no. 1 (2012): 127–140.

——. *Nourishing Terrains: Australian Aboriginal Views of Landscape and Wilderness.* Canberra: Australian Heritage Commission, 1996.

——. 'On History, Trees, and Ethical Proximity', *Postcolonial Studies* 11, no. 2 (2008): 157–167.

——. *Reports from a Wild Country: Ethics for Decolonisation.* Sydney: University of New South Wales Press, 2004.

——. 'Rhythms, Patterns, Connectivities: Indigenous Concepts of Seasons and Change, Victoria River District, NT', in *A Change in the Weather: Climate and Culture in Australia*, eds. Tim Sherratt, Tom Griffiths and Libby Robin. Canberra: National Museum of Australia, 2005, pp. 32–41.

——. 'Val Plumwood's Philosophical Animism: Attentive Interactions in the Sentient World', *Environmental Humanities* 3 (2013), 104.

——. 'When the Rainbow Walks', in *Windows on Meteorology: Australian Perspective*, ed. Eric K. Webb. Melbourne: CSIRO Publishing, 1997, pp. 1–6.

——. *Wild Dog Dreaming: Love and Extinction.* Charlottesville and London: University of Virginia Press, 2011.

Rose, Deborah Bird and Libby Robin. 'The Ecological Humanities in Action: An Invitation', *Australian Humanities Review* 31–32 (April 2004), www.australian humanitiesreview.org/archive/Issue-April-2004/rose.html.

Rowlands, Mark. 'Environmental Epistemology', *Ethics and the Environment* 10, no. 2 (2005): 5–27.

——. *Externalism: Putting Mind and World Back Together Again.* Chesham: Acumen Publishing, 2003.

Ryan, John and J. S. Tregurtha. 'Standing at the Array: A Celtic Tradition Re-enacted at Glen Innes, New South Wales', *Australian Folklore* 7 (1992): 69–76.

Ryan, Simon. *The Cartographic Eye: How Explorers Saw Australia.* Cambridge: Cambridge University Press, 1996.

Saint-Exupéry, Antoine de. *The Little Prince.* 1943. Reprint. Trans. T. V. F. Cuffe. London: Penguin, 2000.

Schlunke, Katrina. *Bluff Rock: Autobiography of a Massacre.* Fremantle: Curtin University Books, 2005.

——. 'Dumb Places', *Balayi: Culture, Law and Colonialism* 6 (2004): 72–81.

——. 'Sovereign Hospitalities?', *Borderlands* 1, no. 2 (2002), www.borderlands.net.au/vol1no2_2002/schlunke_hospitalities.html.

——. 'One Strange Colonial Thing: Materian Remembering and the Bark Shield of Botany Bay', *Continuum: Journal of Media & Cultural Studies* 27, no. 1 (2013): 18–29.

Shepard, Paul. *The Others: How Animals Made Us Human.* Washington, DC: Island Press/ Shearwater Books, 1996.

Shiva, Vandana. *Water Wars: Privatization, Pollution, and Profit.* London: Pluto Press, 2002.

Simpson, Catherine, Renata Murawska and Anthony Lambert. 'Introduction: Rethinking Diasporas – Australian Cinema, History and Society', in *Diasporas of Australian Cinema*, eds. Catherine Simpson, Renata Murawska and Anthony Lambert. Bristol & Chicago: Intellect, 2009, pp. 15–27.

Smith, J. M. B. *Further Ecological Comparisons Between Pine Plantations and Native Forests, Clouds Creek, NSW.* Armidale: University of New England, 1997.

Smith, J. M. B., S. Borgis and V. Seifert. 'Studies in Urban Ecology: The First Wave of Biological Invasion by *Pistacia Chinensis* in Armidale, New South Wales, Australia', *Australian Geographical Studies* 38, no. 3 (2000): 263–274.

Smith, Mick. 'Dis(appearance): Earth, Ethics and Apparently (In)Significant Others', in 'Unloved Others: Death of the Disregarded in the Time of Extinctions', eds. Deborah Bird Rose and Thom van Dooren. Special issue, *Australian Humanities Review* 50 (2011): 23–44.

——. 'Ecological Community, the Sense of the World, and Senseless Extinction', *Environmental Humanities* 2 (2013): 21–41.

Smith, Nicholas. 'Thank Your Mother for the Rabbits: Bilbies, Bunnies and Redemptive Ecology', *Australian Zoologist* 33, no. 3 (2000): 369–378.

Somerville, Margaret. *Body/Landscape Journals*. North Melbourne: Spinifex Press, 1999.

——. 'Towards Universities for the Twenty-First Century', *Higher Education in Europe* 16, no. 1 (1991): 79–86.

Steffen, Will, Paul J. Crutzen and John R. McNeill. 'The Anthropocene: Are Humans Now Overwhelming the Great Forces of Nature?', *Ambio* 36, no. 8 (2007): 614–621.

Stengers, Isabelle. 'A Constructivist Reading of Process and Reality', *Theory, Culture, and Society* 25, no. 4 (2008): 91–110.

——. 'The Cosmopolitical Proposal', in *Making Things Public*, eds. Bruno Latour & Peter Weibel. Cambridge: MIT Press, 2005, pp. 994–1003

Stratton, John and Ien Ang. 'Multicultural Imagined Communities: Cultural Difference and National Identity in Australia and the USA', *Continuum: The Australian Journal of Media and Culture* 8, no. 2 (1994), wwwmcc.murdoch.edu.au/ReadingRoom/8.2/Stratton.html, accessed 15 November 2012.

Sutton, John. 'Remembering', in *The Cambridge Handbook of Situated Cognition*, eds. Philip Robbins and Murat Aydede. Cambridge: Cambridge University Press, 2009, pp. 217–235.

Tenterfield and District Visitors' Association. *Bluff Rock: Location and History*. Tenterfield: Tenterfield and District Visitors' Association, no date.

Thoreau, Henry David. *Autumnal Tints*. Massachusetts: Applewood Books, 1862.

Torbay, Richard. 'Armidale Pine Forest', 2004.

——. 'Armidale Pine Forest', private member's statement, 22 October 2008, www.richardtorbay.com.au/parliamentary/armidale-pine-forest.php.

——. 'Volunteers Helping to Bring Armidale Pine Forest Back to Life', 2009.

Tredinnick, Mark. *The Blue Plateau: A Landscape Memoir*. Brisbane: University of Queensland Press, 2009.

Trigg, Dylan. 'The Place of Trauma: Memory, Hauntings, and the Temporality of Ruins', *Memory Studies* 2, no. 1 (2009): 87–101.

Tsing, Anna. 'Arts of Inclusion, Or, How to Love a Mushroom', in 'Unloved Others: Death of the Disregarded in the Time of Extinctions', eds. Deborah Bird Rose and Thom van Dooren. Special issue, *Australian Humanities Review* 50 (May 2011): 5–21.

——. 'Unruly Edges: Mushrooms as Companion Species', *Environmental Humanities* 1 (2012): 141–154.

Tumarkin, Maria. 'Secret Life of Wounded Spaces: Traumascapes in the Contemporary Australian Landscape', PhD thesis, University of Melbourne, 2002.

Uman, M. *Lightning: Physics and Effects*. Cambridge: Cambridge University Press, 1986.

Van Dooren, Thom. *Flight Ways: Life and Loss at the Edge of Extinction*. New York & Sussex: Columbia University Press, 2014.

——. 'Invasive Species in Penguin Worlds: An Ethical Taxonomy of Killing for Conservation', *Conservation and Society* 9, no. 4 (2011): 286–298.

——. 'Vultures and their People in India: Equity and Entanglement in a Time of Extinctions' *Australian Humanities Review* 50 (2011), www.australianhumanitiesreview. org/archive/Issue-May-2011/vandooren.html.

Virilio, Paul and John Armitage. 'The Kosovo War Took Place in Orbital Space: Paul Virilio in Conversation', trans. Patrice Riemans. *CTheory* (18 October 2000): www. ctheory.net/articles.aspx?id=132.

Walker, Janet. *Trauma Cinema: Documenting Incest and the Holocaust.* Berkeley & Los Angeles: University of California Press, 2005.

Wallach, A., C. N. Johnson, E. G. Ritchie and A. J. O'Neill. 'Predator Control Promotes Invasive Dominated Ecological States', *Biological Conservation* 142 (2009): 43–52.

Warburton, Bruce and B. G. Norton. 'Towards a Knowledge-Based Ethic for Lethal Control of Nuisance Wildlife', *The Journal of Wildlife Management* 73, no. 1 (2009): 158–164.

Ward, Russel. 'Massacre at Myall Creek', in 'The Good Weekend', *Sydney Morning Herald*, 5 November 1977.

Weir, Jessica K. 'Connectivity', *Australian Humanities Review* 45 (November 2008): 153–164, www.australianhumanitiesreview.org/archive/Issue-November-2008/weir.html.

Whitehead, Alfred North. *The Concept of Nature: The Tarner Lectures Delivered in Trinity College November 1919.* 1919. Reprinted as an eBook through Project Gutenberg (16 July 2006), www.gutenberg.org/files/18835/18835-h/18835-h.htm.

Wiesel, Elie. *From the Kingdom of Memory: Reminiscences.* New York: Summit Books, 1990.

Williams, Moira C. and Glenda M. Wardle. '*Pinus Radiata* Invasion in Australia: Identifying Key Knowledge Gaps and Research Directions', *Austral Ecology* 32, no. 7 (2007): 721.

——. '*Pinus Radiata* Invasion in New South Wales: The Extent of Spread', *Plant Protection Quarterly* 24, no. 4 (2009): 146–156.

Wilson, E. O. *The Creation: An Appeal to Save Life on Earth.* New York: W. W. Norton & Co., 2006.

Wright, Judith. *Collected Poems 1942–1970.* Sydney: Angus & Robertson Publishers, 1971.

——. *Half a Lifetime.* Melbourne: Penguin Books, 1999.

Wright, Kate. 'Becoming-With', *Living Lexicon for the Environmental Humanities*, 5 (2014): 277–281.

Wright, Sarah, Kate Lloyd, Sandie Suchet-Pearson, Laklak Burrarwanga and Matalena Tofa. 'Telling Stories in, through and with Country: Engaging with Indigenous and More-than-Human Methodologies at Bawaka, NE Australia', *Journal of Cultural Geography* 29, no. 1 (2012).

Wright, Tamra, Peter Hughes and Alison Ainley. 'The Paradox of Morality: An Interview with Emmanuel Levinas', trans. Andrew Benjamin and Tamra Wright, in *The Provocation of Levinas: Rethinking the Other*, eds. Robert Bernasconi and David Wood. London and New York: Routledge, 1988, pp. 168–180.

Zalasiewicz, Jan, Mark Williams, Will Steffen and Paul Crutzen. 'The New World of the Anthropocene', *Environmental Science & Technology* 44.7 (2010): 2228–2231.

——. 'Stratigraphy of the Anthropocene', *Philosophical Transactions of the Royal Society* 369 (2011): 1035–1055.

Index